What is *Critical* Social Research? Volume 1

– Babak Fozooni –

An environmentally friendly book printed and bound in England by
www.printondemand-worldwide.com

Mixed Sources
Product group from well-managed
forests, and other controlled sources
www.fsc.org Cert no. TT-COC-002641
FSC © 1996 Forest Stewardship Council

PEFC Certified
This product is
from sustainably
managed forests
and controlled
sources
PEFC
PEFC/16-33-415   www.pefc.org

This book is made entirely of chain-of-custody materials

www.fast-print.net/store.php

What is *Critical* Social Research? Volume I
Copyright © Babak Fozooni 2012

A catalogue record for this book is available from the British Library

ISBN 978-178035-279-4

1. Social Science – Sociology – Social Theory
2. Psychology – Social Psychology

First published 2012 by
FASTPRINT PUBLISHING
Peterborough, England.

Acknowledgements

I am grateful for permission to reprint the following essays, and acknowledge here their sources:

Fozooni, B. (2004) Kiarostami debunked! *New Cinemas: Journal of Contemporary Film*. Vol. 2, Issue 2, 71-89.

Fozooni, B. (2005) Review: Janet Walker: Trauma Cinema: Documenting Incest and the Holocaust. *Feminism & Psychology*, Vol. 18, No. 1, 144-148.

Fozooni, B. (2006) Towards a critique of the Iranian psy-complex. *Annual Review of Critical Psychology*, Issue 5, 69-88.

Fozooni, B. (2008) Iranian women and football. *Cultural Studies*, Vol. 22, Issue 1, 114-133.

Fozooni, B. (2010) Cognitive Analytic Therapy: a sympathetic critique. *Psychotherapy and Politics International*, Vol. 8, Issue 2, 128-145.

Fozooni, B. (2012, in print) The politics and parables of encyclopaedias. *Journal of Critical Education Policy Studies*.

CONTENTS

Preface

Convention demands of academic books the dutiful performance of a pre-arranged pirouette. More often than not a clever quote opens up the move, a hefty introduction 'contextualises' it, upcoming chapters are sign-posted, and in a rather obsequious nod to the Oscars, a long list of relatives and colleagues acknowledged in a bid to perform humility before academic arrogance can take its rightful place.

All the while the author remains mindful of the fact that s/he is dancing with an unpredictable troupe that can turn nasty with as little warning as a horde of drunken Klingons. The skilful choreography of this ballet is essential for success within academia. After all, careers are to be made, heads of departments are to be charmed, potential funding bodies impressed, students dazzled and unfriendly colleagues turned green with envy. An academic tome, therefore, contains within it more than a use-value and a *definable* exchange-value. It also possesses *indefinable* units of cultural capital that when invested sagaciously, yield untold riches.

For all these reasons and more, I deplore academia. I despise the funny handshakes to be learnt for advancement within exclusive lodges populated by careerists, the games people play to publicise themselves, the mind-numbing stupor of lecturers availing themselves of a captive audience, the tupperwaring of reactionary ideologies wrapped up in fluffy 'progressive' discourse, the departmental politics that fails to rise above public bath-house gossip and the bureaucratic machinery that has become the diseased underbelly of administration.

In short, universities throughout the world suffer from too many inherent and structural defects. The latest wave of neoliberal attacks has merely accentuated the *bourgeois essence of universities*. Although it remains highly improbable that the present state of affairs can humanise itself, it is not beyond the realm of imagination that universities will one day be devoid of institutional racism, sexism, disablism and homophobia. However, even in this unlikely scenario, I would argue that as bourgeois institutions, they will always retain their anti-working class character. Since the working class represents the overwhelming majority of people in society, universities expose their elitist agenda even as they graciously allow more youths from a working class background to enter their hallowed portals in search of 'bourgeois edification' (I say the 'working classes' are the overwhelming majority without trying to measure this as a quantitative unit since I fail to be impressed by the 'We are the 99%' slogan. The slogan has its roots in an American sociological understanding of wealth differentiation, which quite intentionally ignores class differences amongst anti-capitalist demonstrators. It also reifies through quantification the basically qualitative category of social class).

The present work must therefore be viewed in Hegelian terms as an effort to simultaneously suppress and supersede the bourgeois university and its various artificial disciplines: suppressing the negative elements whilst preserving the positive within a new synthesis. In short, the abolition of universities and the construction of something else, something ... better- *qualitatively* so!

Introduction

If I could have a dollar (or hedging my bets in these precarious days for capitalism, a dollar, a pound, a euro or a yuan) for every time a student has screwed up the courage to ask me: 'But what *exactly* is this thing you call *criticality*?' then I would be able to spend my twilight days summering in the Bahamas, wintering in Scotland, springing in Egypt and autumning in front of an ostentatiously large 3D TV! There are just so many times one can prevaricate when confronted with the scepticism of students regarding the cornerstone of emancipatory social research. Yes, a very valid question: what exactly is this criticality some academics treasure so much and why is it so hard to pin down? In this short introduction I will attempt to provide a simple answer, hopefully one that skews jargon and pretentiousness, two enduring characteristics of academia.

Traditionally there have been three main approaches to defining criticality: technical, etymological and political. The *technical* approach focuses on mechanisms and techniques for delivering critical evaluation. These are based on a rather restricted notion of rationality and may include 'compare and contrast' tasks as well as the weighing up of evidence 'for and against'. Whilst not dismissing them out of hand, I will be arguing that at best these techniques represent a rudimentary form of criticality and at worst they are opaquely overburdened with 'common sense' ideology.

The second approach is an *etymological* method which seeks to harness our fascination with words to embark on a journey starting with the ancient Greeks (or for the culturally literate, the ancient Egyptians), taking in a scientific detour around Renaissance (with figures such as Da Vinci, Galileo, Bacon and Newton), followed by a philosophic pilgrimage (revolved around Descartes, Kant, Hegel and Marx). The journey usually ends with a modernist and/or postmodernist 'updating' of criticality. As a method it has a great deal to offer: it is sound, cautious and informative whilst enabling the novice to get a conceptual handle on criticality. It also has a number of drawbacks which I will discuss below.

The final approach to criticality has an overt *political* dimension and considers itself a form of *praxis* (see below). It veers constantly between two poles: 'what is' and 'what could be'. On the one hand, it sees its project as a critical assessment of the status quo and on the other it offers an alternative as solution to society's ills. This approach too has limitations even though it represents the most profound interpretation of criticality.

TECHNICAL APPROACH TO CRITICALITY

This is the most common approach to criticality. Students are taught a number of 'skills' including observation, inference and analysis and encouraged to see the problem in pragmatic terms. Logical relations are noted and variables assigned as a prelude to experimentation and (the illusion of) control. Solutions for doing criticality are marshalled as a list of 'to do things'. At its worst, this approach becomes a listing of ideal character traits the researcher must display in order to be deemed morally acceptable (traits such as open-mindedness, individualism, fairness, sound judgment and neutrality). In short, criticality becomes a box ticking exercise:

i.   Compare and contrast Mussolini, Hitler and Franco's position on race? Tick.
ii.   What general conclusions would you draw from the US nation-building practice in Afghanistan? Tick.
iii. Design a solution to the water-shortage problem in Sierra Leone. Tick.

Employing a number of epistemologies, criticality is quite intentionally restricted in these questions and turned into a technical problem-solving exercise. In the process it is also conveniently depoliticised.

The first question perpetuates the myth of 'race' (a naive form of empiricism), whilst critical social scientists have been at pains to show its constructedness. It also reduces fascism to a 'racial' policy and further simplifies it by exaggerating the significance of individual leaders - a very common ploy amongst mainstream historians. One could also speculate that fascism in this question is restricted to its classical continental variety, as if to imply it is a problem distanced from us both temporally and spatially. Finally, by using the term 'position' the question suggests bigotry is a matter of intellect -something arrived at after deliberation and reasoning- and nothing to do with emotion. Rationalism is flagged whilst irrationalism is suppressed. The way the question is constructed may even encourage students to ignore the difference between 'discrimination', 'hatred' and 'bigotry' and how these forms of racism contain different emotional content.

In *The Politics and Parables of Encyclopaedias* I have discussed these issues at some length and demonstrated how even the most innocuous of utterances carries a heavy ideological burden. There are important political factors why *Encyclopaedia Britannica* narrates the story of fascism one way and *Wikipedia* chooses to do it another way. Whilst exercising 'compare and contrast' and 'strengths and weaknesses' techniques in this article, I have also tried to go beyond their limitations by unearthing the politics of encyclopaedia production.

The second question encourages students to first generalise (and this is usually a practice embarked upon far too hastily within academia), and to then apply these general conclusions outside the provisional soil from which it emerged (a necessary but risky business). Those familiar with the often obtuse vocabulary of research methodology may also recognise unstated assumptions such as falsifiability and replicability in the question. Worryingly, question 2 also perpetuates the mythological status of *imagined communities* - this time the myth of 'nations' as exemplified by normalised designations such as the USA and Afghanistan. It delinks the military phase of conquest from the peaceful stage of development and nation-building. Finally, it conceals the politics of aid and development by portraying them as neutral and unproblematic.

The article, *Magnus Hirschfeld's Contribution to Sexual Politics and the Nazi Backlash*, was written mindful of these potential pitfalls. It cautiously offers only two generalisations which were postulated after months of immersion in Hirschfeld's work and times. The first generalisation suggests he was attacked not just by Nazis after 1933 but was also constantly undermined by a variety of political and scientific actors within the Weimar Republic who found his defence of homosexuality troublesome (as contemporary neo-liberalism and neo-social democracy flirt with neo-fascist movements in Europe and elsewhere, this generalisation becomes premonitory). And secondly, his work is placed on a continuum ranging from the reductionism pole of *biomedicine* to the multi-dimensional pole represented by *biopsychosocial* research. Sexuality is viewed as a complicated, unfinalizable process and sexual emancipation is hitched onto the wagon of political and economic freedoms. In overcoming the artificial separation of categories, the text displays one of the key ingredients of criticality.

The third problem seems innocuous enough. Many people in the world are denied access to clean and free water. To engineer the problem away through well-construction and damn-building is, naturally, a highly tempting solution. However, as aid agencies and NGOs have gradually discovered sometimes rushing in to help people creates more serious long-term problems. In fact, critical aid-workers have recently reversed the classical motto of aid agencies to read, 'Don't just do something, stand there'! The construction of a local well for people in a Sierra Leonean village may inadvertently exacerbate tensions in the area since it impacts power relations. It may even initiate armed conflict or strengthen reactionary landowners at the expense of farmers. It may create dependence on outside aid-agencies and marginalise traditional skills such as canal construction.

The text *Cognitive Analytic Therapy: A Sympathetic Critique* deals with the same problem of intervention. The urge on the part of therapists and counsellors to aid clients in distress is sometimes overwhelming. And yet just like critical aid-workers, the critically minded therapist must balance the pros and cons of early intervention. After all, the therapist's biggest responsibility is 'to do no harm' and sometimes that means non-intervention until things have become clearer.

In summary, the technical approach imposes severe restrictions on the domain and efficacy of criticality. History and politics are filtered out as a matter of course whilst the dead labour power congealed in tools (wells, computers, medicine, etc.) is concealed. Tools can then be offered as neutral and objective solutions to complex problems. This approach encourages students to make an artificial separation between the researcher and researched and to think about intellect and emotion in dualistic terms. Finally, self-reflexivity (understanding one's impact on the knowledge-creation process and directing some of that precious critical gaze inward to foreground the research agenda) is not so much denied as marginalised by this approach. The transmission-based teaching that takes place within the confines of technical criticality tends to be superficial and over-specialised.

ETYMOLOGICAL APPROACH TO CRITICALITY

This approach focuses on how the etymology and philosophy of criticality has changed over time. It provides a social history for scientific thinking. Most ancient philosophies (including Greek Socratic tradition and Buddhist teaching), have employed probing questions to determine the logical consistency and clarity of knowledge-claims. They also introduced some basic forms of reflection and scepticism for probing common beliefs and explanations.

Different accounts then either move onto the Middle Ages (the likes of Thomas Aquinas are recruited for continuing the genealogy) or bypass the Middle Ages to go straight to the Renaissance (usually categorised as between the 14th to 17th centuries). Both the 'Middle Ages' and 'Renaissance' have been questioned as useful terms by contemporary historians who argue the continuities of these timeframes with preceding centuries far outweigh any differences. Nevertheless for our purposes they represent incremental improvements in looking at religion, art, law, science and politics with a combination of rational and empirical tools.

Today it is customary to be dismissive of these achievements, especially the dualism inherent in the works of someone like Descartes, but at the time it represented a cardinal break with modes of thinking mired in superstition and self-serving propaganda. Descartes, for instance, articulated the need for systematic, precise thinking and the testing of every stage of the research process. In the parallel field of political thought another Renaissance figure, Machiavelli, has become a byword for treachery and immorality. However, his work laid the foundation for humanist republicanism and sought to create self-governing cities where the elite and the citizenry were jointly responsible for political decisions. Descartes, Machiavelli and fellow thinkers such as Galileo and Newton were instrumental in investigating the links between what later philosophers would call 'essence' and 'appearance'. They may not have had all the answers but they can be credited with asking some of the right questions.

In turning a review of a complex book into a genealogy of trauma the text *Reviewing Trauma Cinema* attempts to show how superficial similarities between historical and personal trauma (as exemplified by the Holocaust and sexual abuse respectively), conflate two fundamentally different entities. By questioning every aspect of this analogy, I was able to conclude that the clarity lost in such a project exceeds any potential gain. Many of the concepts employed for this evaluation owe their origins to the tradition of hermeneutics (initiated in the Middle Ages) and rationalism and empirical data gathering (established by Renaissance thinkers). Nowadays, far too frequently a clichéd critique of dualism ignores the great debt we owe to past masters.

Fuck Critical Psychology takes one of the abiding aspects of Renaissance criticality, that of reflection, and turns its gaze inwards in order to interrogate Critical Psychology. I felt at the time (in a sense I still do) that this relatively new subset of psychology has made enormous contributions to our understanding of the history and politics of psychology. However, it was also evident that key assumptions of Critical Psychology were not being challenged from within. My public talk was aimed at jolting both old and new participants into becoming more critical of Critical Psychology and treating it more as a way of seeing and doing than as a sub-discipline of psychology!

POLITICAL APPROACH TO CRITICALITY

The explicitly political take on criticality may plunder certain techniques from the technical approach and lavish attention on the etymological evolution of key words in a discourse, but ultimately it is about demystifying commonsense ideology and offering an alternative interpretation. It is more ambitious and radical in its desire to unearth hidden linkages between phenomena and conversely to expose certain constructed links between events as bogus. It postulates a critical perspective from below.

Criticality in this context is about overcoming dualism. *Objectivity* and *subjectivity* are not perceived as neatly demarcated fields but intimately connected. *Theory* and *practice* are part of the same process and inseparable at every level of investigation. Likewise *intellect* and *emotions* are not essentialised in gendered terms but viewed as an integral part of the pre-production, production and post-production phases of research. Criticality respects both *abstract* (formal) knowing and *everyday* (informal) knowing. The truly critical researcher does not dwell exclusively on *information* (decontexualised units of date) as some empiricists do, or *knowledge* (the narrative framework for interpreting the information) as some constructionists are prone to, but fuses them dialectically. Nor does she get hung up on championing paradigms like *modernism* and *postmodernism,* which quite frankly have had their day in the sun and should now have the courtesy to make way for something better. Likewise, the infantile sniping of advocates of quantitative and qualitative methodologies is a game the critical researcher has long consigned to irrelevance, since every phenomenon displays both a quantitative and a qualitative dimension. The trick is to know how to combine them effectively.

The key to transcending these binaries is *praxis-* the conscious putting into practice of theory, which leads to better theory and in turn paves the way for more successful practice. But stated in such bland and dry terminology, praxis lacks the passion that gives it zest. Praxis is an active and (by and large) conscious advocacy of a position. Through praxis the critical researcher proves to us the flaws of the status quo and offer radical rupture as the only way out. In this day and age, criticality can hardly mean anything other than devising a social rupture with capitalism and everything it entails. Anything less would simply be inadequate.

Cognitive Analytic Therapy: A Sympathetic Critique is written from the viewpoint of a non-practitioner. I am neither a therapist nor an analyst. In order to understand Cognitive Analytic Therapy (CAT) I immersed myself in its literature and attended a weekend seminar. I watched videos and listened to public talks. All this did not make an expert out of me, but it did facilitate my uptake of its philosophy and practice. The article became part of a wider debate between CAT practitioners regarding future directions and in turn sharpened my understanding of certain areas of CAT hitherto unknown to me.

Kiarostami debunked! is an even better illustration of praxis since at the time of writing I was dabbling in independent (low-budget) filmmaking. I was dividing my time between attending filmmaking courses and studying for a theoretical masters' degree in film and video-making. On top of all this I was employed as an interpreter for actors and directors who were being screened at the *British Film Institute* and the *National Film Theatre*. I was in short (and here is that word again) *immersed* in film culture and meeting some of its practitioners. After meeting Abbas Kiarostami and interpreting for him over a two-day period, I decided to research his films more thoroughly and that is how the article came about.

The political approach to criticality is therefore more than an analytical application of skills for evaluating a text or solving basic problems. It is even more than illustrating the evolution of ideas/events. Perhaps it even goes beyond establishing the social history of phenomena. It is, in my view, about fusing the past and future inside the present, instead of focusing on a snapshot. Ultimately, it is about taking sides, participating in one's own research and dialectically improving practice and theory. It is about going to the roots of an issue and laying it bear for all to see and discuss. It is about dialogue between researcher and researched, rather than a monologic interpretation of subjects. Real criticality is collective meaning-making in the process of changing the world.

Cognitive Analytic Therapy:
A Sympathetic Critique

INTRODUCTION

Since capitalism transformed into a hyphenated entity variously prefixed as *post-modern* (Lyotard, 1984), *late* (Mandel, 1975), *neoliberal* (Rüstow, 1980), *post-industrial* (Bell, 1973) or *post-Fordist* (Negri, 1988), a corresponding subject has been taking shape. This new subject is a more fluid and knowledgeable worker who seems at the same time to be more vulnerable and atomized than her earlier incarnations. Moreover, the needs, desires and anxieties of this new worker have also multiplied thus requiring a more nuanced psychotherapeutic service to repair the damage done to its multi-faceted labour power. At the same time, an increasingly radicalized generation of therapists has attempted new projects using the equalizing paradigm to ensure equality along class, race, age, power and gender variables (Chaplin, 2005). One product of these transformations has been the development of 'Cognitive Analytic Therapy' (CAT) and it is the purpose of this paper to assess its credentials to heal damaged labour power.

Since the subject matter of this paper is a dialogic form of therapy, I feel a brief self-reflexive confessional would be an appropriate place to start. I began what turned out to be a rather inauspicious 'career' in psychology many years ago with the firm conviction of qualifying as a clinical psychologist. In the mid 1980s clinical psychology was still a very small profession (approximately 1100 UK practitioners in 1982), living in the shadow of its more illustrious cousins – psychiatry, psychoanalysis and psychotherapy.

Clinical psychology's fate was from the outset inexorably linked with 'behaviour therapy' and later on with 'cognitive behavioural therapy' (Reavley, 1982, 26). It is precisely this uncritical relationship that compelled me to re-evaluate my initial sympathies toward clinical psychology. On closer examination, the assessment part of clinical psychology seemed a recipe for stigmatization, the therapy element proved haphazard at best and reductionist at worst, and the research agenda became disconcertingly self-serving. To paraphrase Joel Kovel, 'I began to wonder then whether [clinical psychology] had not been created in order to trivialize history'

(Kovel, 1981, 19). I thus said my goodbyes to a career in clinical psychology and embarked on a different route that finally ended in the stupor of academia. What has kept me going within this vacuous and conservative field of intellectual endeavour has been the occasional spark of brilliance discovered in the works of Lev Vygotsky, Michael Bakhtin and, more generally, critical psychology. Through these critical currents I have once again become acquainted with radical forms of therapy and counselling, which contextualize the individual within her social environment and promote emancipation. One such current *may* prove to be cognitive analytic therapy (CAT). The present work is an attempt to assess whether CAT is a genuinely novel form of radical therapy or a pseudo-radical intervention aimed at the rapid repair and return of the subject to the workplace and the joys of wage-slavery!

FIRST CONTACT

I first came across CAT during a weekend training course at Birkbeck College, University of London, which ran on 30–31 January 2009 (supervised by two qualified CAT trainers, Steve Potter and Annalee Curran). The aim was to provide a group of participant counsellors, psychiatric nurses, social workers, clinical psychologists and the odd non-practising mole (me!) the opportunity to evaluate the principles and practice of CAT.

The initial sales' pitch was rather low-key and dignified. We were informed how CAT was developed over the past 30 years through the work of Anthony Ryle and his associates. Their aim was to 'create a brief, focused and effective psychotherapy that could be delivered by front-line staff to large numbers of patients in the public sector' (Llewelyn, 2003, 502). In the process, they worked on transforming the monologic discourse of psychoanalysis *about* the patient to a dialogic (and simplified) discourse created in collaboration *with* the patient. Initially CAT was employed with 'neurotic' problems within an out-patient psychiatric context although more recently it has been applied to a wide variety of 'psychotic' issues including major mental illness (Kerr, 2001).

There was no attempt to aggrandise Ryle's role in CAT's creation story, which is a refreshing change from other forms of psychodynamic or humanistic psychotherapy still reliant on the aura of the bourgeois-progenitor. The conceptual tools of CAT were described through a brief talk and a video depicting a fictional therapy session. Two further tools (the *diagram* and the *letter* which will be discussed below) were then introduced for the *reformulation* of the client's life-story.

The second day focused on seminal pressure points during the therapeutic process, various 'difficult' and 'breakthrough' moments. The *good-bye letter,* which traditionally ends the therapeutic relationship, was elaborated and the programme came to a close with a discussion of multidisciplinary work with the client and community mental health teams (CMHT). In fact, working with CMHTs seems to be a conscious strategy on the part of advocates of cognitive analytic therapy in an effort to gain a foothold within the world of psychotherapy. Community mental health teams consisting of social workers, psychiatric nurses, clinical psychologists, counsellors and therapists are increasingly used in the UK to provide a consistent and long-term service for people with complex difficulties, especially those with childhood trauma who manifest a high level of distress and self-harm. Cognitive analytic therapy's emphasis on relations and communication with significant others, it is claimed, places it in a superior position to help these patients compared to either cognitive or psychoanalytic models (Thompson et al., 2008, 132). Furthermore, CAT can provide members of CMHTs with a 'shared common language' and a coherent ideological framework of analysis (Thompson et al., 2008, 131).

THE LANGUAGE OF CAT

In line with any novel treatment, CAT promotes its own discursive practice, which on closer inspection turns out to be influenced by three imperatives: (1) a rejection of previous discourse, especially the 'archaic and confusing language of' classical psychoanalysis (Llewelyn, 2003, 502); (2) a re-accentuation of older modes of expressing mental illness, especially those connected with object relations; and (3) a new vocabulary for capturing the nuances missed by other therapeutic models.

Like so many practitioners before them, cognitive analytic therapists began by rejecting and/or de-emphasizing certain dimensions of Freudianism. As Bateman et al. (2007, 51) inform us,

'CAT originated in part from the attempt to restate key psychoanalytic object relations ideas in an essentially cognitive language and in the extensive use of repertory grid techniques to investigate psychodynamic therapy.' The early emphasis on object relations was part of the move away from the Freudian notion of universal unconscious conflicts. However, when object relations itself proved inadequate to the healing task, a major rethink was prompted, leading to the import of Vygotskian and Bakhtinian concepts.

Throughout these changes, some key aspects of CAT have remained constant. For example, CAT insists on conceptualizing 'the patient in non-static, systemic terms whereby actions and relationships are understood as both causal and caused by each other' (Llewelyn, 2003, 503). Moreover, the interaction between therapist and patient is from the outset collaborative and mindful of asymmetries of power. All this gives CAT a theoretical flexibility and relational dynamism that more bureaucratised forms of therapy have forsaken over the course of their co-option.

The notion of a series of symptoms constituting a 'disorder', as favoured by The Diagnostic and Statistical Manual of Mental Disorders (DSM), is replaced by the *procedure*. The original definition of a procedure was close to schema. If Fredrick Bartlett saw schema as an active organization of the past in order to give people orientation for future behaviour (Bartlett, 1932), then Ryle described the procedure as a 'linked chain of mental processes and actions involved in the execution of aim-directed acts' (Ryle, 1985, quoted in Llewelyn, 2003, 503). Procedures, however, are more than schemas since they 'include external and mental phenomena and unite cognitive, affective and behavioural components and communication' (Bateman et al. 2007, 53). Most of us use procedures effectively most of the time in our endeavour to function in the world. However, people with psychological distress become tangled up in a cycle of dysfunctional and distressing procedures.

It is crucial to view procedures relationally. 'Our early experience in reciprocation with our all-powerful carers invites a number of . . . *reciprocal role procedures* (RRP)' where *roles* describe how we interpret others or the internalized voices within (McCormick, 2008, 33). Role procedures aim for a response from others but also regulate the individual once they become internalized voices. Certain influences are evident in the notion of reciprocal role procedures: the influence of Trevarthen who studied early post-natal experience through infant-carer engagement; D. W. Winnicott who believed 'there's no such thing as a bad baby' (i.e., baby grows with others); Bowlby's attachment theory with its focus on 'the shared world outside rather than the private world inside' (Moghaddam, 2007, 162); George Kelly's insistence on getting to know the client's life story in order to empathize more easily (Bannister et al., 1994, 74); and, finally, Bakhtin's dialogism with its desire to understand the speaker and her intent.

In healthy individuals there is a wide range of dichotomous role procedures, such as care-dependency or control-submission or demand-striving, which are internalized. These internalized patterns help to maintain the self in the social world. In individuals suffering from psychological disorders, therapists identify a narrow repertoire of role procedures and/or exaggeration in one of the poles of the RRP. For instance, one could discover deficiencies of care in the care-dependency RRP, excess of control in the control-dependency RRP or excess of demand in the demand-striving RRP (Bateman et al, 2007, 54). A borderline personality who is trapped in an abused-abuser pattern can come to play both roles of this RRP. Sometimes just remembering or talking about past traumatic experiences can provoke state switch. So in CAT the emphasis is not so much on the cause of the original trauma and the cathartic re-living of it (Miltenburg and Singer, 1999a, 1). According to Ryle and Fawkes (2007, 166) and in a nod to Vygotsky, '[i]nterpersonal and intrapersonal patterns are often parallel, as when a childhood experience of *striving to please* parents who are *critical* is repeated both in self-criticism and in criticalness of others'.

Faulty or maladaptive procedures are classified into three main types: traps, dilemmas and snags. Briefly put, *traps* are repetitive cycles of behaviour with a loop-back mechanism where consequences feed back into their perpetuation. For example, a depressed patient acts in ways that 'make failure and defeat more likely', leading to more depression (Denman, 2001, 244). *Dilemmas* refer to false choices or unduly narrow options, which lead to self-despised behaviour on the part of the patient who then becomes cross with himself and switches to an opposite procedure. For instance, an individual who initially acts by placating people around her, may become angry with herself, and switch to being overaggressive towards everyone. Finally, *snags* are 'anticipations of future consequences of action ... so negative that they are capable of halting a procedure before it ever runs' (Denman, 2001, 244). Denman gives the example of a gay man so frightened of coming out that he prefers to live a lie.

Cognitive analytic therapy supersedes existential forms of therapy such as logotherapy where 'choice' is sometimes elevated to an idealistic principle as a determinant of individual behaviour (cf. Frankl, 2004). In contrast, CAT recognizes the limitations imposed on individuals by social, economic and cultural factors. The narrowing of procedural repertoires discussed above may be caused alternatively by 'impoverished environmental opportunities', 'deliberate attempts by caregivers to restrict procedural repertoires', or previous faulty learning (Denman, 2001, 245).

STAGES OF THERAPY

Cognitive analytic therapy proposes that neurosis is characterized by *diminished* or *dysfunctional multiplicity* whereas in more extreme cases of childhood abuse this becomes a psychotic dissociation represented by *pathological multiplicity*. The therapeutic process aims to 'support the patient's capacity for self-reflection' by overcoming diminished and pathological RRPs (Ryle and Fawkes, 2007, 166). Change depends on the extent of this self-reflective process and the control of difficult memories/feelings. Unhelpful procedures are identified and alternatives explored. Here the therapist helps by becoming 'a new internal voice' and by avoiding reciprocation of dysfunctional RRPs (Ryle and Fawkes, 2007, 167). In line with Bakhtinian therapy, CAT acknowledges multiplicity while maintaining the essential unity of 'the self'.

Therapy is divided into three overlapping phases, namely, reformulation, active therapy, and termination. The whole process usually lasts between 16–24 sessions. This time limit is not absolute. Ryle acknowledges that for some clients, long-term therapy and more intensive care may be of value (Ryle, 1997, 160). However, it is also worth pointing out that time-limited therapies can in fact be more intensive than extensive long-term therapies (Ryle and Kerr, 2002, xvi). For those interested in the origins of CAT's interest in time-limited therapy see James Mann (1973).

During the *reformulation* phase the patient's difficulties are collaboratively located within a model of the self. The patient is asked to carry out 'homework' in the form of reading the Psychotherapy File which describes traps, dilemmas and snags. The homework is intended to help patients recognize patterns of thinking, feeling and acting and how to control their dysfunctional elements. The patient is assured that through changing dysfunctional patterns, they can also change the way other people behave towards them. The last part of the File is a questionnaire that aims to discover difficult and unstable states of mind. Usually by the fourth session a reformulation letter and a sequential diagram are collaboratively worked out and discussed.

The active part of the therapy begins by encouraging the use of the reformulation letter and sequential diagram to recognize dysfunctional RRPs. Hopefully the safety of the therapeutic environment will encourage previously denied and avoided memories to be discussed openly. Cognitive analytic therapists believe that the mere naming and accepting of these negative expressions have a major therapeutic effect. This is a common belief amongst most schools of therapy and the cynic may seek to trace its roots to the ancients' belief that naming a plague was half-way to battling its ills.

The therapist spends a considerable amount of time preparing the patient for the end of therapy, which 'is seldom accepted without some disappointment or anger' (Ryle and Fawkes, 2007, 168). The experience of losing the therapeutic alliance can bring back painful feelings of betrayal and loss. 'Good-bye letters' are one form of mitigating the negative effects of these feeling but also an accurate appraisal of the gains and failures of therapy. Unlike psychoanalytic and some forms of humanistic therapy, CAT 'does not seek to make major characterological changes, but rather, attempts to un-stick a stuck system' (Llewelyn, 2003, 504). To my mind, this is an affirmative feature of CAT which distinguishes it from fluffier forms of therapy that attempt to engineer 'clean closures'.

VYGOTSKY AND BAKHTIN ADD THEORETICAL COHERENCE

An outsider may form the impression that CAT has been subjected to major theoretical overhauls at seminal junctions during its development, usually in response to pragmatic concerns. For example, at its outset, CAT deliberately distanced itself first from Freudian defence mechanisms in symptom formation and later from Klein/Bion's explanation of borderline personality disorder as psychic disintegration (Denman, 2001, 249). Then there was a temporary move towards Kelly's personal construct theory, whose traces can still be detected in CAT's predilection for scientific problem solving (e.g., setting homework for patients). However, more recently the focus on individual processes, so privileged by cognitive psychology, has been supplanted by the ideas of Vygotsky and Bakhtin. In fact, the Patient File Questionnaire could be viewed as a Bakhtinian-influenced version of Kelly's repertory grid.

Jerome Bruner's work on 'scaffolding' (an extension of Vygotsky's learning techniques) was an early influence on the development of CAT (Ryle, 1994). The educational scaffolding that occurs in the classroom acts as a model for the handing over of control and conceptual thinking that takes place within therapy. Bruner has also described two forms of knowledge, namely 'narrative' and 'paradigmatic', arguing that both can be used to persuade. Critical psychologists would recognize these as falling within the domain of narrative therapy (cf. Law, 1999) and rhetorical psychology (cf. Billig, 1996) respectively. Cognitive analytic psychology uses both narrative and paradigmatic discourses to shift the balance of discussion from a restrictive Freudian past to a retelling of the patient's experiences from alternative perspectives. The reformulation letter discussed above is based on narrative discourse whilst the RRPs and diagram are examples of paradigmatic thinking, since they employ abstract, verifiable descriptions (Ryle, 1994). Collectively these two modes of discourse help create a 'zone of proximal development' (ZPD) where therapist and patient can jointly create conceptual tools for enhancing self-knowledge (Ryle, 1994).

Following the import of Bruner's ideas, CAT also benefited from the pioneering work of Leiman (1997, 2002), who employs Vygotskian and Bakhtinian ideas in therapy. In fact, the relationship between Leiman and Ryle is best described as reciprocal, since Leiman has derived his *dialogical sequence analysis* from RRP. This is a technique intended to describe the moment-by-moment details of the therapeutic process and the 'interpersonal patterns that clients repeatedly enact in life' (Leiman and Stiles, 2001, 314). Crucially it incorporates therapist utterances as well as client utterances in identifying issues of concern.

Leiman has shown through his case studies how clients can 'advance more than one level within a single session' within the zone of proximal development (Leiman and Stiles, 2001, 315). Once trust is established within the ZPD, partly hidden and painful signs/words can be gradually rediscovered. Likewise new, jointly created signs/words will emerge facilitating comprehension (Leiman, 2002, 228).

UNDERUTILIZED IDEAS FROM VYGOTSKY AND BAKHTIN

If the section above signposted the deliberate and direct utilization of Vygotsky and Bakhtin by Ryle and co-thinkers, there is also an untapped reservoir of Vygotskian and Bakhtinian ideas with, at best, a tangential relationship to CAT. This section attempts to foreground these potential links in the hope of a richer engagement.

De-classification

We can begin by mentioning Seikkula (2003) who as a clinical psychologist and family therapist influenced by Bakhtin is keen to get away from the limitations of clinical diagnosis. He suggests that for most orthodox practitioners the labelling of a patient as 'schizophrenic' means 'an end to the interest of this research problem' but for those engaged in a dialogic interaction this definition triggers an avalanche of new meaning (Seikkula, 2003, 88). This is sensible counsel for a faction within the CAT movement who seem to have developed an uncritical stance towards diagnostic classification. In the assessment part of their seminal book for example, Ryle and Kerr express the mildest form of concern when they concede the 'state-trait' distinction is 'not always clear' (Ryle and Kerr, 2002, 72). It is true that they criticize labelling as, at times, 'arbitrary and reductive' (Ryle and Kerr, 2002, 132) but, by and large, the existence of mental illness and the distinction between Axis I and Axis II in DSM are taken for granted with undue haste.

　We must constantly remind ourselves that 'the original DSM [Diagnostic and Statistical Manual: Mental Disorders] listed about 60 disorders, while the latest has about five times as many' (Singer, 2006, 6). The focus on the more bizarre attempts to create illness (e.g., *accidie* which was believed to arise from a failure to do one's duty to God in medieval England or the stigmatization of *homosexuality* as deviance) serves to detract attention from the sheer ubiquity of classification. Cognitive analytical therapy does not reject classification so much as *re-accentuate* it through introducing a dialogic element (Bakhtin, 2000, 423). This is a valid tactic for resistance, when used as part of a wider repertoire, but I would argue quite inadequate on its own.

Therapy as teaching

Therapy as education and self-development has a long history. Erich Fromm urged the analyst to ask herself constantly, 'What is new that the person learned this hour or this week?' (Thomson, 2009, 82). He also believed, 'the teacher is taught by his students, the actor is stimulated by his audience, the psychoanalyst is cured by his patients: provided they do not treat each other as objects, but are related to each other genuinely and productively' (quoted in Thomson, 2009, 90). What was in Fromm a vague humanistic technique of interaction has more recently found a coherent theoretical expression in neo-Vygotskian therapy.

Roland Tharp suggests '[p]ychotherapy-as-education is a concept that has been slowly rooting for some decades, but its ripening has awaited the application of analytic tools with the explanatory and guiding power of sociocultural/activity theory' (Tharp, 1999, 18). Cognitive analytic therapy has wisely decided to hitch its wagon to this movement. Both Vygotskian and CAT practitioners would agree that therapist and client should negotiate the *meaning* and *sense* of words in the course of therapy and interpret events jointly. Unlike phenomenology, *epoché* is not elevated to a fetishized ideal and in contradistinction to Freudianism *insight* alone is not credited with breakthroughs. Again in distinction to most forms of phenomenology, rooted in the here and now, CAT uses language historically. Whether it does do with the same depth as psychodynamic therapy or the breadth of Marxism is an issue beyond the scope of this text.

Family and group therapy

In line with Seikkula above, Tharp has also extended Vygotskian techniques into family therapy. If Vygotsky was correct in suggesting that the task of development is the dialectical synthesis of everyday/informal knowledge with abstract/formal concepts, then the role of family and 'community' becomes indispensable. This is especially true 'for members of cultures of which the therapist is not thoroughly knowledgeable' (Tharp, 1999, 22). This manoeuvre from Freud's 'stuffy consulting office through to group, family and network therapies' is *by and large* a positive expansion of psychological problems into wider social relations.

There are significant exceptions to this rule when the inclusion of family members and larger network members would be counterproductive. For instance, issues involving child abuse, insoluble family antagonisms and some forms of eating disorders. Part of the therapist's task is to ascertain which family member would enhance the therapeutic process and when to retain a one-to-one relationship with the client. Related to this issue is CAT's uneasy relationship with the 'unconscious'. Is it really appropriate for CAT practitioners to refuse interpreting the unconscious and merely focus on 'what can be seen or has been reported' (Ryle and Kerr, 2002, 11–12)? Does this attitude include ignoring 'invisible' capitalist social relations? Do we have to downplay them too because they may have their roots in the past and be concealed from view most of the time?

Jones and Skaife (2009) have even shown how the political and personal can be fused within a masters' degree course in art therapy. They explain the aims of their course at Goldsmiths College as follows:

> The purpose of the art therapy large group is to teach students about art therapy processes, which become magnified in the large group context, and to consider the existential, political and social issues that are raised in becoming a professional art therapist (Jones & Skaife, 2009, 23). [They argue that even within the present constraints of neoliberal capitalism, this approach] 'helped students gain a new understanding of their political agency and about the power of acting collectively to represent their interest ... (Jones & Skaife, 2009, 25) [my additions]

It would be ironic if CAT became complicit in reversing this trend. In this context the current minimal group interventions of CAT seems to be a limitation that time will overcome (cf. Ryle and Kerr, 2002, 174).

Dealing with trauma

An excellent example of overlap in therapeutic conceptualization between neo-Vygotskians and CAT is the work of Miltenburg and Singer (1999b), who question the orthodox therapeutic practice of forcing the client to relive traumatic experiences. They believe this could reinforce dissociation, reify clients, and 'destroy the client's spontaneous compensatory system' (Miltenburg and Singer, 1999b, 541). Moreover, 'not every client needs or is willing to relive these experiences, nor is equal to the task' (Miltenburg and Singer, 1999b, 541). Moreover, 'survivors cannot afford to give up their survival strategies as long as there are no alternatives available' (Miltenburg and Singer, 1999a, 2). The behaviours and feelings that the client wishes to change are not always 'dysfunctional'. They may at the same time be necessary for client survival.

It would also be sensible to ensure CAT's focus on 'states' remains dialogic and flexible. Concepts like 'states' are not usually suitable for demonstrating development and interaction. They also tend to treat 'psychic processes as reified entities, *things*' (Miltenburg and Singer, 1999b, 545). That is why Vygotsky put so much emphasis on 'human plasticity' and understanding the 'internal logic' of subjects (Miltenburg and Singer, 1999a, 8). It also explains why Shotter is at pains to warn us of the dangers of a Cartesian monological concept of mind, which would have us believe that 'the mind is not just contained inside the head of the self-contained individual, but is *radically hidden* in there' (Shotter, 1999, 72). Has CAT taken sufficient precaution to avoid these errors? I believe it has but the potential for reification exists whilst 'states' remain a crucial part of CAT's discourse.

Perhaps what is really making me uneasy regarding CAT's treatment of trauma is the apolitical stance adopted. In line with a great deal of trauma research, 'the role of capitalism in promoting [. . .] sexual abuse is conspicuous [. . .] by its total absence. Terms such as *posttraumatic stress* disorder and *identity* are employed uncritically throughout' (Fozooni, 2008, 147). As I have commented in the same text, 'I would like to see research on trauma to benefit from the writings of Vygotsky and Bakhtin in the future. For example, Weine (1999) has ably used Bakhtin's notion of *speech genre* to discover the *Forgotten History* of traumatic events during psychotherapy . . . And Zittoun (2004) has used a Vygotsky-inspired semiotic interpretation to investigate the relationship between trauma, memorials and politics' (Fozooni, 2008, 147).

Dialogic self

The next idea that could benefit CAT comes courtesy of Hermans and Kempen (1993). They understand the self as a multiplicity of positions, called a Personal Position Repertoire (PPR) which brings to mind Ryle's Reciprocal Role Procedures (RRP). In Hermans and Kempen's account the self comprises various social roles incorporated by an individual ('internal positions'), together with representations of significant others ('external positions'). The positions are endowed with a 'voice' through which they engage in dialogues (Geiser, 2006, 444). The dialogic self should be seen as a network of power with power relationships as catalysts for change (Valsiner, 2002, 262).

Geiser in applying this model to shape-shifters from Sierra Leone touches on a vital issue. What is the link between the 'healthy' losing of self during shape-shifting or shamanistic trances on the one hand and dissociations experienced during 'psychotic' episodes? Is this 'losing of the self' a skill that can be developed? Or perhaps a 're-awakening of skills we all had as children' (Geiser, 2006, 447)? Is the changing body-image experienced by Wiccan witches during a state of 'losing of self' similar to perceptual distortions associated with most forms of eating disorders? Is multiple personality disorder an extreme form of the kind of shape-shifting most of us employ in everyday life? If so then the task of the therapist is to mobilize the 'adult' part of the client to develop communication tools for contacting the 'angry' part of the dialogic self (Miltenburg and Singer, 1999a, 11). Instead of dismissing the 'angry' part of self as 'dysfunctional', or 'maladaptive', the therapist comes to appreciate its survival functionality and gradually reassures the self to do without it or employ it more wisely.

Cross-cultural contributions

Ultimately what is interesting about Geiser's work is twofold: firstly, this and similar projects could act as a cross-cultural contribution to the burgeoning research being carried out on CAT, thus enforcing its self-reflexive dimension. As Rogoff and Morelli (1989) have pointed out '[a]n important function of cross-cultural research has been to allow [Western] investigators to look at their own belief systems (folk psychology) on scientific theories and research paradigm' (Rogoff and Morelli, 1989, cited in Messer and Dockrell, 1998, 310). Secondly, such Bakhtinian approaches can interpret client's religious beliefs sympathetically without colluding with what the therapist may strongly disagree with.

Of course it is perfectly legitimate to point out that in today's complex and dynamic world, cultural variations within a society may prove as significant as cross-cultural variations. In that case, I would suggest Bakhtin's distinction between *official* and *unofficial* cultures should become a more integral part of CAT's interpretative repertoire. The patient's unofficial culture is often at odds with the official culture imposed from above. The tension may be a primary cause of mental anguish and alienation.

Polyphonic travelling and chronotopes

If Geiser uses Bakhtin's notion of polyphony to address the 'surplus of visions' experienced by shape-shifters, the related work of Peter Good (2001) employs Bakhtin's concept of a *polyphonic traveller* to reinterpret the psychiatric landscape. In this outstanding contribution, Good argues that to 'engage with the voices that play on the [psychiatric] landscape requires more than a simple intellectual shift ... Polyphony demands a physical change to one's own bodily standing' (Good, 2001, x). Good rails against the separation between healer and sufferer institutionalized by official psychiatry. He identifies two principle *chronotopes* (time-space bonds) that populate the psychiatric landscape: the care chronotope and the patient chronotope. The care chronotope is distinguished 'by the sheer speed of its time flow' (Good, 2001, 25). It represents psychiatry's vision and is always addressed to an idealized future 'capable of dealing with the inevitable disappointments of the present and the shame of the past' (Good, 2001, 26). Time, in the patient chronotope, has a 'much more unstable quality ... given to sudden accelerations or alarming tangents' (Good, 2001, 27). The most common feature of time in this chronotope is its 'slowed-down almost viscous quality' (Good, 2001, 27). Good expands on this basic antagonism between the two chronotopes to reinterpret psychiatry – its mode of surveillance and regulation as well as moments of resistance and autonomy exerted by patients. This is an approach that can enhance CAT's rather perfunctory critique of institutionalized psychiatry and add a new dimension to the collaborative dialogue at the heart of CAT.

The antagonism between care and patient chronotopes should conclude in synthesis rather than mere negation of the former. Paré and Lysack (2004) pose a similar problem: how to balance client knowledge with therapist knowledge? How can clients feel free to express themselves, and at times 'adopt certain ways of making meaning around problems' without feeling overwhelmed and hemmed in by therapeutic discourse? The issue is not a simple case of ensuring an even wicket or empowering the client to withstand monologic discourse. The process should aim for a dialectical synthesis of scientific (therapist) and everyday (client) discourses, whilst minimizing the harmful effects of official discourse. The process must also be cognizant of moments of client vulnerability when empowerment is willingly handed over to the therapist in return for peace of mind.

Power relations

According to Paré and Lysack (2004, 10) the 'intention [of therapy] is to disrupt and disempower the taken-for-granted *truths* or constraints, so that more empowering and open *voices* may enter into the conversation'. Following Bruner, they use scaffolding to manoeuvre the therapeutic discourse from monologue to dialogue. Talk, and problems, are externalised during scaffolding or to use Bruner's terminology a 'loan of consciousness' takes place (Bruner, 1986, 74). Of course, I am aware of the problems with this approach: firstly, the post-structuralist reader may rightly object to the structuralist taste of such metaphors, and secondly, externalising problems may not be applicable in certain cultures (e.g., Japanese culture), which prefer compromise to confrontation (Paré and Lysack, 2004, 15). Finally, one indicator of resistance and disengagement could be non-verbal communication. This is an aspect of therapy usually consigned to intuition, whereas ideas from Bakhtin can sensitize us to the subtle nuances of non-verbals within a coherent theoretical framework.

Activity and performance

Whilst wary of imposing the Leninist political philosophy of Fred Newman and Lois Holzman (1997) on the reader, there are certain parallels between *Social Therapy* and CAT that need to be drawn out. To quote: 'Basic to social therapy (and to building community) are two human capacities that engage alienation: *activity* and *performance*' (LaCerva et al., 2002). Activity is defined as 'revolutionary, practical-critical activity' (Marx, 1974, 121), the relevant ontological unit for psychotherapy. Performance is a particular form of this general activity, 'the human capacity to ... be both *who we are* and *who we are becoming/who we are not*' (LaCerva et al., 2002, 31).

In a departure from CAT, the focus in social therapy is not to solve individual problems but 'rather ... to help groups of people create environments for getting better' (LaCerva et al., 2002, 32). This group approach, and a genuine desire to avoid victimology, are two positive aspects of social therapy that could strengthen CAT. It may even be worthwhile pointing out that both CAT and social therapy's usage of performance can be improved if they take on board Bakhtin's notion of the 'emancipatory laughter' – a sadly neglected aspect of therapy even within Bakhtinian circles.

RAISING CONCERNS WITH CRITICAL PSYCHOLOGY/PSYCHOTHERAPY

The final section of my paper attempts to use the substantial, and growing, resources of critical psychology/psychotherapy/counselling to raise issues that have caused concern as I delved deeper into CAT. I hasten to add that I view these issues as deficiencies that could be overcome in time. Given the fact that I am neither a CAT insider nor a qualified therapist, it is perfectly conceivable that the list below is more a manifestation of my ignorance than an accurate picture of the state of play. I trust my criticisms will be received as positive and constructive rather than an exercise in nitpicking.

Capitalism and class

We live in a capitalist world which gorges itself on the entrails of the overwhelming majority in the interest of a tiny minority. This, for me, is the most basic, fundamental truth of our times which no amount of modernist humanism or postmodernist relativism can conceal (Fozooni, 2006). Any therapeutic intervention, aiming to ease suffering until the social relations propping up the system have been superseded, must take onboard this elemental truth.

There is very little in CAT writing that can be described as the political economy of psychotherapy or a class analysis of psychological illness. As Walkerdine (2007, 24) has suggested regarding psychoanalytic psychotherapy, it is conceivable that '[t]here is, in a Foucauldian sense, not an absence of clinical engagement with class, but a very specific engagement with the working class as an object of a surveillant social-work gaze.' In other words, class may be present in CAT discourse *implicitly*. I accept this possibility. And it may also be the case that actual clinical work, especially carried out by therapists from a working-class background, are far more responsive to class issues. However, my reading so far suggests this is a low priority topic for CAT.

Whether this absence is by accident or design I cannot say but I do view it as a major deficiency. Unless therapy gives class emancipation centrality, and that means dealing with the issue *explicitly*, it will fail to help the sufferer or subvert bourgeois social relations. Psychotherapy is a commodity that, like any other, contains both a use-value and an exchange value. Singer's analysis of the political economy of psychotherapy in the US, for instance, has ably demonstrated how 'huge insurance companies call the shots in the mental health field' (Singer, 2006, 1). Medication 'therapy' becomes the treatment of choice for insurance companies. This has engendered a cosy relationship between them and pharmaceutical companies leading to a situation when, in 2002, 'the combined profits of the ten drug companies in the Fortune 500 were more than the profits of all the other 490 firms put together' (Singer, 2006, 3). The promotion of 'disease' and 'illness' to fit new drugs (Angell, 2004) is a relatively new phenomenon that any radical psychotherapy has to challenge if its efforts are not to be institutionalized. At present I see little sign, and perhaps more worryingly little desire, of that in CAT.

As Totton has observed, all psychotherapists have a political *agenda*, whether this is admitted to or not: 'all psychotherapy rests on a theory – explicit or implicit, conscious or unconscious – of *how people should be*' (Totton, 2006, xiv). And as Parker rightly adds, it is not a question of finding the right 'balance' between psychotherapy and politics in some sort of false homage to the ancient Greek notion of 'equilibrium' but the realization that every action, discourse and desire is already saturated by politics (Parker, 2008, 96).

In practice this should amount to an open discussion with the client regarding the bourgeois origins of the 'psy-complex' (Rose, 1985). It is not sufficient to carry out a 'dialogic interaction' (Bakhtin, 2000) without the historical tool of therapy being jointly demystified (Vygotsky, 1978). For instance, if it is true that the bourgeois and petty-bourgeois background of most therapists hinders the therapeutic relationship (Hannon et al., 2001, 142), should not this be a topic for discussion between therapist and client? If Hannon et al. (2001, 143) are correct in asserting that '[c]lassism is institutionalized in counsellor education programmes' (and I believe if anything they are understating their case) then isn't CAT's refusal to discuss class tantamount to collaboration with capitalism?

What makes the issue of class even more urgent is the fact that 'much of what is frequently discussed under the rubric of race or ethnicity [and I would add gender, sexual orientation and disability] may be better explained by social class' (Davis and Proctor, 1989, cited in Hannon et al, 2001, 140). Anne Kearney, herself both a counsellor and a trainer, has put it well: ' ... class is far more important an influence on counselling than any other social grouping, and that each of the other groupings is mediated by class' (Kearney, 1996, 47).

We are witnessing massive transformations in psychotherapy and counselling. Part of this shift is intellectual as more and more practitioners become influenced by critical, constructionist and Vygotskian currents. However, there are two negative factors worthy of consideration: professionalization and regulation. Ehrenreich (1989) has shown how the 'professionalization' of therapy/counselling has been used as a cloak to buttress petty-bourgeois interest and exclude working-class candidates. And Parker argues that 'the British government is preparing to regulate the activity of counsellors and psychotherapists through the Health Professions Council.' This he speculates is about normalizing a set of principles and practices that will reduce therapy to 'procedures, techniques and targets to roll through as many people as quickly as possible' (Parker, 2009). It would be unfortunate if CAT's desire for professional recognition from official bodies and its preference for short-term therapy were to make it a convenient cost-cutting measure for the state.

Poverty and depression

John Cromby (2004) demonstrates convincingly that depression and social inequality are associated. This poses an immediate challenge to all those forms of therapy that view depression as maladaptive behaviour or a disorder with organic roots. It also challenges therapies to explain why the effects of social inequality do not impact uniformly upon individuals.

CAT is capable of dealing with the latter problem but tends to ignore the social aspects of depression. Occasionally lip-service is paid to external realities such as unemployment and poverty and their adverse impact on self-esteem but one feels these issues play an insignificant part in the course of cognitive analytic therapy (cf. Ryle and Kerr, 2002, 57). Where, for example, is CAT's critique of medicine and the pharmaceutical industries, or for that matter the impact of alienation on depression? McCormick, for instance, encourages the severely depressed to trust 'medical or psychiatric advice' (2008, 23). Her depiction of the 'depressed thinking trap' seems only marginally superior to agony column homilies (McCormick, 2008, 76–79). There is little or no political interrogation of science, medicine or the notion of progress. In its desire to make friends with everyone, CAT ceases to question power relations and the financial advantage accruing to certain segments of psychiatry as a result of drugs like Prozac (cf. Lewis, 2003).

In this context CAT's humanistic philosophy can seem inadequate to the task at hand: '[CAT therapists] seek to remove the *roadblocks* which have maintained restrictions and distress and have prevented the patient's further growth and we assist in the development of more adequate route maps' (Ryle and Kerr, 2002, 14).

The trend is worrisome, especially since a great deal of positive work has been done in recent years to get away from 'outcome research'. For example, John Marzillier (2004, 392) has warned us '... psychotherapists, anxious to prove that what they do works, have bought into a medicalised way of defining psychological experience. They act as though it is correct to state that people have depression or anxiety or schizophrenia like they *have* measles or diabetes or heart disease.' It is also worrisome because it has parallels with CAT's non-resistance to bourgeois morality. In what I consider a distortion of Vygotsky, CAT has a tendency to fetishize early caregiver-child dyadic relationships and downplay formal bourgeois cultural restrictions imposed on us throughout life: 'Formal rules of conduct and explicit social norms have a small and late impact compared to the indirect transmission of values and assumptions about the world and self through the child's joint activities with others in the early years' (Ryle and Kerr, 2002, 42). This leads to the unfortunate paraphrasing of Vygotsky, which strikes me as flawed as well as dogmatic: 'what the child does not do or say with the adult today she will not do or say on her own tomorrow' (Ryle and Kerr, 2002, 43).

Finally, MacDonagh reminds us that 'those with depression are ... not always able to see the illocutionary aspect of speech - what words are expressing and the emotions and intents lying behind them' (MacDonagh, 2008, 58). They also find it difficult to fuse past, present and future dimensions of their personal narrative and it then becomes the task of the therapist to facilitate this process. The problem is a time-limited form of therapy is not always able to achieve these complex aims leaving the client's narrative arch incomplete.

Temperament and neurobiology

The de-emphasising of politics and class antagonisms in society by CAT is made worse by its predilection for notions of 'temperament' and its uncritical import of behavioural genetics and developmental neurobiology (cf. Ryle and Kerr, 2002, 26–8). It is noteworthy that the only criticism of Jung's conception of the self alluded to is the neglect of the social dimension of self (Ryle and Kerr, 2002, 37). Having presented certain clichéd positions regarding genetics and biology as uncontroversial 'facts', Ryle and Kerr go on to make this astonishing concession:

> ... a certain amount of what may be described as personality may be the effects of temperament rather than of developmental experience. As such they may be relatively immutable, raising the question of whether, in that case, the task of psychotherapy may be, in part, to help an individual to

live with and manage their particular temperamental characteristics as well as to make sense of their consequences. (Ryle and Kerr, 2002, 26)

Although sold to us as pragmatic and realistic, this, in fact, is a pre-emptive admission of defeat, which imposes self-limiting boundaries on the therapeutic process.

CONCLUDING REMARKS: TWO PATHS AVAILABLE TO CAT

Totton (2005) makes a distinction between two positions within therapy; one he calls *therapy as an expert system* and the other *therapy as a social critique*. The former 'tends to operate from a cure or adjustment model' (Totton, 2005, 86). It is concerned with establishing its credentials as a profession by finding a niche, erecting an enclosure around it and claiming the knowledge generated inside the enclosure as its private property. The enclosure is then further parcelled out according to a technical division of labour that aims to increase production. It has its own seminal texts, lodge masters and bureaucrats. This is, of course, therapy as exchange value.

Therapy as social critique or social resistance aims instead to demystify the relations (economic, cultural, political and personal) that perpetuate exploitation and alienation. If a therapy cannot politically interrogate capitalism its usefulness must be seriously curtailed. Vygotsky, and to a greater extent Bakhtin, would refute the notion of a body of expert knowledge that therapists could lay claim to (Pollard, 2008, 209). The problem with CAT's import of political figures such as Vygotsky and Bakhtin is that ultimately they have been tamed and sanitised and perhaps even used instrumentally. Their radicalism has been transformed into woolly humanism and liberal sentimentalism. I believe Pollard makes a similar point in her excellent study of Bakhtin and psychotherapy (Pollard, 2008, 1). Which position would CAT have the greatest affinity with: therapy as an expert system or therapy as social critique/resistance? I suspect different practitioners in this field would respond to the question differently and I also suspect that most practise a kind of therapy that borrows elements from both poles.

Related to this is the substance of socio-economic factors influencing individuals, a dimension usually neglected by CAT. Despite Vygotskian influences, one feels CAT lacks an activity theory for navigating the wider issues of concern that may fall within the extra-psychological domain but are nonetheless crucial for successful intervention in psychotherapy. There is little attempt to connect personal distress and the structures of a system based on capitalist exploitation, patriarchy and racism (cf. Jacoby, 1997; Kovel, 1987; Ralph, 1983). In this sense CAT is a regression from the gains of the 1970s and 1980s. On the other hand, in its incorporation of Vygotsky and Bakhtin, its innovative treatment of 'neurotic' and 'psychotic' patients and its desire to open up its methods and practice to inspection by all and sundry, CAT is justifiably winning admirers in the therapeutic community.

In assessing CAT I have had to overcome my own deep-seated scepticism about the efficacy of therapeutic treatment. I have come to accept CAT as a genuinely integrative approach, which is still expanding and finding its feet. There is a great deal in CAT worthy of serious consideration: I like the way its time-limited nature reduces dangers of overdependence; I like its Vygotskian and Bakhtinian elements and would prefer it to develop further along these lines; I like CAT's ambition in helping the most 'difficult' clients (although on the other hand CAT selects its clientele very carefully, filtering out those with suicidal or extreme self-harm tendencies, who are referred to psychiatry, as well as those deemed not sufficiently motivated to benefit from therapy, e.g., addicts); its attempt to base itself on sound, coherent theory instead of settling for a convenient eclecticism; its preference for anti-Cartesian dialogism and its collaborative approach. Finally, I am impressed by CAT's scope and ambition. I believe that if in the future CAT chooses to become a fully fledged therapy as critique/resistance/education rather than therapy as an expert system, its status amongst radical psychologists will be guaranteed.

REFERENCES

Angell, M. (2004) *The Truth about the Drug Companies: How They Deceive Us and What to Do About It.* New York: Random House.

Bakhtin, M. M. (2000) *The Dialogic Imagination: Four Essays.* Austin: University of Texas Press.

Bannister, P., Burman, E., Parker, I., Taylor, M. and Tindall, C. (1994) *Qualitative Methods in Psychology: A Research Guide.* Buckingham and British: The Open University.

Bartlett, F. C. (1932) *Remembering.* Cambridge: Cambridge University Press.

Bateman, A. W., Ryle, A., Fonagy, P. and Kerr, I. B. (2007) Psychotherapy for borderline personality disorder: mentalization based therapy and cognitive analytic therapy compared. *International Review of Psychiatry,* 19(1): 51–62.

Bell, D. (1973) *The Coming of Post-Industrial Society: A venture in social forecasting.* New York: Basic Books.

Billig, M. (1996) *Arguing and Thinking.* Cambridge: Cambridge University Press.

Bruner, J. (1986) *Actual Minds, Possible Worlds.* Cambridge: Harvard University Press.

Chaplin, J. (2005) The Bridge Project: radical psychotherapy for the twenty-first century. Psychotherapy and Politics International, 3(2): 133–9.

Cromby, J. (2004) Depression: embodying social inequality. *Journal of Critical Psychology, Counselling and Psychotherapy,* 4(3): 176–86.

Davis, L. E. and Proctor E. K. (1989) *Race, Gender and Class: Guidelines for Practice with Individuals, Families, and Groups.* Englewood Cliffs, NJ: Prentice Hall.

Denman, C. (2001) *Cognitive-analytic therapy. Advances in Psychiatric Treatment,* 7: 243–56.

Ehrenreich, B. (1989) *Fear of Falling: The Inner Life of the Middle Class.* New York: Pantheon Books.

Fozooni, B. (2006) Towards a critique of the Iranian psy-complex. *Annual Review of Critical Psychology,* 5: 69–88, http://www.discourseunit.com/arcp/5 (accessed 12 September 2009).

Fozooni, B. (2008) Review: Janet Walker: trauma cinema: documenting incest and the Holocaust. *Feminism and Psychology,* 18(1): 144–8.

Frankl, V. (2004) *Man's Search for Meaning.* London: Rider.

Geiser, T. (2006) How to transform into goddesses and elephants: exploring the potentiality of the dialogic self. *Culture and Psychology,* 12: 443–59.

Good, P. (2001) *Language for Those Who Have Nothing: Michael Bakhtin and the Landscape of Psychiatry.* New York: Kluwer Academic/Plenum Publishers.

Hannon, J. W., Ritchie, M. and Rye, D. R. (2001) Class: the missing discourse in counselling and counsellor education in the United States of America. *The Journal of Critical Psychology, Counselling and Psychotherapy*, 1(3): 137–54.

Hermans, H. and Kempen, H. (1993) *The Dialogic Self: Meaning as Movement*. San Diego, CA: Academic Press.

Jacoby, R. (1997) *Social Amnesia: A Critique of Contemporary Psychology*. New Brunswick and London: Transactions Publishers.

Jones, K. and Skaife, S. (2009) Under the cobblestones, the beach: the politics and possibilities of the art therapy large group. *Psychotherapy and Politics International*, 7: 18–27.

Kearney, A. (1996) *Counselling, Class and Politics: Undeclared Influences in Therapy*. Manchester: PCCS Books.

Kerr, I. (2001) Brief cognitive analytic therapy for post-acute manic psychosis on a psychiatric intensive care unit. *Clinical Psychology and Psychotherapy*, 8: 117–29.

Kovel, J. (1981) *The Age of Desire: Case Histories of a Radical Psychoanalyst*. New York: Pantheon Books.

Kovel, J. (1987) *A Complete Guide to Therapy: From Psychoanalysis to Behaviour Modification*. London: Penguin Books.

LaCerva, C., Holzman, L., Braun, B., Pearl, D. and Steinberg, K. (2002) The performance of therapy after September 11. *Journal of Systemic Therapies*, 21(3): 30–8.

Law, I. (1999) A discursive approach to therapy with men. In Ian Parker (ed.) *Deconstructing Psychotherapy*. London: Sage.

Leiman M. (1997) Procedures as Dialogical Sequences: a revised version of the fundamental concept in cognitive analytic therapy. *British Journal of Medical Psychology*, 70: 193–207.

Leiman, M. (2001) Toward Semiotic dialogism: the role of sign mediation in the dialogical self. *Theory and Psychology*, 12(2): 221–36.

Leiman, M., Stiles, W. B. (2001) Dialogical sequence analysis and the zone of proximal development as conceptual enhancement to the assimilation model: the case of Jan revisited. *Psychotherapy Research*, 11(3): 311–30.

Lewis, B. E. (2003) Prozac and the post-human politics of cyborgs. *Journal of Medical Humanities*, 24(1/2): 49–63.

Llewlyn, S. (2003) Cognitive analytic therapy: time and process. *Psychodynamic Practice*, 9(4): 501–20.

Lyotard, J-F. (1984) *The Postmodern Condition: A report on knowledge*. Manchester: Manchester University Press.

MacDonagh, J. (2008) 'Every Meaning Will Have Its Homecoming Festival': Providing New Possibilities for Meaning in clients' Dialogue. *History & Philosophy of Psychology*, 10(2): 56-63.

Mandel, E. (1975) *Late Capitalism*. London: New Left Books.

Mann, J. (1973) *Time-limited Psychotherapy*. Cambridge, MA: Harvard University Press.

Marx, K. (1974) Theses on Feuerbach. In K. Marx and E. Engels, *The German Ideology*. New York: International Publishers.

Marzillier, J. (2004) The myth of evidence-based psychotherapy. *The Psychologist*, 17(7): 392–95.

McCormick, E. W. (2008) Change for the Better: Self-help through Practical Psychotherapy. Los Angeles, London, New Delhi, Singapore, Washington DC: Sage.

Miltenburg, R. and Singer E. A. (1999a) Culturally mediated learning and the development of self-regulation by survivors of child abuse: a Vygotskian approach to the support of survivors of child abuse. *Human Development*, 42: 1–17.

Miltenburg, R. and Singer, E. A. (1999b) Dissociative identity disorder is a developmental accomplishment: reply to Van der Hart and Steele. *Theory and Psychology*, 9(4): 541–9.

Moghaddam, F. M. (2007) *Great Ideas in Psychology: A Cultural and Historical Introduction*. Oxford: Oneworld.

Negri, A. (1988) *Revolution Retrieved: Selected Writings on Marx, Keynes, Capitalist Crisis and New Social Subjects 1967–83*. London: Red Notes.

Newman, F. and Holzman, L. (1997) *The End of Knowing: A New Developmental Way of Learning*. New York: Routledge.

Paré, D. and Lysack, M. (2004) The willow and the oak: from monologue to dialogue in the scaffolding of therapeutic conversations. *Journal of Systemic Therapies*, 23(1): 6–20.

Parker, I. (2008) Politics versus psychotherapy. *Psychotherapy and Politics International*, 6(2): 91–7.

Parker, I. (2009) State regulation of counselling and psychotherapy – for or against? Socialist Resistance, http://socialistresistance.org/?p=653 (accessed 10 September 2009).

Pollard, R. (2008) *Dialogue and Desire: Mikhail Bakhtin and the Linguistic Turn in Psychotherapy*. London: Karnac Books Ltd.

Ralph, D. (1983) *Work and Madness: The Rise of Community Psychiatry*. Montréal: Black Rose Books.

Reavley, W. (1982) Clinical Psychology in Practice. In S Canter and D Canter (eds) *Psychology in Practice: Perspectives on Professional Psychology*. Chichester: John Wiley & Sons, Ltd.

Rogoff, B. and Morelli, G. (1998) Perspectives on children's development from cultural psychology. Reprinted in David Messer and Julie Dockrell, *Developmental Psychology: A Reader*. London: Arnold, 309–20.

Rose, N. (1985) *The Psychological Complex: Psychology, Politics and Society in England 1869–1939*. London: Routledge & Kegan Paul.

Rüstow, A. (1980) *Freedom and Domination: A Historical Critique of Civilization*. Princeton: Princeton University Press.

Ryle, A. (1985) Cognitive theory, object relations and the self. *British Journal of Medical Psychology*, 58: 1–7.

Ryle, A. (1994) Persuasion or education? The role of reformulation in cognitive analytic therapy. *International Journal of Short-Term Psychotherapy*, 9(2/3): 111–18.

Ryle, A. (1997) *Cognitive Analytic Therapy and Borderline Disorders: The Model and the Method.* Chichester: John Wiley & Sons, Ltd.

Ryle, A. and Fawkes, L. (2007) Multiplicity of self and others: cognitive analytic therapy. *Journal of Clinical Psychology: In Session*, 63(2): 165–74.

Ryle, A. and Kerr, I. B. (2002) *Introducing Cognitive Analytic Therapy: Principles and Practice.* Chichester: John Wiley & Sons, Ltd.

Shotter, J.(1999) Life inside dialogically structured mentalities: Bakhtin's and Voloshinov's account of our mental activities as out in the world between us. In John Rowan and Mick Cooper (eds.) *The Plural Self: Multiplicity in Everyday Life.* Sage Publications: London, Thousand Oaks, New Delhi.

Singer, D. (2006) The Political Economy of Psychotherapy. *New Politics*, xi(1), summer, http://www.wpunj.edu/newpol/issue41/Singer41.htm (accessed 8 September 2009).

Tharp, R. G. (1999) Therapist as teacher: a developmental model of psychotherapy. *Human Development*, 42: 18–25.

Thompson, A. R., Donnison, J., Warnock-Parkes, E., Turpin, G., Turner, J. and Kerr, B. (2008) Multidisciplinary community mental health team staff's experience of a 'skilled level' training course in cognitive analytic therapy. *International Journal of Mental Health Nursing*,17: 131–7.

Thomson, A. (2009) *Erich Fromm: Explorer of the Human Condition.* London: Palgrave Macmillan.

Totton, N. (2005) Can psychotherapy help make a better future? *Psychotherapy and Politics International*, 3(2): 83–95.

Totton, N. (2006) Introduction. In N. Totton (ed.) *The Politics of Psychotherapy: New Perspectives.* Maidenhead: Open University Press, xiii–xx.

Valsiner, J. (2002) Forms of dialogical relations and semiotic autoregulation within the self. *Theory and Psychology*, 12: 251–65.

Vygotsky, L. S. (1978) *Mind in Society: The Development of Higher Psychological Processes.* Cambridge, Massachusetts and London, England: Harvard University Press.

Walkerdine, V. (2007) Class in the consulting room. *Psychotherapy and Politics International*, 5(1): 23–8.

Weine, S. (1999) 'A forgotten history' and related risks for speech genre in trauma mental health: a commentary. *Journal of Contemporary Psychotherapy*, 29(4): 267–81.

Zittoun, T. (2004) Memorials and semiotic dynamics. *Culture and Psychology*, 10(4): 477–95.

Reviewing Trauma Cinema

Trauma is big business. Nowadays it has its own army of practitioners, its barely contested official diagnostic profile and its numerous representations within the (mainly modernist) TV/film industry as well as the (mainly postmodernist) documentary field. Janet Walker's book, *Trauma Cinema: Documenting Incest and the Holocaust* (2005), is described as 'an apologia for the role played by mistaken memory in understanding catastrophic past events' (p. 189). In it she attempts to show how films and videos about the Holocaust and incest advance our understanding of trauma. 'Trauma cinema' is thus defined by Walker as a transnational group of films that 'deal with a world-shattering event ... whether public or personal' (p. 19). I would like to begin this review by foregrounding some of the valuable contributions of the book because I do not wish my later critical comments to deter the reader from engaging with this thoughtful work.

Walker warns us at the outset that her approach for understanding trauma and memory skews consoling binary explanations found in juridical and social work discourses. It is argued that neither of these two discourses 'have a language capable of distinguishing between a desire and a want' (p. 10). She believes 'recourse to empirically based realist historiography ... cannot adequately address the vicissitudes of historical representation and memory' (p. xviii). This literalist approach makes a fetish of believing the accuser and assumes that all memories are 'flashbacks' and not inventions. Equally, she rejects the 'social constructionist approach', which ignores the accuser's avowals and puts the emphasis on 'psychic reality' (p. 11). So in relation to both incest and the Holocaust, 'nothing will be learned if internally generated memory formations are either dismissed out of hand or taken at face value' (p. 6). Instead, she proposes a model of memory 'ranged along a continuum, with extremely veridical memories to the right, false memories to the left, and fantasies propped on reality but not perfectly reflective of it in the center' (p. 12). This conjuring of past mental images, altered in certain aspects, she calls *disremembering*. For her, disremembering 'is a common feature of traumatic memory rather than [an] anomaly' (p. 17).

This is a book with a healthy distrust of positivist and objectivist notions of representation. For example, her qualitative approach values the kind of (auto)biographical documentary that breaches 'the strict positivist conventions of Holocaust documentaries' (p. 29). In such works, eyewitness testimonies and oral historical evidence are not treated as 'unimpeachable building blocks of history' (p. 140). These unconventional works, she suggests, may reach a deeper level of understanding of trauma and memory. There is throughout her analysis sympathy for representations that deliberately combine genuine and fictive footage.

She is also fully aware that the documentation of trauma can be (and perhaps at times should be) confrontational. For example, she mentions how a central feature of *Shoah* (Dir: Lanzmann 1985) is to return Holocaust survivors to 'their childhood towns to trigger memories for the interview process and, importantly, to confront the remaining non-Jewish townspeople' (p. 108). She describes how this deliberate act of confrontation 'causes the Polish peasants not only to express but actually to enact the anti-Semitism that led them to both deny and profit from the killings in their midst' (p. 108).

Regardless of the reader's position on memory formation, all should find the discussion about the False Memory Syndrome Foundation valuable (p. 64). Walker first describes the Foundation's refutation of abused women's memories and then mounts a challenge. While acknowledging that some forms of therapy such as 'regression', 'detachment' and 'rage' therapies may lead to manipulation and the inducement of false memories, Walker exposes the hidden script framing the Foundation's accusations. She does not mince words when it comes to the role of institutional religion in abuse: '... when it comes to the relationship between fathers and daughters, religious tenets combine with social organization to discount crimes and disarm testimony' (p. 107).

Trauma Cinema is unequally divided between incest and the Holocaust. Three chapters are dedicated to incest and only two to the Holocaust. Chapter 2 investigates how the subject of incest is omitted from Hollywood cinema and how, when it does make an appearance, it is marginalized and distorted. For instance, incest was almost completely excised from seminal movies such as *Kings Row* (Dir: Wood, 1942) and *Freud* (Dir: Huston, 1962). These classic films only allude indirectly to a subject viewed as taboo until more recent times. Walker discusses how post-Freudians have found it difficult to accept Freud's later denial of father–daughter incest (p. 42).

Chapter 3 discusses the representations of incest in TV movies such as *Sybil* (Dir: Petrie, 1976) and *Shattered Trust: The Shari*

Karney Story (Dir: Corcoran, 1993). Walker explains how in the final analysis 'the television movie presentation of incest is restricted by its positivist approach' (p. 49). These films engage in a fantasy of knowing and since 'neither inaccurate nor false memories are pictured, we are left with the impression that all abuse memories are wholly true and that parental denial is wholly wrong' (p. 59). These TV movies are concerned with the achievement of proof and therefore treat memory 'as an artifact buried by the sediments of time' (p. 84). They set themselves the task of excavating these memory traces and having them authenticated by legal and therapeutic institutions. This chapter also contains a brief critique of Alfred Kinsey's work on sexuality. Walker accuses Kinsey of exonerating the perpetrators of incestuous abuse. She sees Kinsey's defence of men accused by 'hysterical girls' as prefiguring the rhetoric of the False Memory Syndrome Foundation by four decades (p. 51).

In Chapter 4, Walker looks at incest in trauma documentaries. *Just, Melvin: Just Evil* (Dir: Whitney, 2000) and *Capturing the Friedmans* (Dir: Jarecki, 2003) are perhaps the two best known examples of the genre. *Just, Melvin* is described as a 'genealogy of incest' and the '*Shoah* of incest documentaries' (p. 103). Pre-empting criticism of this comparison, Walker immediately adds that she 'is not *equating* the incest perpetrated by one man on his families with ... the Holocaust ... Rather, [she is] saying that the two films representing these different events may be compared in style and structure' (p. 103). What impresses Walker about *Just, Melvin* is the skill with which the director skews the quantification of incest in favour of depicting 'the texture and color of specific incidents' (p. 104). When specifics are mentioned, there is always a point to the description. In this way, the twin strategy of voyeuristic titillation and indignant disgust that characterizes the treatment of incest in the mainstream media is avoided.

Capturing the Friedmans is viewed by Walker as a documentary about epistemology. Given the unreliability of memory, it asks how we know anything and why we think we do. It is a film 'about the tricks a person's mind can play, not to fabricate trauma where there is none, but rather to survive traumatic events that are all too real' (p. 116). Trauma documentaries of the type discussed in this chapter employ home movies, interviews and re-enacted sequences in order to assess the past. In so far as they have taken on board the lessons of postmodernism, these documentaries 'recognise the ultimate inaccessibility of perfect historical truth but aim nevertheless at the truth that lies on the cusp of a *receding horizon*' (p. 85).

The next two chapters shift the attention onto filmic representations of the Holocaust. Chapter 5 begins by explaining how the advanced age of Holocaust survivors and the growing number of Holocaust deniers have prompted a 'zeal for archiving' (p. 125). Walker then discusses *Shoah* and how some critics have accused it of 'retraumatizing' survivors 'so as to traumatise secondary witnesses – the film's spectators' (p. 131). Moreover, Lanzmann (the director of *Shoah*) clandestinely filmed an ex-SS officer during the making of the documentary even though he had promised the latter anonymity. Walker debates the ethics of this subterfuge and comes down in favour of Lanzmann. With *The March* (Dir: Ravett, 1999) we are looking at a different kind of remembering, one that is 'fragmentary but also halting, repetitive, presented in dribs and drabs over a period of years and punctuated by resistance and forgetting' (p. 145).

Chapter 6 analyses second-generation depictions of the Holocaust. These sons and daughters of survivors are referred to as 'memorial candles' of the Holocaust with all the burden the designation inflicts upon them. It is also the most therapy-oriented section of the book because it talks about *disremembering* as a way of working through painful events. In this context, disremembering is the expression of fleeting and ephemeral images of the past that the individual can release from the tyranny of trauma through experimental videos and documentaries. A variety of novel techniques are used in these daring second-generation visualizations, techniques such as posthumous 'interviews' and cartoon drawings. The sacred representations of the Holocaust are thus challenged by second-generation film-makers in a bid to reassess the traumatic impact of the Holocaust on both victims and survivors. There is a great deal in this ambitious book worthy of serious consideration. The interested reader may wish to read Walker's book in conjunction with Kaplan and Wang's (2003) thematically similar offering. However, I wish to end my review by listing a number of substantial disagreements with Walker's methodology and political positions and briefly foreground alternative ways of looking at trauma from the perspective of critical psychology.

My most immediate concern is that lumping incest and Holocaust into a 'genre' of film-making is based on formalist criteria that ignore the sociocultural psychology of these two vastly disparate phenomena. By emphasizing various filmic techniques or psychological symptoms common to both themes, Walker is creating an abstraction – *Trauma Cinema* – which conceals far more than it illuminates. The roots of the term trauma in medicine and psychiatry are never adequately explicated. The promised insight into the 'aetiology and sequelae of trauma' that is supposed to be gained by the comparison simply does not materialize. I do not believe this approach to be an advance on the intricate dialectics of personal and historical meaning making.

Although Walker seems familiar with qualitative methodology and postmodernist writings on film-making, I feel she has squandered the vast literature within critical psychology and more radical forms of film analysis. By reducing the themes of incest and the Holocaust to the notion of trauma, she is guilty of the same error found in advocates of the 'risk society'. A trendy label is invoked as an alternative to the complicated historical, sociological and psychological analysis essential for comprehension. The role of capitalism in promoting genocide and sexual abuse is conspicuous in her analysis by its total absence. Terms such as 'post-traumatic stress disorder' and 'identity' are employed uncritically throughout (cf. McLaughlin 2003). Walker seems unaware of the role these films, and for that matter her own book, play in the discursive construction of concepts such as 'trauma' and 'survivors' (see Devlin 2005). And although I find her treatment of the False Memory Syndrome Foundation of interest, it ultimately fails to break new grounds because it lacks the sharp analytical rigour found in other feminist critiques of the 'False Memory' debate (cf. Brown and Burman 1997; Burman 1997; Schuman and Galvez 1996).

The book is severely hampered by its rejection of historical knowledge, especially with regard to the Holocaust. It is as if these films are produced in a vacuum. At times this leads to a fetishization of non-explanation and incomprehension. Furthermore, throughout the book there is an unproblematic acceptance of the bourgeois notions of 'crime' and 'law' that concedes far too much to the status quo.

On a personal note, I would like to see research on trauma to benefit from the writings of Vygotsky and Bakhtin in the future. For example, Weine (1999) has ably used Bakhtin's notion of 'speech genre' to discover the 'Forgotten History' of traumatic events during psychotherapy. Miltenburg and Singer (1999) use Vygotskian therapy for supporting survivors of child abuse. And Zittoun (2004) has used a Vygotsky-inspired semiotic interpretation to investigate the relationship between trauma, memorials and politics.

In conclusion, readers will appreciate Walker's astute observations on memory formation and trauma through a filmic topography filled with fascinating mainstream and experimental representations. The more critical reader will find Walker's bourgeois epistemology limiting but still benefit from her analysis of catastrophic past events. Psychologists, historians and film analysts would be the natural audience for this complex work.

REFERENCES

Brown, L. S. and Burman, E. (1997) Feminist Responses to the 'False Memory' Debate. *Feminism & Psychology,* 7(1): 7–16.

Burman, E. (1997) Telling Stories: Psychologists, Children and the Production of 'False Memories'. *Theory & Psychology,* 7(3): 291–309.

Devlin, M. (2005) 'Teenage Traumas': The Discursive Construction of Young People as a 'Problem' in Irish Radio Documentary. *Young: Nordic Journal of Youth Research,* 13(2): 167–84.

Kaplan, E. A. and Wang, B. (eds) (2003) *Trauma and Cinema: Cross-Cultural Explorations.* Hong Kong: Hong Kong University Press.

McLaughlin, K. (2003) Identities: Should we Survive or Surpass Them? *Journal of Critical Psychology, Counselling and Psychotherapy,* 3(1): 48–58.

Miltenburg, R. and Singer, E. (1999) Culturally Mediated Learning and the Development of Self-Regulation by Survivors of Child Abuse: A Vygotskian Approach to the Support of Survivors of Child Abuse. *Human Development,* 42: 1–17.

Schuman, J. and Galvez, M. (1996) A Meta/Multi-Discursive Reading of 'False Memory Syndrome'. *Feminism & Psychology,* 6(1): 7–29.

Weine, S. (1999) 'A Forgotten History' and Related Risks for Speech Genre in Trauma Mental Health: A Commentary. *Journal of Contemporary Psychotherapy,* 29(4): 267–81.

Zittoun, T. (2004) Memorials and Semiotic Dynamics. *Culture & Psychology,* 10(4): 477–95.

Sand-Nigger Psychology: Towards a Critique of the Iranian Psy-Complex[1]

INTRODUCTION

Consider the intelligence of the average American [or Iranian psychologist]. Then consider the fact that half of them aren't even that smart.
- with apologies to Mark Twain
(Quoted in Graeber, 2005, 5).

Oh, boy! This is gonna be a tough one! All things considered I would rather be writing the fifth volume of Marx's *Das Kapital* or the genealogy of lesbianism in the Khomeini clan than a critique of the Iranian *psy-complex*.[2] And since the nemesis of this psy-complex (i.e., Iranian Critical Psychology) does not yet exist as a coherent body of thought and action, I have no choice but to conjure it up as we go along.

My thankless task in this article is to begin with a potted history of Iranian psychology, its key figures and landmarks. This will entail investigating Iranian psychology's conscious re-animation of premodern Irano-Islamic thought, the even more uncritical import of (US) modernist psychology and, finally, its more recent flirtations with (West European) postmodernist psychology.[3]

---

[1] I would like to thank the guest editors of the *Annual Review of Critical Psychology* for their encouraging comments. I am especially grateful to Professor Erica Burman for reviewing my article. Her criticisms improved the text greatly.

[2] The term is defined by Nikolas Rose as 'a complex of discourses, practices, agents and techniques, deployed within schools, clinics, the judicial and penal processes, the factories and the army- which [provides] the basis for the generalisation and development of *applied* and *clinical* psychology ...' (Rose, 1985, 9).

[3] I do not care for terms like *premodernism, modernism* or *postmodernism* and try to avoid using them wherever possible. It is not the fact that they mean different things to different people, since all terms are sites of contestation (cf. Vološinov, 1929[1986]). Nor is the problem their constructedness, since truth need not be captured through an *organic*

In the second section, I look at the eclectic applications of this psy-complex, including favoured psychotherapies and established clinical sub-disciplines. I will then discuss some of its seminal themes and demonstrate how most of them conspire to maintain the hegemony of the bourgeoisie. Having critiqued this *sand-nigger psychology*, I end the article by calling for a Radical 'Iranian' Critical Psychology (R'I'CP) which will articulate and cement the opposition between *house-sand-niggers* and *field-sand-niggers*. The former consists of all those Iranian psychologists, psychiatrists, psychoanalysts, social workers and academics who maintain and strengthen the grip of their bourgeois masters, whilst the latter consists of those organising an open conspiracy against the present state of affairs.

Radical 'Iranian' Critical Psychology will be shaped by current proletarian struggles against capitalism and marked by rejuvenated feminist and atheistic currents. Whilst foolishly rushing in where previous angels have feared to tread, R'I'CP also aims to supersede the limitations of both 'western' and 'eastern' versions of critical psychology. After all, there would be no point in dislodging the psy-complex for a fluffier version of the beast.

CONTEXTUALISING THE IRANIAN PSY-COMPLEX

When religion and politics travel in the same cart, the riders believe nothing can stand in their way. The movement becomes headlong-faster and faster and faster. They put aside all thoughts of obstacles and forget that a precipice does not show itself to a man in a blind rush until it's too late.
- Frank Herbert, *Dune* (1988, 441).

Since the consolidation of the Islamic counter-revolution (1979-1981), every book published in Iran regardless of subject matter, has

---

vocabulary. My concern is that they do not serve the interests of the working class and as such should be considered suspect. However, for the sake of brevity and since so many agents within the psy-complex perceive of their actions in terms of such concepts, I felt *obliged* to follow convention. As a critical psychologist, therefore, I am as much hostage to *obligation* as anyone else (see footnote 4).

been obliged to begin with the self-serving Koranic gambit, 'In the name of Allah, the Compassionate, the Merciful'. This includes most psychology textbooks. In a society where the private-public divide is teetering on the verge of complete collapse and where an entire belief system is imploding under atheistic pressures from below, even this obligatory ritual is now routinely flouted by plucky translators/publishers (cf. Foucault, 2000; Marx, 1871[1993]; Trotsky, 2001).

Obligation, however, continues to play a pivotal role within the Iranian psy-complex.[4] This includes the obligation of children to their parents, the wife to her husband, the worker to his/her boss and the 'inmate' to society at large. This atavistic demiurge has condemned it to fall badly behind the rest of society. Its predilection for torturing unresponsive patients with ECT and the (almost) wholesale medicalistion of psychotherapy is the unsightly modernist underbelly of an authoritarian premodern mindset.[5] In a quest for legitimacy its self-appointed narrators seek 'native' heroes in place of foreign pioneers of psychology. Thus every account of the emergence of psychology in Iran begins with a mandatory homage to either ancient prophets (e.g., Zarathushtra) or scholars of the Middle Ages (e.g., Avicenna, Razi and even Ibn Khaldun).

---

[4] Obligation in this context is an example of what Raymond Williams referred to as 'residual cultural artifacts' (Williams, 1973, 41). It is a set of values and practices from a previous social formation (e.g. feudalism) which continue to shape human interaction within the psy-complex.

[5] I do not wish to give the impression that ECT is administered only in *underdeveloped* and *authoritarian* parts of the globe. According to Johnstone (2003, 236) '[ECT] was given to approximately 11,340 patients in England in 1999, compared with a peak of around 28,000 in 1985'. Likewise, Rejali (2001, 101) has shown that 'the spread of electric torture is part and parcel of the spread of democratization', probably because electric torture does not leave a mark on the victim. Also it is worth remembering that 'the CIA expressed considerable interest in ECT devices. During World War II, a chief CIA psychologist advised John Foster Dulles that each surviving German over the age of twelve should receive a short course of electroshock treatment to burn out any remaining vestige of Nazism' (Rejali, 2001, 102). The point I am trying to make is that in other parts of the world there is at least a debate about ECT. In Iran there is only a debate about electric torture administered to *political* prisoners. Psychiatric patients are left at the mercy of reactionary psychiatrists with no qualms about using ECT as either treatment or punishment.

According to Birashk (2004, 381) in the earliest times, 'people with mental illness were believed to be entrapped by wicked ghosts'. The treatment of choice was seclusion, restraint, torture, burning and *trepanation* (making a hole in the skull in order to release the resident poltergeist). Zarathushtra, by introducing the first monotheistic world religion, moralised the relationship in terms of the battle of Ahura Mazda [Light] against Ahriman [Darkness] (Cohn, 1993).

The humanistic dimension of Zarathushtra's message gradually produced a different set of treatments for mental illness. Ghosts were now treated by the application of syrups, plants, concoction and spells (Birashk, 2004, 382). Misdeeds were not encouraged to fester in the psyche, meshing with guilt and eventually transforming into sins. Good deeds and not ascetic self-torment redeemed wrong-doing. Zarathushtra had sought a god that laughed and danced joyously. Sadness and gloom he associated with Darkness. However, with the advent of the Achaemenian dynasty (550-330 B.C.) and the later Sasanian (242-641 A.D.), Zarathushtra was institutionalised, his radicalism co-opted (Perlman, 1983). Magi (clergymen) came to monopolise the fight against mental illness. Since they were already the guardians of the state against subversion, the line between mental illness and rebellion became increasingly blurred.

The trail goes cold until the Middle Ages when 'psychology' (*ilm-o-nafs*) was studied in a philosophical/theological context. Personality development was now conceived of as a journey culminating in spiritual perfection (Kamarzarin, 2002, 5). Avicenna studied the interaction of mind and body in terms of psychology and neurology. 'He believed that many disorders resulted from a lack of harmony between the brain and the body' (Birashk, 2004, 382). Another Islamic physician, Razi, discussed medical ethics and employed crude conditioned reflexes in treating mental disorders. Birashk refers to him as the first Islamic 'behaviour therapist' (Birashk, 2004, 382). Jorjani's description of psychiatric symptoms, such as delusion, hallucination and affective conditions, is considered very close to modern standards (Mohit, 2001, 342). The existence of the famous Jondi Shapoor (established 271 A.D. as a teaching hospital) and Dar al-Shafa (also known as *house of insane*) hospitals catalysed psychological/psychiatric interventions.[6]

---

[6] In fact, it is fair to say that since Islamic Humanism enjoyed its heyday some 300 years prior to its European counterpart, psychiatric hospitals in the Middle East were also more advanced in terms of treatment (Mohit, 2001,

But perhaps the most relevant premodern figure for our purposes remains Ibn Khaldun (1332-1406). Over the years, the work of this Tunisian Muslim thinker has gained the status of progenitor of modern ideas in historical materialism and group psychology (Al-Azmeh, 1990, vii). A cross between Machiavelli and Vico, Ibn Khaldun gave history (as the narrative of human habitation of the world) a crude primacy- the kind of crudeness that would centuries later impress Engels but not Marx. Ibn Khaldun discussed psychology by introducing the concept of *asabiyya*, which is usually defined as social cohesion or group solidarity. However, this was a remarkably absolutist concept which denied the possibility of contestation by dissenters. In Bakhtinian terminology, one could accuse Ibn Khaldun of privileging 'official culture' over 'unofficial culture'. A recent promoter of Ibn Khaldun describes asabiyya in these terms:

> Asabiyya binds groups together through a common language, culture, and code of behaviour and when there is conscious approximation of behaviour to an idea of the ideal, at different levels, family, clan, tribe, and kingdom or nation … Asabiyya is what traditional societies possess … but which is broken down in urbanised society (Ahmed, 2002, 27).

This distrust of urbanisation and its corrupting influence on morality and 'psychic welfare' is a recurring theme of many reactionary ideologies and not confined to (certain brands of) Islam but in them it finds its most ardent champions.[7]

---

342). This relative superiority did not last very long and gradually patient care and psychiatry in general fell into decline. By the 17th century keeping patients chained up was quite common in Iran (Mohit, 2001, 343).

[7] I say 'certain brands of Islam' because according to some scholars, orthodox Islam was very much an urban movement. In fact, Arabistan in the seventh century consisted of a myriad of social formations ranging from Bedouin tribes, agricultural settlers, slaves and slave-owners, urban elites and merchants (Mir Fetrous, 1989, 13; Tokarev, 1989, 370; Rodinson, 1973, 36). Mohammad was a shrewd enough political operator to maintain the allegiances of all these factions but his reforms and those of the Caliphs who succeeded him were mostly in favour of further urbanisation. Modern Islamism is, with the exception of Afghanistan and one or two other cases, a mostly urban inspired movement. This is certainly true of its Iranian variant. And yet despite this *objective* interest in urbanisation, there remains a

Once sufficient obligatory praise is heaped upon ancient prophets and scholars of the Middle Ages, little else can be added regarding their contribution. The narration then usually hurls itself forward to the beginning of the twentieth century in search of modern Iranian psychology. Here all pretence of originality and native genius gives way to a rather meek and uncritical recounting of how modernist (mostly US) psychology was imported into Iran. The major mechanism in the early decades of the twentieth century was the translation of 'western' textbooks.

Ironically for a society renowned for its patriarchal tendencies, one of the very first psychology pamphlets was published in 1930 by a woman called Badr-ol-molook (Kamarzarin, 2002, 5).[8] The Minister of Culture ordered the establishment of the first psychology laboratory in 1933 under the supervision of A. A. Siassi. The first IQ tests were administered soon after in 1935 by M. B. Hushyar who was also responsible for publishing the first Iranian experimental psychology textbook in 1938 (Pereira, 2001). Until the 1940s 'lunatic' asylums (*dar-ol-majanin*) 'with poor conditions existed in Tehran, Hamadan, Shiraz and Isfahan' (Yasamy *et al.*, 2001, 381). From the 1940s onwards 'medical schools were established and psychiatry gradually emerged from them as a branch of modern medicine' (Yasamy *et al.*, 2001, 381). By 1950 a psychology programme was founded at Tehran University but the first psychology department was set up only in 1959 at the *National Teacher's College* in Tehran (Pereira, 2001).

The Psychological Association of Iran was established in 1968 under the Shah's regime but stopped its activities after the Islamic 'revolution'. In the 1970s a series of epidemiological research projects were initiated, new psychiatric hospitals built and the Tehran Psychiatric Institute formed in 1979, in the midst of the upheavals (Yasamy *et al.*, 2001, 382). The war with Iraq during the 1980s acted as a catalyst for the establishment of a comprehensive National

---

subjective undercurrent within Islamic thought deeply suspicious of cities and city mores.

[8] I have taken great care to cross-reference the dates mentioned in this section. However, since there is a certain amount of discrepancy in the original sources these dates should be treated as approximate tendencies and not absolute cut-off points. Since I have never been a practitioner within the Iranian psy-complex, I lay no claim to special insight. My critique has been generated from a distance and at times betrays its limitations.

Programme of Mental Health which was then integrated into the primary health care system in pursuit of 'efficiency' (Yasamy *et al.*, 2001, 381-382). At present there exists, to my knowledge, four nongovernmental psychology bodies which have taken over from the Shah's Psychological Association of Iran. A somewhat hazy division of labour has been engineered so that different professionals, such as clinical psychologists, counsellors and educational psychologists, can run their respective guilds (Birashk, 2004, 384).

This modernist psy-complex has been successful in marginalising premodern rivals such as shamans and traditional healers. For instance, 'seeking help from traditional healers as first contact has shifted from 40.2% in 1990 to ... 15.6% in 2000' (Yasamy *et al.*, 2001, 383). Rapid urbanisation may be seen as a corrupting influence on people but the psy-complex is also aware of its potential windfalls for expanding its power-base. Whereas rural areas have a 'community' based approach to mental health, urban areas rely more on the private sector and NGOs. Recently the creation of catchments areas around university hospitals with psychiatry services has been promoted in a bid to co-ordinate intervention (Yasamy *et al.*, 2001, 383). Despite such concessions to the private sector, the state remains in overall charge of the nation's 'mental health', since the reproduction of labour power is a central plank of the regime's survival strategy. From 1985 onwards, one week at the end of October has been designated 'mental health week' (Yasamy *et al.*, 2001, 385). In a society where national calendars are instrumentals in imposing 'official culture' (Bakhtin) on the proletariat, this represents both recognition of the scale of the problem and a feather in the cap of the psy-complex's lobbyists. Yasamy *et al.* (2001, 385), for instance, claims that 'during the mental health week in 2001, 245 mental health meetings and seminars and 4100 training sessions were held, and widespread news coverage of the week was found on national radio, televisions and other media'.

Although the majority of Muslim state officials have their roots in the natural sciences, the social sciences have witnessed a tremendous expansion in recent years. According to Birashk (2004, 385) there are currently about 17,650 students studying psychology. Around 4500 new students are accepted each academic year. As far as gender differences are concerned, 'there are four female students at the BA level for every male student; however, there are no significant differences in the number of female and male students at the MA and PhD levels' (Birashk, 2004, 385). The government still controls the course syllabi[9] but internet and satellite access has forced modifications.

Without wishing to overwhelm the reader with statistics, let me just add the following note in order to give a more coherent picture of the Iranian psy-complex: Overall there are 9.3 psychologists for every 100,000 people in Iran (Ghobari and Bolhari, 2001). Most clinical psychologists or psychotherapists 'prefer rational-emotive behaviour therapy (REBT), cognitive-behavioural, client-centred, or analytical approaches' (Birashk, 2004, 390). Psychiatrists are accredited with more organisational power than their 'inferior' psychologist colleagues and this is bitterly resented by the latter. This power imbalance is partly due to psychiatrists' greater numbers. There are around 735 psychiatrists in Iran and 50 new ones graduate each year (Mehrabi *et al.*, 2000). By contrast there are only 25 clinical psychologists with doctorates and 389 with master's degrees. In total around 7850 beds are earmarked for psychiatric patients (Yasamy *et al.*, 2001).[10]

THE OCTOPUS'S TENTACLES

Well, you see, Mr Skaggs, none are so dull as the people who think
they think.
- Paul Laurence Dunbar, *The Sport of the Gods* (1901[2005], 255).

Just like its marine brethren, the psy-complex has tentacles with which it engulfs its terrified victims, paralysing them with stinging poison. When feeling threatened it releases a black jet as cover for a fast getaway. I aim to look at some of its many tentacles in this section.

Birashk (2004, 385) insists that Iranian psychology has seven branches. He then goes on to list them: general (taught at 16 universities), educational (8 universities), clinical (13 universities), exceptional (7 universities), industrial and measurement (3 universities), and health psychology (at 1 university). These are

---

[9] In addition, 'students must pass a course entitled *Muslim Scholars' Views on Psychology*' (Birashk, 2004, 386).
[10] Mohit gives the figure of 9,200 for psychiatric beds and 1000 for psychiatrists (Mohit, 2001, 345).

regulated by two government ministries. To this list we should add psychiatry, social work and psychotherapy/counselling. Together they form the ten tentacles of the beast. Below I critically discuss some of them.

The psy-complex retained its sand-nigger status both under the Shah and the Ayatollahs. There was, however, a concerted attempt to *islamicise* all branches of the psy-complex after the consolidation of Islamic Fascism. These moves have been partially countered in recent times by secular critics but psychotherapy and counselling are still heavily tinged by an Islamic imperative. Overall religion does sadly permeate most other fields of the psy-complex, especially social work. Islamic therapists openly borrow from that other *cul-de-sac* of thought and reflection- Christian therapy.

The great charade carried out by psycho-religious therapy is threefold. First, psycho-religious therapy erects metaphysical entities such as *morality* instead of investigating the socio-economic background of mental problems. During the second move, it links morality with religion until the two become indistinguishable and, finally, it imposes this religious morality on the *patient*. Whilst Christian therapists have years of experience in expressing these manoeuvrings with subtlety, their Islamic counterparts dispense with all diplomacy and tact.[11] Hashemian (n.d.) is a typical example. He writes: 'there are close links between morality and religion … morality is valuing and seeking certain goals rather than others, obeying certain rules, being able to resist temptations … religions reinforce natural moral tendencies …'. Ominously Hashemian (n.d., 3) warns that 'religion can affect behaviours via fear of punishment …'.

Rebellion is conceived as 'incompleteness' or 'transgression' from the divine and this separation brings the rebel pain and suffering. Therapeutic techniques such as 'free-association,

---

[11] Of course not all Christian reactionaries express their dogma with subtlety. Promise Keepers, for instance, is a right wing Christian organisation founded in 1990 which blatantly calls for active male leadership to overcome women's increasing autonomy (Hepburn, 2003, 98). Their Iranian counterparts cite verses from the Koran as ideological justification for various psychological techniques. For example, behaviour control and modification apparently find legitimation in the following Koranic verse: 'Surely we have prepared for the unbelievers chains, fetters and a Blaze' (Mohammad, n.d. [1974], Man [76: 2-22]).

structured interviewing, persuasion, dream interpretation, hypnosis, psychodrama and role play' are then used to help the patient rediscover his/her 'inner feelings' (Hashemian, n.d., 7). Prayer and confession are also staple techniques of securing the power of the religious therapist/counsellor over the patient. Psycho-religious therapy is considered particularly useful for alcoholism, drug addiction, behaviour modification, conflict resolution and neurosis.

Having explained that most forms of therapy are imported from the US, Shamloo (n.d., 4) goes on to describe certain native forms of therapy. The technique of storytelling is all about reading a story relevant to the problems faced by the patient and using it to offer insights and possible solutions.[12] Poetry too is often used with the same aim. Iranian psychotherapists claim positive clinical evidence for this method (Farvardin, 1984). Meditation and mantras have also become fashionable relaxation techniques in some quarters (Rizvi, 1988).

One of the most hideous examples of therapy is the use of 'integration therapy' in prisons.[13] Tehrani (1997, 92) describes his version of integration therapy as follows: 'This therapy, based on humanistic psychological theory and the Islamic theory of the Unity of God and of all creation, recognizes that the healthy human can achieve harmonious integration of different subsystems'. Tehrani takes pride in foregrounding his anti-working class credentials. The following is a representative example of his viewpoint: 'A human being in prison is a human being in conflict with the rules of society.

---

[12] Whether storytelling therapies 'work' or not depends on whether these stories are contextualised to take on board wider social and political issues. It also depends on the motivation of the therapist. Most Iranian therapists use storytelling as an extension of preaching during which the patient is imbued with a set of reactionary values and role models. Critical examples of storytelling by Iranian subjects for effecting change and producing new knowledge are rare. Dossa's work with Iranian women in Vancouver (British Columbia) may represent one such example (Dossa, 2002).
[13] I do not claim to know much about the 'integrative movement in psychotherapy'. It is my understanding that it has its origins in the works of Russian scholars, V. V. Makarov and R. D. Tukaev (n.d.). It is an eclectic synthesis of past forms of therapy including cognitive-behavioural and psychoanalytic therapies. Its attraction for (some) Iranian psychotherapists seems to be its 'spiritual dimension' and the fact that 'native' therapies can find a home within foreign forms of therapy. I suspect Tehrani's version of integrative psychotherapy is a far cry from the original proposition.

Conflict with the environment often reflects a conflict within the self, marked by emotional turmoil, irrational thoughts, erratic (maladaptive) behaviours, and spiritual distress' (Tehrani, 1997, 92).

Tehrani claims support from earlier works on 'quest for meaning' (Jung, 1933), 'trust in God' (Frankl, 1969), and the need to reverse the youth's rejection of religion (cf. Seligman, 1988). Synthesising these writers with his own Islamic predilections, he states, 'Not submitting to God not only eliminates all hope of perfection, but brings about disharmony and disintegration' (Tehrani, 1997, 96). He even has the effrontery to claim, 'our acceptance of faith in the power of spirituality and religious belief ... in no way means that we preach, coerce, or unduly try to influence the inmates' (Tehrani, 1997, 101). There is worse to come. 'The inmates and staff', he patronisingly reassures his readers, 'tend to exist together in an atmosphere of care and sympathy' (Tehrani, 1997, 102). The fact that this fatuous, disingenuous Islamic fascist discourse (with a human face) is given credibility by a prestigious journal such as *The Journal of Humanistic Psychology* is indicative of how the mighty have fallen.

Far more realistic are accounts by investigators such as Baghai (2004) from a Vygotskian perspective about the incarceration of children and their mothers. He has looked at three groups: children born in prisons to 'politically active' mothers, toddlers moved to prison when the mother is arrested and those children arrested for political activity such as distributing leaflets or anti-government graffiti. Baghai rightly points out how these children are in effect hostages. In many cases the intended target is the father who has fled or living underground fearing immediate execution. Their *misbehaviour* is politicised by a regime which views all transgressions as 'westoxication'.[14] Anecdotal evidence suggests that

---

[14] 'Westoxication' (*gharbzadegi*) or 'West-stricken-ness' or even 'Euromania' is a term popularised by a reactionary fourth rate intellectual called Jalal Al-e Ahmad. 'I say that *gharbzadegi*', he writes, 'is like cholera [or] frostbite. But no. It is at least as bad as sawflies in the wheat fields. Have you ever seen how they infest wheat? From within. There's a healthy skin in places, but it's only a skin, just like the shell of a cicada on a tree' (quoted in Mottahedeh, 1987, 296). Al-e Ahmad hid his 'anti-modernist', petty-bourgeois Islamic rants under a pseudo-Fanon discourse. Most Iranian intellectuals (both religious and secular) were initially impressed by such

~ 54 ~

children around the age 5-6 suffer most of all, since they are old enough to sense the limitations of prison but too young to comprehend the reasons for their captivity (Baghai, 2004, 5). This is an excerpt from an inmate's account of a game children play in the dungeons of the Islamic Republic: 'the kids apply anti-septic balm on each other's feet and bandage [imaginary] wounds, then nurse each other to health' (Baghai, 2004, 6).

Due to their lack of contact with the outside world, some of these children do not comprehend the meaning of everyday concepts such as 'sandwich', 'ice-cream', and 'park'. Since sometimes the mother's interrogations lasts for months on end, the child is placed in solitary confinement. This is the hell Tehrani and the *Journal of Humanistic Psychology* attempt to sanitise.

Understandably the torrid times experienced by both incarcerated and non-incarcerated children in the Islamic Republic have led to the emergence of a loose *childsaving movement*. This is by and large a modernist secular response, although it also contains a minor religious reformist faction exemplified by the 2003 Noble Prize winner Shirin Ebadi, and filmmaker Samir Makhmalbaf's social work documentaries. It unites both internal and external dissidents who find in the plight of the child a useful site for contesting absolutist Islamic injunctions. Filmmakers such as Kiarostami document the lack of choice and opportunity for Iranian children (Fozooni, 2004, 86). Academics such as Darius Rejali (1994) brilliantly chart the moral geography of Iran and demonstrate how institutions are geared toward socialising working class children and saving upper and middle class children from sin and corruption. Lawyer-activists such as Mehrangiz Kar foreground and criticise the extensive networks of child labour which produce considerable profits for the clergy. Leftist political organisations abroad concentrate on exposing the sexual exploitation of children, whether this exploitation is carried out under the auspices of Shari'a law or not.

However, it is not in the interest of this childsaving movement to question either the concept of *childhood* or the sub-discipline of developmental psychology.[15] In fact the images of suffering children

---

xenophobic nonsense. Its influence lingers on in certain parts of the psy-complex.

[15] The only exceptions I can find to this generalisation are the works of Darius Rejali from a post-Foucauldian perspective (cf. 1994) and the

serve to reinforce precisely those qualities of powerlessness, passivity and dependence that define childhood (cf. Burman, 1994, 30). Iranian Leftist organisations abroad redefine the deprivation of childhood as a violation of 'human right'. Thus a bourgeois concept is consciously imported into discourse in pursuit of short term political expediency. This is exacerbated through the occasional (and usually politically motivated) charity campaigns launched by *Iranians* abroad in response to earthquakes, floods and drug addiction amongst the youth 'back home'. Here the discourse of childsaving is riding the crest of an earlier paternalistic discourse based on the *poor*.[16] The secular childsaving movement, therefore, is as zealous in its desire to see the entrenchment of schooling, social work, medicine and health psychology as its religious counterpart. Critical perspectives are easily squeezed out as impractical and quixotic.

Other sub-disciplines of the psy-complex have enjoyed a boost to their public portfolio and received generous budget allocations thanks to extraordinary events. For instance, neuropsychology gained prominence only after war broke out between Iran and Iraq in 1980 (Roozbehani, 2003, 1). This led to the first neuropsychology symposium in 1986 and closer ties to psychometrics and child and educational psychology thereafter (Roozbehani, 2003, 2). There is as yet only one dedicated neuropsychology research centre in Iran and only around 11% of psychology masters submitted are neuropsychology related but interestingly 'the most emphasized neuropsychology textbooks were those of Alexander Luria and Lev Vygotsky' (Roozbehani, 2003, 2).

Another sub-discipline enjoying a revival as a result of having to deal with a huge number of physically impaired war veterans is occupational therapy. Its origins in Iran are to be found in a World

---

translation of works by Vygotsky by a number of Iranian psychologists/academics (cf. Vygotsky, 1999).

[16] 'Children' and the 'poor' (sometimes as a synonym for *lumpenproletariat*) are fused discursively in other ways. They are both considered 'unproductive' (even parasitic) and politically dangerous since unpredictable (cf. Hardt and Negri, 2004, 130). Significantly the same emotional responses poverty-stricken children elicit in us through charity ads (cf. Burman, 1994) couched in terms of sympathy, guilt and disgust are also encouraged by political discourse regarding the poor. This constant, insatiable demand on 'our goodwill' is instrumental in arousing feelings of sadism against both children and the poor (Holland, 1992, 154).

Health Organisation initiative in 1971. There are now training courses in occupational, speech and physical therapies although trainees tend to complete their education abroad (Fallahpour, 2004, 1). It is claimed there are some 2,000 graduates in occupational therapy (Fallahpour, 2004, 1). The website for the Iranian Occupational Therapy Association (http://www.irota.org/index.htm) mentions Leuret in approving terms. Leuret's *Moral Treatment* (1840) was a mixture of paternal charisma and individual accountability usually backed up with narcotics such as morphine and opium.

To my knowledge Iranian occupational therapists have not shown any interest in the social model of disability which distinguishes between 'impairment' (i.e. the loss or lack of some functioning part of the body) and 'disability' (the way society turns impairment into exclusion, disadvantage and discrimination). In relation to Britain Chappell *et al.* (2001, 46) write, 'great efforts have been put into dividing disabled people from each other as they are channelled into segregated services aimed at specific impairment. By contrast, the social model emphasizes the re-casting of disability by disabled people and the importance of collective action'.

Most Iranian occupational therapists collude with authorities in concealing the political economy of disablement. Russell (2001, 87) has shown how 'industrial capitalism imposed disablement upon those nonconforming bodies deemed less or not exploitable by the owners of the means of production. The prevailing rate of exploitation of labor determines who is *disabled* and who is not'. The poverty rate amongst 'disabled' working class people has been increasing even in rich parts of the world such as the USA (Russell, 2001, 88). Their plight is even more acute in Iran, despite the fact that many constitute the regime's power-base. This is nowadays mostly a financial and no longer an ideological dependence. However, the co-option of impaired veterans through limited social services and sporting spectacles can no longer be taken for granted. Once *disabled* people begin collective protest, the clergy will lose a great deal of its remaining legitimacy.

Overall the Iranian psy-complex, therefore, seems to be a mostly imported US octopus. This rather uncritical transfer of psychological knowledge from one *fundamentalist* society to another should not surprise us unduly (cf. Moghaddam, 1987). Iran and the USA have a great deal of commonality. Both societies display a number of extreme divisions: the widening division between the ruling class and the proletariat; the increasingly unsustainable division between the private and public spheres of living and the evermore antagonistic division between religion and atheism. In both societies the same value-ridden politics (cf. Graeber, 2005) creates a monologic discourse well suited to maintaining *authoritarian* bourgeois hegemony. The proletariat, however, is capable of creating its own dialogic, multi-voiced discourse. There is, naturally, far more information about the resistance of US proletarians to the psy-complex (manifested through the rejection of drugs, therapy, incarceration and ideology) than its Iranian counterpart. The following section attempts to foreground some of the emergent themes of the Iranian psy-complex. The importance attached to these themes is loosely commensurate with the subversive threat they pose for the regime.

THE IRANIAN PSY-COMPLEX: SOME THEMES AND CREVICES

America is a great country with good people living in it. For this reason alone, I am optimistic that the necessary reforms will be embraced and our civilization renewed. However, as my grandmother taught me, God helps those who help themselves.
- Newt Gingrich, *To Renew America* (1995, 6).

Kirk: Spock, you want to know something? Everybody's human.
Spock: I find that remark ... insulting.
- (*Star Trek*, quoted in Bernardi, 1998, 69).

Lately the Iranian psy-complex has been waving its tentacles frantically. There are few taboo subjects beyond its reach nowadays. The Iran Statistical Centre has conducted studies in contraception usage and family planning. Abortion has been frowned upon since the emergence of the Islamic Republic and 'population growth' was ignored until 1988 when the government became concerned about long-term trends (Aghajanian, 1994, 67). Family planning, including contraceptive supplies, is now a major plank of the government's educational policy. False advertising is condemned by psychologists for undermining consumer confidence. These condemnations are posited in skull-numbing ethical discourse. For instance, one consumer psychologist advises 'Before advertising a product make sure you actually have it in stock'! (Mohammadian, 2005). The eating habits of teenagers are classified according to western notions of 'obsessive compulsive' behaviour and dieting (Mohammadi, *et al.*, 2004). Ironic since in the 'West' anorexia was considered a theological matter until the Georgian and Victorian eras when medicine created its own discourse around the subject (Hepburn, 2003, 112). Iranian psychologists abroad concentrate on how women immigrants adapt better to new circumstances than their husbands and discuss marital conflict and second-generation cultural conflicts (Darvishpour, 2002). Although these are all topics worthy of further investigation, I have chosen to foreground the following themes since they seem to be of greater urgency to the psy-complex itself.

Personal relations

Pop psychology plays an inordinately vital role in shaping the agenda of the Iranian psy-complex. In a way, pop psychology is merely courting and then mediating the concerns of real people in the same manner the media employs *vox pop* techniques to gather intelligence whilst strengthening the grip of (bourgeois) *common sense*. At the top of pop psychology's list of concerns is the issue of personal relations. In most other societies this would be a subject unworthy of serious attention. But the lack of public forums and civil societal modes of expression makes it an essential conduit of information in the Iranian context.

Take a reactionary pap like *Men Are From Mars, Women Are From Venus* (Gray, 1992). According to a recent report this is a bestseller in Iran with most of its 60,000 copies being purchased by 18- to 24-year-olds (Psychology Today, 2005). Fathali M. Moghaddam maintains that although most of the readers consider themselves part of the 'secular educated class, the idea of relationship self-help is an integral part of Islam' (Psychology Today, 2005). He also points out an irony we have already alluded to above- that whilst Iran's universities were being purged of 'Western-educated psychologists after the revolution, [today], American psychology is more dominant than before the revolution … In addition, more than half of the psych professors are women' (Psychology Today, 2005).

The clerical ruling elite comprehends the need to regulate and police affective labor and since it has already fetishized women as unique repositories of affective labor, it stands to reason that it should employ them for the delicate task of managing personal relations. Not surprisingly in a society where men hide their inadequacies behind Islamic laws and patriarchal traditions, another pop psychology bestseller, *All Men Are Jerks Until Proven Otherwise* (Schwartz, 1999) was banned by the Ministry of Culture and Islamic Guidance.

Islamic discourse moralises every aspect of personal relationships, from lonely heart ads (which have lost some of their business-like stuffiness and become as playful as their western examples perhaps due to the influence of the Net), to prostitution (which is attacked periodically as part of the regime's anti-women, anti-gay and anti-working class moral crusades). In fact, it could (and has) been argued that Islam whilst coming down hard on open prostitution and paedophilia, has institutionalised both within a strict set of protocols. The Islamic attitude toward prostitution and paedophilia not only goes to the heart of its hypocrisy but it also exposes the fascist ideals at the heart of regime's scholars.[17] University Professor, Mohammad Hussein Farjad is a particularly odious example. In an interview he provides us with the following nuggets of wisdom:

> Prostitution is an anti-social phenomenon threatening the health of the individual, family and the whole society ... Sometimes, mental disorders in men and women lay the groundwork for the scourge of prostitution ... poverty does not lead to prostitution ... social welfare may result in prostitution ... City Hall [...] should air music and stage plays and films [for the youth in order to discharge their energies positively] ... Prostitution is the major reason for AIDS ... (Entekhab, 2002).

This vile attack on sex-workers is related to the rulers' loss of control over *undesirable* sexual liaisons. A new liberated verbal and gestural language of desires is being forged in contemporary Iran. The attacks on prostitution and homosexuality are in reality attempts to curb this

---

[17] See interview with Marieme Hélie-Lucas in *Trouble & Strife* (2002, 46-53) for an interesting Algerian perspective on Islamic Fascism.

emerging sexuality.[18] The resistance of sex-workers and gay proletarians to draconian Islamic prescriptions ought to serve as a source of inspiration for the rest of the class. I would even go as far as claiming that the Islamic theocracy fights against the very notion of 'joy'. Ehrenreich's work sensitises us to the historic battle between joyful proletarian carnivals and ritualistic authoritarian spectacles (Ehrenreich, 2007). The recent threat to fine, ban and publically flog two popular Footballers for 'over-celebrating' and 'inappropriate behaviour' on the pitch (The Freethinker, 2011) is a stark reminder of the Islamic spectacle's need to control capitalist social relations through images.

A few dissident voices here and there are trying to give voice to this oppositional sexuality. For example, the Scandinavian–based journal *Homan* (http://www.homanla.org/) defends the rights of Iranian gays and lesbians with informative well-researched articles from a (mostly) social-democratic perspective. The German-based *Shahrzad* specialises in erotic Persian literature and poetry and from a modernist Feminist-Leninist perspective (which is to say atavistic) magazines like *Medusa* (http://www.medusa2000.com/) chart the relationship between religion and prostitution. There are also gay and lesbian Iranian groups in the USA and West European countries. These groups, by and large, confine their activities to *educating* other Iranians about homosexuality, domestic violence, honour killings, exposing some of the myths circulated by reactionary propagandists (both religious and secular), lobbying and the occasional public demonstration.

Authoritarian vs. democratic personality

Another discursive theme that permeates the fabric of society is the clash between the *authoritarian* personality and its *democratic* opposite. This discourse began life as a translation project focusing on the Frankfurt school. It then found a resonance within discussions of Fanon, colonialism, dependency, conspiracy theory and paranoia in the 1960s and 70s. Today it can be observed in the strangest of crevices, especially as it seems to be in a symbiotic relationship with the renewed interest in Freudian sexuality.

---

[18] For a fascinating clash of opinion about homosexuality in the Netherlands between Muslims and the host society see Hekma (2002).

Even pop psychology is getting on the act. Ashtiani (2003) compares the *authoritarian personality* and the uncritical reverence such an individual may feel for the leader with the respect the child bestows upon the parent. This cross-fertilisation between social and developmental psychology may seem atavistic and methodologically unsound by the standards of 'western critical psychology' but it is noteworthy how readily even such banalities can generate political ramifications in present-day Iran. The *democratic* person, Ashtiani (2003) goes on to explain, is akin to a rebellious teenager who emphasises group decision making in order to disempower the Father.

At a higher level of academic rigour there has always been a general interest in writers such as Freud, Fromm, Adorno, Horkheimer, Benjamin, Brecht, Korsch, Marcuse, Habermas, Sartre and Merleau-Ponty. The recent additions to this canon are also illuminating: Reich, Foucault and Wittgenstein. Reich's work on fascism and sexuality has been debated for perhaps the first time amongst Iranian intellectuals and Foucault[19] and Wittgenstein have inserted a postmodernist note on debates surrounding incarceration, absolute knowledge, word-games and the expansive definition of freedom. In my view, the addition of Michael Billig's early work on fascism (1978) and more recent investigation into 'banal nationalism' (1995) would be a great way of updating this debate. From a different perspective the translation of works by Vygotsky, Bakhtin and Todorov has created a whirlpool of relevant ideas. Chomsky is read both as a linguist and a libertarian socialist and Negri's warm reception in Iran during a recent conference is indicative of ideological affinities (Power, 2005). Last but by no means least, one should mention the excellent translation of Marx and a number of anarchists whose output was either unknown or studied through biased intermediaries.

The *authoritarian vs. democratic* personality debate has had at least three interesting side-effects. Firstly, certain criticisms that would not have been tolerated by the regime in any other context have been aired under the auspices of the psy-complex. The reasons for such a manoeuvre are unclear to me. Clearly the reformist wing of the ruling class has been trying to liberalise society as a matter of

---

[19] The attention bestowed upon Foucault is a decidedly double-edged sword considering his naïve dalliance with Islamic fascism (cf. Afray and Anderson, 2005).

survival. This recent 'tolerance' may be part of the same top-down process of liberalisation witnessed in other fields. Alternatively, one should never underestimate the intellectual tardiness of the Islamic elite. It could very well be that their censorial radar is simply too crude to pick up on various subtle critical discourses circulating in and around this debate.

Secondly, critics of Iranian racism directed against Afghani, Kurdish and Arab citizens and foreigners in general have also been active in this debate through promoting the *democratic personality* as an ideal worthy of pursuit. If would be interesting to see whether this debate within the psy-complex can catalyse a more radical critique of Iranian racism in the future.[20]

Finally, it is crucial to remember that the debate has not been an unbridled success for the advocates of *democratic personality*. Both Nietzsche and Jung have been mobilised (sometimes unfairly) in order to cement the arguments of the other camp which still believes passionately in divine authority, hierarchy, patriarchy and charismatic leadership.

Drugs, self-burning and suicide

Youth has pushed its way up the list of issues causing concern to the ruling class. A great deal of paternalistic energy is consumed in defining, guiding, educating and disciplining the *youth*. The so-called opposition reaffirms this constituency through epidemiology and statistics and in the process positions itself as the youth's natural ally.

---

[20] Even well-intentioned Iranian psychologists are beginning to objectify 'foreign minorities' such as Afghans (cf. Kalafi *et al.*, 2002) in a rerun of the way the American psy-complex treated descendants of slaves. *We cannot ignore Iranian racism simply because Iranians themselves have become the sand-niggers of the world.* Iranian racism must be combated not only because it is wrong but also because it undermines the class struggle. In my view, it has at least three distinct roots which occasionally forge an unofficial alliance to better assault the victim. These three ideological roots are: 1) the Islamic doctrine which bases its racism on cultural and religious discrimination; 2) the Zoroastrian religion as misinterpreted by Monarchists with its pretensions of Aryan supremacy; and, 3) parts of the secular-Left which employs crude 'scientific socialism' in order to conceal their anti-foreign prejudices.

The majority of the *youth* are, of course, young proletarians as alienated from the product of their labour as they are from theocracy. Their rejection of the present state of affairs seems total: football fans that use the game to destroy government properties; students who refuse religious accounts of history; party animals who live through a haze of 'recreational' drugs, music and sex; youngsters who run away from home instead of tolerating sexual abuse; those who reject Islamic dress-codes, Friday prayers and military service; and finally those who 'drop out' by either using stronger drugs or through the ultimate act of defiance- suicide.

The same hypocrisy at the heart of 'Western' attitudes toward drugs is to be found amongst the clergy. Whilst drugs such as opium and nicotine have been socialised and distributed through mafia-like cartels supported by some elements from within the regime, alcohol is associated with 'Western decadence' and *prohibited*. The bravado is as farcical as the 1920 US prohibition and has proved a bonanza for a number of Islamic *families*.

The role of the psy-complex in dealing with *addiction*, with considerable help from foreign NGOs and UN agencies one might add, has been threefold: First, there has been a concerted effort to bamboozle the public with figures and statistics as opposed to the mullah-bourgeoisie's preferred tactics of suppressing relevant information; second, the psy-complex acts to de-contextualise drug usage by suppressing the economic, cultural and political reasons behind the 'turn to drugs'[21]; and third, the psy-complex offers a range of reductionist and instrumentalist therapies as a way of earning its keep.

The above criticisms should not be read as an attempt to belittle the scale of the problem. According to (ideologically loaded) figures

---

[21] Occasionally a reductionist, sociological connection may be made with high levels of unemployment the way second-rate 'western' sociologists have habitually explained away the rise of fascism. The other traditional method of explaining away heavy drug use is to blame everything on the 'other', in this case Afghani drug dealers. As an aside I would like to add that I have been briefly stopped and searched as a suspected drug dealer in both Tehran and London. (OK, there was also that time when I was picked up as a possible 'card-boy' in Kings Cross, but we won't go into that!) What struck me was the superiority of the political discussion that ensued with my Iranian interrogators. They seemed so much better informed and politically sophisticated compared to their swinish London brethrens.

from a 2005 UN report, Iran is the highest ranking country in terms of drug addiction (some 2.8% of the 70 million population are classified as addicts). The number of 'youth' considered 'addicted' to heroin is around 200,000 (Kayhan, 2005). Opium is used by 37% of the 'addict population', followed by cannabis and heroin with rates of 21% and 19% respectively (Yasamy *et al.*, 2002, 385).

At the beginning of the reign of the mullahs, government policy was geared towards supply-reduction strategies. When it became apparent that such a strategy was as effective as drug policies in neighbouring Afghanistan, supply-reduction was complimented with demand-reduction programmes. There are now about 130 outpatient clinics and some 300 beds reserved for the treatment of drug users and a concurrent Narcotics (semi)Anonymous self-help group with 10,000 members (Yasamy *et al.*, 2002, 385). One does not wish to be flippant about a serious issue but it is becoming increasingly apparent that these demand-reduction strategies too are proving as helpful as Nancy (Just Say No) Reagan's 1980s PR campaign. Capitalism, whether *western* or *eastern*, does not possess the desire, the theoretical know-how or the practical resources to come to terms with this complex problem.

What the psy-complex euphemistically calls 'self-harm' finds another macabre manifestation in the practice of self-burning. In the Mazandaran province alone (adjacent to the Caspian Sea) there were 318 recorded cases of self-burning in a 3 year period. The average age was 27 and 83% of victims were female. The major motive was described by the investigators as 'marital conflict' (Zarghami *et al.*, 2002, 115). Once the problem is identified as 'self-harm' due to 'marital conflict' the psy-complex then takes refuge in inane positivist investigation which have already *proved* the high correlation between Islamic counselling (independent variable) and marital adjustment (dependent variable) (Danesh, n.d.). Before leaving the subject it is worth speculating how many of these cases are acts of 'self-burning' and how many are, in fact, murders committed by hateful husbands/in-laws dressed up as suicide. For the present we are unable to establish a more accurate picture.

Unnatural disasters: Earthquakes and traffic accidents

Hurricane Katrina exposed many things, chief amongst them the increasing gulf between the collective *consciousness* and *humanity* of the US proletariat and their bourgeois masters. The frequent tectonic eruptions experienced by Iran, especially the disastrous 2003 Bam earthquake played a similar function. Whilst the proletariat understood the culpability of capitalism in failing to warn, take preventive measures, treat the injured and reconstruct shattered lives, the rulers responded with a nauseating mixture of religious fatalism, pie in the sky platitudes and psycho-babble.

The psycho-babble became an opportunity for Iranian psy-complex to find a new niche for itself. Its professionals descended on the hapless equipped with their 'multi-stage stratified sampling methods' and 'General Health Questioannire-12 measures' to ingeniously conclude that people with old age, females, less educated individuals, divorced or widowed and unemployed respondents, and those with loss of more family members in the earthquake reported more severe psychological distress (Montazeri *et al.*, 2005).

The sceptic reader might interject that the volume of Methadone shipped to Bam (apparently 30% of the survivors are on Methadone-Kayhan, 2005) was a clear enough indication of levels of distress. One must expect future disasters to further enhance psy-complex's profile. Whether the depoliticised, asinine interventions earthquake victims have had to endure thus far will continue unabated or not remains to be seen.

Another problem that has attracted the attention of Iranian psychologists is traffic accidents. Seventy people are killed in traffic accidents on a daily basis, giving Iran another notorious world top ranking (BBC.Persian.com, 2005). Some 75% of these accidents are apparently due to 'driver error' with car problems and dangerous roads accounting for 14% and 11% respectively (Note that none of these deaths are accredited to capitalism!). The capital (Tehran) is a world-beater when it comes to the number of motorcycles on the road, currently standing at around 2,000,000. Naturally enough, cognitive psychologists have found this a lucrative field of endeavour.

A RADICAL 'IRANIAN' CRITICAL PSYCHOLOGY?

The voice of our complaint implies a vengeance.
- Ottobah Cuguoano, in Sakolsky and Koehnline, *Gone to Croatan*
(1993, 148).

> *You think I have visions*
> *Because I am an Indian.*
> *I have visions because*
> *There are visions to be seen.*
> - Buffy Sainte-Marie, in Zinn, *A People's History of the United*
> *States* (2003, 536).

I am a sand-nigger. This much I know since almost every time a Tony Blair, a David Cameron, a Donald Rumsfeld, a Hilary Clinton, a Barack Obama or a Condoleezza Rice open their mouth, I find my sand-nigger status reaffirmed. Similarly, the Iranian psy-complex in its present state is no more than sand-nigger psychology- derided, dependent, infantilised, subservient and second-class. The preceding pages have charted its evolution and the collusion of its practitioners with dominant modes of psychology. Whether this collusion is practiced intentionally or inadvertently is in many ways a moot point.

However, no official culture is monologic enough to be able to dispense indefinitely with proletarian re-accentuation. In this context I choose to re-accentuate this unsolicited identity by polarising sand-niggers into two camps: *house-sand-niggers* and *field-sand-niggers*.[22] I despise the former and belong to the latter. This much I can do since the contours of this antagonism are already with us. House-sand-niggers are apologists for Islamic capitalism who preside over the Iranian psy-complex (their American and European counterparts endeavour to defend the original European psy-complex). Field-sand-niggers comprise all 'professionals' and 'users' within and outwith the psy-complex who have a stake in subverting its activities. The term 'sand-nigger psychology' is thus the perfect description and

---

[22] This is a political distinction and must not be mistaken for a geographical or occupational differentiation. In other words, I am *not* saying that Iranian psychologists living in Iran are house-sand-niggers and those of us living abroad are field-sand-niggers. No! I am introducing a *political* distinction between those who wish to perpetuate Islamic or Christian capitalism and those who stand in opposition. According to this criterion, the overwhelming majority of Iranian-American psychologists for example are also house-sand-niggers (whether they know it or not). As Harriet Tubman would say: 'I freed a thousand slaves, I could have freed a thousand more if only they knew they were slaves'.

analysis of the status quo. In its re-accentuated form, it also provides us with a fight-back strategy.

Precisely because 'Iranian' Critical Psychology is emerging with a time lag compared to its counterparts in other parts of the globe, it must aim to be better, much better. All the more so since the class struggle in Iran is approaching the point of no return. This much is self-evident to me.

I wish to end this article by proposing an alternative to the status quo. Without wishing to pre-empt the nascent Radical 'Iranian' Critical Psychology (R'I'CP), the following general characteristics strike me as a sensible starting point:

1. R'I'CP should be nurtured from the most radical social struggles being waged against the psy-complex, whether in Iran or elsewhere. These struggles will benefit from Luria's notion of *living spontaneity* (Luria, 1961) and Vygotsky's concept of *joint action* (Vygotsky, 1962). As such R'I'CP recognises no artificial national boundaries and welcomes contributors from all fields and nationalities. It does, however, aim to concentrate on Iran in the hope that gains in that part of the world would enhance Critical Psychology worldwide.

2. R'I'CP should not limit itself to mere *criticism* which can only humanise the psy-complex but a fully-fledged practical *critique* (cf. Korsch, 1971). Likewise, R'I'CP should not limit itself to mere deconstruction but aim from the outset to reconstruct human relations based on a post-capitalist human *community* (cf. Camatte, 1978 and 1995).

3. R'I'CP should reject the false choice offered critical psychologists between pre-modernism, modernism and post-modernism. Although willing to learn from any source that strengthens our praxis, we should remain deeply suspicious of *ideologies* not created by the world proletariat in the course of its struggle against wage-slavery and the state.

4. R'I'CP should not only expose the positivist, empiricist, individualistic, dualistic, reductionist and instrumentalist practice of the Iranian psy-complex but engage with all those topics deemed taboo: religion as a form of abuse and/or mystification; capitalist alienation and exploitation and its connection to mental problems;

Iranian racism against 'minorities'; the connection between the Mosque and paedophilia; sexual oppression and the inherent heterosexism of monotheistic religions (here the body of work on gay and lesbian issues in the 'West' will be of immense value); the function of politeness, shame and etiquette in repressing controversial issues from everyday discourse and the role played by drug companies and psychiatry in pacifying discontent.

A victory for R'I'CP in the midst of a more general social revolution would have a tremendous impact on Critical Psychology worldwide. It will provide us with an opportunity to reject profit-seeking and alienation in favour of a reconstituted set of human relations based on genuine need and desire.

REFERENCES

Afray, J. and Anderson, K. B. (2005) *Foucault and the Iranian Revolution, Gender and the Seduction of Islamism.* Chicago: University of Chicago.

Aghajanian, A. (1994) Family Planning and Contraceptive Use in Iran, 1967-1992. *International Family Planning Perspectives,* June, 20(2): 66-69.

Ahmed, A. S. (2002) Ibn Khaldun's understanding of civilization and the dilemmas of Islam and the West today. *The Middle East Journal,* winter, 56(1): 20-46.

Al-Azmeh, A. (1990) *Ibn Khaldun.* London and New York: Routledge.

Ashtiani, A. F. (2003) The Root Psychology of Democracy. *Social Psychology*, no. 1, [Farsi]. http://www.jamee-psy.com/official/jameepsy/view.asp?ID=84056 (accessed 13 August 2005).

آشتیانی، علی فتحی (1382) ریشه های روانشناختی دمکراسی. *روانشناسی جامعه.* شماره 1.

Baghai (2004) *Prison and its effect on children's development.* [Farsi]. http://bidaran.com/article.php3?id_article=49 (accessed 11 August 2005).

بقایی، غلامرضا (1383) *زندان و تاثیر آن بر رشد کودکان: طرح یک تحقیق پیرامون کودکان زندانی در زندانهای سیاسی جمهوری اسلامی در دهه ی شصت خورشیدی.*

BBC.Persian.com (2005) Iranian programme for reducing road accidents. [Farsi]. http://www.bbc.co.uk/persian/business/story/2005/09/050911_ra-ka-iran-road-accidents.shtml (accessed 2 October 2005).

برنامه های ایران برای کاهش تلفات و هزینه های (2005) BBC.Persian.com
تصادف. کاوه امیدوار.

Bernardi, D. L. (1998) *Star Trek and History: Race-ing toward a white future.* New Brunswick, New Jersey and London: Rutgers University Press.

Billig, M. (1978) *Fascists: A social psychological view of the National Front.* London: Academic Press.

Billig, M. (1995) *Banal Nationalism.* London: Sage.

Birashk, B. (2004) Psychology in Iran. In K. Pawlik and M. Rosezweig (eds) *The Handbook of International Psychology.* London: Sage. Chapter 23: 381-394.

Burman, E. (1994) poor children: charity appeals and ideologies of childhood. *Changes,* 12: 29-36.

Camatte, J. (1978) *Community and Communism in Russia.* London: Unpopular Books.

Camatte, J. (1995) *This World We Must Leave and Other Essays.* New York: Autonomedia.

Chappell, A. L., Goodley, D., and Lawthom, R. (2001) Making connections: the relevance of the social model of disability for people with learning difficulties. *British Journal of Learning Disabilities,* June, 29(2): 45.

Cohen, N. (1993) *Cosmos, Chaos and the World to Come: The Ancient Roots of Apocalyptic Faith.* New Haven and London: Yale University Press.

Danesh, E. (n.d.) *The efficacy of Islamic counselling on improving marital adjustment levels of incompatible couples.* http://www.iranpa.org/pdf/054.pdf (accessed 23 august 2005).

Darvishpour, M. (2002) Immigrant women challenge the role of men: how the changing power relationship within Iranian families in Sweden intensifies family conflicts after immigration. *Journal of Comparative Family Studies,* Spring, 33(2): 271-301.

Dunbar, P. L. (1901[2005]) *The Sport of the God: and Other Essential Writings.* Modern Library.

Ehrenreich, B. (2007) *Dancing in the Streets: A History of Collective Joy.* London: Granta Books.

Entekhab (2002) Prostitution in Iran: An interview with Professor Mohammad Hossein Farjad. *Entekhab* (Persian Morning Daily), Tuesday, June 11, Vol. 4, No. 898.

Farvardin, A. (1984) *Poetry Therapy.* Dehkhoda Press.

Fozooni, B. (2004) Kiarostami debunked! *New Cinemas: Journal of Contemporary Film,* 2(2): 73-89.

Fallahpour, M. (2004) *A Review of Occupational Therapy in Iran.* http://www.uswr.ac.ir/IRJ/Lpublished/Areview.htm (accessed 23 September 2005).

Foucault, M. (2000) *Iran: The Spirit of a World without Spirit and 9 Other Interviews.* [Farsi]. Tehran: Nay Publications.

فوکو، میشل (1379) *ایران: روح یک جهان بی روح و 9 گفتگوی دیگر.* ترجمه نیکو سرخوش و افشین جهاندیده. تهران: نشر نی.

Frankl, V. (1969) *The will to meaning.* New York: New American Library.

Ghobari, B. and Bolhari, J. (2001) The current state of medical psychology in the Islamic Republic of Iran. *Journal of clinical psychology in medical settings,* 8(1): 39-43.

Gingrich, N. (1995) *To Renew America.* New York: HarperCollins Publishers.

Graeber, D. (2005) Preface: Spring 2005. *thecommoner: a web journal for other values,* 10: 4-65. www.thecommoner.org (accessed 26 August 2005).

Gray, J. (1992) *Men Are from Mars, Women Are from Venus: A Practical Guide for Improving Communication and Getting What You Want in Your Relationships.* HarperCollins Publishers.

Hardt, M. and Negri, A. (2004) *Multitude: War and Democracy in the Age of Empire.* New York: The Penguin Press.

Hashemian, K. (n.d.) *A Comparative Analysis of Islamic and Christian Psychotherapies.* http://www.iranpa.org/pdf/042.pdf (accessed 21 September 2005).

Hekma, G. (2002) Imams and Homosexuality: A Post-gay Debate in the Netherlands. *Sexualities,* 5(2): 237-248.

Hepburn, A. (2003) *An Introduction to Critical Social Psychology.* London, Thousand Oaks and New Delhi: Sage Publication in association with Open University.

Herbert, F. (1965[1988]) *Dune.* London: Hodder & Stoughton.

Holland, P. (1992) *What is a child? Popular images of childhood.* London: Pandora Press.

Johnstone, L. (2003) A shocking treatment? *The Psychologist,* 16(5): 236-239.

Jung, C. G. (1933) *Modern man in search of a soul.* New York: Harcourt Brace & World.

Kalafi, Y., Hagh-Shenas, H. and Ostovar, A. (2002) Mental health among Afghan refugees settled in Shiraz, Iran. *Psychological Report,* February, 90(1): 262-266.

Kamarzarin, H. (2002) Country Profile: Iran. *Psychology International, American Psychological Association Office of International Affairs,* winter, 13(1): 5.

Kayhan (2005) *Based on the number of addicts, Iran becomes the highest ranking country in the world.* [Farsi].

کیهان (1384) *از لحاظ تعداد معتادان، ایران در جهان اول شد.* شماره 1075، 13 مهر ماه 1384 خورشیدی، صفحه 3

Korsch, K. (1971) *Three Essays on Marxism.* London: Pluto.

Leuret, F. (1840) *Du Traitement Moral de la Folie.* Paris.

Luria, A. R. (1961) *Speech and the Regulation of Behaviour.* London: Pergamon Press.

Makarov, V. V. and Tukaev, R. D. (n.d.) *The integrative movement in psychotherapy.* http://www.iranpa.org/pdf/095.pdf (accessed 24 August 2005).

Marx, K. (1871[1993]) *The Civil War in France.* [Farsi]. New York: International Publishers.

مارکس، کارل (1380) جنگ داخلی در فرانسه. ترجمه باقرپرهام. تهران: نشر مرکز.

Mir-Fetrous, A. (1989) *Contribution Aux Études Islamiques.* [Farsi]. Montréal : Farhang.

میرفطروس، علی (1368) اسلامشناسی: پرتوی در مطالعات اسلامی. مونترال: انتشارات فرهنگ.

Mehrabi, F., Bayanzadeh, S. A., Atef-Vahid, M. K., Bolhari, J., Shahmohammadi, D. and Vaezi, S. A. (2000) Mental health in Iran. In I. Al-Issa (ed) *Al-Junun: Mental Illness in the Islamic World* (pp. 139-161). Madison, CT: International Universities Press.

M. J. (1998) Men are from Tehran ... women are from Isfahan. *Psychology Today.* http://cms.psychologytoday.com/articles/pto-19980501-000002.html (accessed 14 October 2005).

Moghaddam, F. M. (1987) Psychology in the three worlds: as reflected by the crisis in social psychology and the move toward indigenous third world psychology. *American Psychologist,* 42: 912-920.

Mohammad (n.d. [1974]) *The Koran.* London: Penguin Books.

Mohammadi, M. R. *et al.* (2004) Prevalence of obsessive-compulsive disorder in Iran. *BMC Psychiatry,* 4: 2.

Mohammadian, M. (2003) False advertising. *Social Psychology,* no. 1, [Farsi]. http://www.jamee-psy.com/official/jameepsy/view.asp?ID=84179 (accessed 6 July 2005).

محمدیان، محمود (1382) کجروی ها و انحرافات در تبلیغ. روانشناسی جامعه. شماره 1.

Mohit, A. (2001) Mental health and psychiatry in the Middle East: historical development. *Eastern Mediterranean Health Journal,* 7(3): 336-347.

Montazeri, A. *et al.* (2005). Psychological distress among Bam earthquake survivors in Iran: a population-based study. *BMC Public Health,* 5: 4.

Mottahedeh, R. (1987) *The Mantle of the Prophet: Religion and Politics in Iran.* Peregrine Books.

Pereira, M. E. (2001) History of the Psychology: A TimeLine of Psychological Ideas. http://www.geocities.com/Athens/Delphi/6061/en_linha2.htm (accessed 14 July 2005).

Perlman, F. (1983) *Against His-story, Against Leviathan!* Detroit: Black & Red.

Power, N. (2005) Persian Empire. *Radical Philosophy,* March-April, Issue 130. http://www.radicalphilosophy.com/default.asp?channel_id=2193&editorial_id=17194 (accessed 10 July 2005).

Rejali, D. (2001) Electricity: The Global History of a Torture Technology. Originally appeared in *art.politics.theory.practice,* June, 101-109. Also

available at
http://academic.reed.edu/poli_sci/faculty/rejali/rejali/articles/History_of_
Electric_Torture.htm (accessed 10 September 2005).
Rejali, D. (1994) *Torture & Modernity: Self, Society and State in Modern Iran.* Boulder, San Francisco, Oxford: Westview Press.
Rizvi, S. A. A. (1988) *Muslim Tradition in Psychotherapy.* Lahore: Institute of Islamic Culture.
Rodinson, M. (1973) *Mohammed.* London: Penguin Books.
Roozbehani, A. (2003) Neuropsychology in Iran. *International Neuropsychological Society Liaison Committee Newsletter,* summer, 12: 1.
Rose, N. (1985) *The psychological complex: Psychology, politics and society in England 1869-1939.* London, Boston, Melbourne and Henley: Routledge & Kegan Paul.
Russell, M. (2001) Disablement, Oppression, and the Political Economy. *Journal of Disability Policy Studies,* Fall, 12(2): 87.
Sakolsky, R. and Koehnline, J. (1993) *Gone to Croatan: origins of North American dropout culture.* New York and Edinburgh: Autonomedia and AK Press.
Schwartz, D. D. (1999) *All Men Are Jerks Until Proven Otherwise: A Woman's Guide to Understanding Men.* Adams Media Corporation.
Seligman, M. E. P. (1988) Boomer blues. *Psychology Today,* October, 50-55.
Shamloo, S. (n.d.) Psychotherapy in Iran. http://www.iranpa.org/pdf/007.pdf (accessed 12 October 2005).
The Freethinker (2011) Iranian footballers face a flogging after televised bottom-pinching incident. http://freethinker.co.uk/2011/11/05/iranian-footballers-face-a-flogging-after-televised-bottom-pinching-incident/ (accessed 6 November 2011).
Tokarev, S. (1989) *History of Religion.* Moscow: Progress Publishers.
Trotsky, L. (2001) *Marxism and Terrorism.* [Farsi]. Pathfinder Press.
تروتسکی، لئون (1380) مارکسیسم و تروریسم. ترجمه مسعود صابری. تهران: نشر طلایه پرسو.
Trouble & Strife (2002) *Fundamentally Fascist,* summer, 43: 46-53.
Vološinov, V. N. (1929[1986]) *Marxism and the Philosophy of Language.* Cambridge, Massachusetts and London, England: Harvard University Press.
Vygotsky, L. S. (1962) *Thought and Language.* Cambridge, MA: MIT Press.
Vygotsky, L. S. (1999) *Mind and Society: The Development of Higher Psychological Processes.* [Farsi]. Translation: Behrooz Azabdaftari. Tehran: Fatemi Press.
ویگوتسکی، لو سیمونوویچ (1378) ذهن و جامعه: رشد فرایندهای روانشناختی عالی. ترجمه بهروز عزبدفتری. تهران: انتشارات فاطمی.

Williams. R. (1973) Base and superstructure in Marxist cultural theory. *New Left Review*, 82, Nov-Dec.

Yasamy, M. T., Shahmohammadi, D., Bagheri Yazdi, S.A., Layeghi, H., Bolhari, J., Razzaghi, E. M., Bina, M. and Mohit, A. (2001) Mental health in the Islamic Republic of Iran: achievements and areas of need. *Eastern Mediterranean health Journal,* May, 7(3): 381-391.

Zarghami, M. and Khalilian, A. (2002) Deliberate self-burning in Mazandaran, Iran. *PubMed*, March, 28(2): 115-119.

Zinn, H. (2003) *A People's History of the United States: 1492-Present.* New York: HarperCollins Publications.

Fuck Critical Psychology! Paper presented at the International Conference on Critical Psychology, 27-31 August 2003, Bath University.

You might have noticed that there is a slight change to the published programme. Firstly, I have chosen to take this opportunity to offer my impressions of the International Conference on Critical Psychology in lieu of my original talk [I was originally slated to talk about Vygotsky and his 'zone of proximal development']. And second, Ian Parker decided at the last minute to dissociate himself from this paper since he could not go along with my alterations [a white lie calculated to make things dramatic, and at the same time ensure any flak from the audience would be directed at me and not my supervisor, Professor Ian Parker].

I wish to make clear that my criticisms of this conference are in no way a reflection on the organisers [Bath University], since I feel they have gone out of their way to make us feel welcomed. I have enjoyed the food, the fishponds, and the city architecture and the digs I have been allocated are far more splendid and spacious than I deserve.

My gripe is with critical psychologists and what they have become. The degeneration of Critical Psychology brings to mind Oscar Wilde's *The Picture of Dorian Gray*. As Dorian Gray's public image gets a makeover, its basement representation goes through various stages of decomposition [in fact, this is also true of a number of sexy-sub-fields within the sciences. The amount of praise neuropsychology, economics and genetic engineering receive from the media is not commensurate with their real progress toward establishing the Arcadian dream of capitalism to have perfect workers producing for a perfectly self-sustaining system.]

Moreover, I feel the frequency of such acts of *sympathetic white magic* [e.g., ritualised conferences such as this gathering or the Oscars ceremony or the Maori Potato Dance- that is any ritual where magic is used to increased productivity and bind the group in anticipation of future crises] and their success in attracting gullible fresh meat and super-star keynote speakers conceals a chronic malaise within this *imagined community*. And let me emphasise that we are dealing with an imagined community in the sense described by Benedict Anderson.

I became acutely aware of this when we were being arm-twisted into joining Valerie Walkerdine's International Network of Critical Psychology [at this stage Professor Walkerdine heckled the proceedings with the words: 'Oh, shut up Babak!' Clearly I did NOT but it was gratifying to know academics are still capable of badgering!]. Valerie's mistake was in assuming there is a coherent 'we', with a shared set of values and principles who wants to and needs to communicate more effectively. Even before deciding on an agreed framework, her so-called autonomist friends were cajoling us into joining yet another bourgeois outfit based on the separation of the executive and legislative branches of power complete with specialist bureaucrats in charge of planning conferences, designing the website and collecting union subs.

Recently the use of the magical term 'non-hierarchal' has become a ritualistic excuse for blindly tail-ending bourgeois modes of organising and communicating. This is as true of Valerie Walkerdine's Network as of reactionary outfits such as Indymedia [If you have noticed Indymedia replicates many of the stylistic and formatting procedures of mainstream media. In terms of content, one has to plough through too many inane, wishy-washy liberal/libertarian pronouncements before finding a radical perspective]. The use of the term 'International' is also problematic since it covers up the backwardness of *inter*-national cooperation in both its Leninist and anarchist versions. Some currents within the 'anti-capitalist movement' have already gone beyond mere *inter*nationalism. Neither the term 'global' nor 'trans-national' fully capture the nuances of this achievement. No doubt a new word will be conjured up once the consciousness of this leap is generalised.

In contrast to Valerie, I feel Ken and Mary Gergen [key proponents of 'postmodernist psychology'] are mindful of blindly tail-ending bourgeois modes of representation. Their performance [a singing and banjo routine preceded their talk] was a courageous attempt to supersede the mundane drudgery of conference speechifying. Since I am tone deaf I cannot comment on their artistic credentials as either actors or banjo players. However, even here two concerns should be raised: Firstly, it seems to me that a host of previous radicals have already provided us with a superior set of tools for subverting bourgeois representation. I have in mind here, amongst others, the Dadaists, Surrealists, Lettrists and Situationists. To try to equip Critical Psychology with a watered down version of such past currents strikes me as both atavistic and self-indulgent.

Secondly, no amount of stylistic innovation can make up for lack of originality in content. Critical Psychology may be able to get along with yesterday's leftovers but the class struggle deserves something better!

Things soon took a turn for the worse. I don't mind admitting that I almost left the conference for the sanity of my London flat after Professor David Canter's contribution. Posited at a fresh level of imbecility, Canter's presentation was a cross between a Tupperware sales' pitch and an exercise in management consultancy. The fact that he was not booed off the stage is testimony to the prevalent atmosphere of liberalism that has always been a part of Critical Psychology but is now shamelessly foregrounding itself.

Talking of booing and heckling and all those transgressive moments of emotive projection, another question comes to mind: why are today's critical psychologists so completely devoid of passion? Apart from Michael Billig and Steve Reicher and one or two other contributors, I have experienced bland, boring, pedantic talk after talk during the last four days. If the researchers can't get turned on by their work, why the hell should I? And is it my imagination or are the younger members of this imagined community even more reactionary and spineless than the Founding Fathers? (Who less we forget 'are very brave and courageous and risked their careers to create a new space for the rest of us'?) [This is how one lackey narrated the creation story of Critical Psychology]!!

And finally, I give fair warning that if I hear one more fucking critical psychologist bullshit moralistically about reconciliation between nation-states (as did Daniel Bar-Tal in relation to Palestine and Israel) or racial reconciliation between races (as in south Africa or Australia), I shall dispense with niceties and really tell you what I think of your profession. As increasing number of proletarians are becoming aware of the reactionary nature of 'nation', 'race' and religion the continued misuse of these terms to provide capitalism with a human face becomes unacceptable. Radical proletarians actively fight for a wage-less, money-less, nation-less world human community. If critical psychologists are too boring and inane to keep up with us, that ought to be your problem. Do not make it ours!

Once I used to say: 'Critical Psychologists, one last effort if you want to be revolutionaries!' How utterly naive of me. Now all I have to say to you is this: 'Slow down this freakin' bandwagon. One or two of us want to get off without breaking an ankle!'

Thank you for your time and enjoy the rest of the conference.

Iranian Women and Football

To the outside world, the periodic dispute surrounding the eligibility of Iranian women to attend football matches may seem atavistic. After all, to have the holocaust-denying President Ahmadinejad paternalistically grant you the right to attend sporting events one day, only to have the decision vetoed by the 'supreme spiritual leader' Khamenei the next, is suggestive of a political climate embroiled in pre-modernity (cf. BBCPersian.com 2006a, 2006b).

The fragility of the regime explains how the most mundane reforms may trigger a political crisis. More concretely it foregrounds some of the tactical tensions between the state-bourgeoisie and the clerical-bourgeoisie. Ahmadinejad's decree was a populist manoeuvre calculated to head-off protests by Iranian feminists in the run up to the 2006 World Cup in Germany as well as an attempt to broaden his government's support base in anticipation of future domestic and foreign challenges. By arguing that change would bring 'chastity' and 'morality' to the stands (Bickerton, 2006), he was perpetuating the essentialist rhetoric of patriarchy. The clerical fatwa was a sharp reminder of his short leash and when even some of his most ardent supporters within the Pasdaran 'Revolutionary' Guards and the pressure group Ansar-e Hizbollah demonstrated against him, the initiative was quietly shelved. It is interesting to note that the same essentialist mindset has been deployed more recently in Turkey with the Turkish Football Federation punishing fan 'misbehaviour' at certain clubs through imposing a 'women and children only' attendance policy (*The Guardian*, 20 September 2011).

Ahmadinejad and a minority of clerics such as Rafsanjani and Khatemi within the ruling elite have been forced to acknowledge the deep-seated frustrations of Iranian women. The huge celebrations that followed Iran's qualification for the 2006 World Cup once again witnessed scores of women and young girls disregarding injunctions about the veil and mingling with the opposite sex. The smaller protests outside the gates of the stadium in Tehran prior to the match involved women carrying placards such as, 'A few steps to freedom' and 'We refuse to remain offside'! In the same year the movie *Offside* (Dir. Panahi) depicted young women who attend football matches by disguising themselves as boys. More recently, a number of struggles against the Islamic hejab and gender segregation in public places including universities and public transport, attempts by feminists to increase the age of consent, access to nurseries, contraceptives, abortion rights, employment opportunities, divorce and inheritance laws, and, last but not least, participation in sports have brought together a vast coalition of women activists from different backgrounds. As Janet Afary (1996) has correctly pointed out,

> ... [Today] independent secular feminist movements are steering a highly dangerous course between Scylla and Charybdis. On the one side is the antifeminist religious opposition offering women a degree of security and protection if they adhere to the strict code of conduct of the Muslim patriarchal culture but denying them their individual rights. On the other side are secular and authoritarian governments giving women a degree of economic and social equality yet denying everyone, including women, autonomous political and civil rights. This was the quagmire Iranian women found themselves in the late 1970s.

It is precisely to evade this false choice that many Iranian women have chosen sport as a site of contestation. It took the ideologues of the Islamic Republic around a decade to grasp the significance of sport as a mechanism of regulation (cf. Sabūri 1996). The nagging ambivalence that persists is rooted in the clergy's recognition that sport, especially football, can easily be transformed from a tool of conformity into an arena of resistance (cf. Chehabi 2002). In an earlier article I suggested football was initially championed by middle-class civil modernizers who were opposed by an authoritarian political elite. The ruling class (first the monarchy and then the mullahs) gradually discovered the financial and political rewards of football and introduced mechanisms by which Taylorism, competition and division of labour could shape the game into a profitable enterprise (Fozooni 2004, 368).

This chapter foregrounds an under-researched area of the women's movement. I claim that the periodic political controversy regarding women's attendance at football matches is indicative of wider social conflicts. I look at Iranian women's participation in football as fans, players and administrators of the game. Relevant examples from Turkey, Argentina, China, Japan and USA are provided as counterpoints. Finally, I demonstrate how this movement is catalysing both Iranian feminism and the wider working-class social movement confronting the clerical-bourgeoisie.

Whilst upper and middle-class Iranian feminists have been articulating their demands at least since the Constitutional Revolution of 1906, working class women have had to tread more judiciously. Football celebrations have permitted the latter to express grievances and link up the private and public spheres of struggle. The present Iranian feminist movement has some commonalities with the tensions that existed within the Pankhurst family and I think it would be instructive to pursue this analogy.

Needless to say, the entire history of political infighting amongst the Pankhursts is not reducible to class issues. However, for my purposes it is sufficient to point out that ideologically speaking, Emmeline, Christabel and Sylvia fall respectively in the upper, middle and working class camps. This is certainly true of the period 1917-1924 when following the radicalizing impact of the Russian revolution and before her sympathetic turn towards national liberation movements, Sylvia Pankhurst represented the best of the British anti-Parliamentarian communist tendencies. Here is Jen Pickard (1982) commenting on the difference between Sylvia and the rest of the family,

> The names of the Pankhurst family are synonymous with the struggle to win the vote for women, but what distinguished Sylvia Pankhurst's approach from that of her mother Emmeline and her sister Christabel were class issues . . . It resulted in the 1920s, after nearly twenty years of struggle, with Emmeline standing as Tory Parliamentary candidate and Sylvia becoming a founder member of the British Communist Party ... The seeds of such a divide were there from the early days of the suffragette organisation ...

In 1901 'women workers in the Lancashire cotton mills linked the right to suffrage to the removal of discrimination and exploitation and presented a petition of 29,000 signatures to Parliament demanding the vote' (Pickard 1982). A century later Iranian working women make the same kind of linkage when they unite their demand to participate in sport with wage claims. Women's spontaneous and anonymous resistance has become widespread. For instance, in 1997 'a group of young women went on the offensive in Tehran when they broke into a stadium which security forces had assigned for men only' (Mojab 2001, 129). The demand to enter stadiums was closely linked to the desire for a looser dress-code and better job prospects.

In a similar vein to Sylvia's criticisms of symbolic militancy (e.g., sacrificial tactics such as hunger strikes), Iranian women workers are also moving away from vanguardist displays of bravado and toward more collective modes of resistance. I am not suggesting hunger strikes are always reactionary. Sometimes they may be the only method of publicizing the imprisonment and torture of radicals by the state. However, the vanguardist and moralistic dimensions of this tactic seem to have been at the forefront of both British suffragettes and bourgeois Iranian feminists. In this sense, a realization and supercession of the limits of such moral forms of education by deed seem to be a positive step in the right direction [for a fuller discussion of the relationship between 'sacrifice' and revolutionary activity see Ken Knabb (1977)].

Whilst upper and middle-class Iranian feminists wax lyrical about the need to synthesize the personal and political, proletarian women actively seek to harmonize victories in the public domain with emancipation in the private sphere. Of course, the boundaries and functioning of the 'private' and 'public' spheres are different in contemporary Iran compared to Europe and the US (cf. Ayubi 1995). The public space seems to be far more tightly controlled, moralistic and ritualistic in Iran and the private sphere is defined by Islamic authorities not in terms of a 'free' privatized realm of conscience but as 'what is left over after the public is defined' (Tajbakhsh 2003, 876). Having said this, it is my contention that in Iran sport plays a similar role to some newspapers and internet websites in pushing back certain taboos by making public what was private. In a society based on absolutist morality and the maintenance of a vast distance between the private and public this move is rightly perceived as a threat to the regime's very existence (cf. Abdo 2003).

Football, occupying a liminal position in this regard, has acted as a crucial bridge. As bourgeois morality also tries to occupy and guard the same space, it was inevitable that football participation would engender moral transgressions. Since sexual revolution and football have become intimately linked, the clergy has tried its utmost to limit both heterosexual and homosexual interactions in sport. It has failed. There are two interrelated issues here.

First, sport provides an opportunity for what the feminist Gayle Rubin has called 'homosocial' relationships (cf. Rubin 1975, Sedgwick 1985). These refer to same-sex relationships that may be charged with eroticism but not necessarily sexual. An example would be the all-male culture of medieval knighthood. Another would be the tendency of corporate executives to fraternize with and promote other men at the expense of (better qualified) women. Contemporary Iranian sporting life would be a stark manifestation of homosocial spaces where internal autonomy is constantly undermined by external patriarchal forces.

Second, sport also provides an opportunity for both homosexual and heterosexual relations to develop in relative 'freedom' from the surveillance apparatus set up to limit sexual liaisons. My position is that Iranian sporting life has always been one of the most liberated and permissive spheres of activity. Under the Islamic Republic and with the imposition of a puritanical view of sexual interaction, this space has been (unsuccessfully) militarised and moralised. The threatened flogging of two Persepolis footballers for 'inappropriate touching' during a goal celebration indicates the insecurity of Islamic masculinity (The Freethinker, 2011). What is interesting is how this relatively liberated regime of gestures, bodily contact and sexual liaison is now percolating into the sporting sub-culture of fans.

This failure to prevent transgressive sexual liaisons has a corollary in the abortive external attempts by foreign (mostly Anglo-American) bourgeois forces to support 'civil society' and 'alternative leadership' within Iran. The privileging of (liberal and social democratic) Iranian women artists and the granting of the 2003 Noble Peace Prize to an Iranian woman lawyer (the reformist Muslim, Shirin Ebadi) fall in this category. The Emmeline and Christable Pankhursts of the Iranian feminist movement fail to exploit this opportunity because most Iranian women have no illusions in reforming either Islam or capitalism. They know, as did Sylvia Pankhurst, that only a root and branch social upheaval is capable of delivering them genuine emancipation. Football has come to play a pivotal role in the process of self-organization of working women and their fight against both religious and secular forms of patriarchy.

ISLAM, SPORTSWOMEN AND CARNIVALESQUE

When it comes to discussing the relationship between Islam and sportswomen, the unintentional wit of Muslim thinkers is side-splittingly delicious. A prominent Muslim scholar, Sayyad Rezā Pāk-Nezhād, opines,

> Frankly, most people do not approve of sportswomen ... experts are of the opinion that sportswomen lose 50% of their femininity, as they have to endure constant and arduous training in order to achieve international standards. Naturally, they grow rough and speak coarsely. They do not even care about men's opinions of them anymore ... Women must not play football or rugby. These are not feminine sports. Instead they should play volleyball, basketball or skiing without losing their feminine charm ... (quoted in Sabūri 1996, 82, own translation)

The author goes on to quote a 'scientific article' in the British *Daily Mirror* to substantiate his claims that 'sporting activities make women unattractive' (Sabūri 1996, 82). Clearly, he does not seem to have grasped the black humour of British tabloids otherwise he would have chosen his scientific evidence with more care.

Related to these admonitions is the bane of all Islamic sport ideologues, namely, 'nakedness' in sport. Nakedness is perceived as one of the most shameful legacies of 'imperialism'. Even Iranian sportsmen are targeted by the regime for 'wearing make-up', colouring their hair and tattooing their skin (BBCPersian.com, 2005). In 2010 Grand Ayatollah Golpayegani declared that female athletes winning sports medals is a form of 'humiliation' [for men and Islam] (Dehghanpisheh, 2011). This prudish facet of Islamic sporting doctrine is close in spirit to Latin American populism and Spanish Francoism.

If Latin America and Iran populisms share similar hegemonic strategies, it is also the case that the proletarians of these two regions follow parallel modes of resistance. Bakhtinian carnivalesque makes a regular appearance in the gamut of defying gestures hurled at the bourgeoisie by both sets of football fans. Pablo Alabarces writes about the carnivalization of Argentinean football and the authorities' project of co-opting its subversive elements,

> The stadium seems to become the place for inverting hierarchies, for realizing the democratic illusion of modernity, and for verifying the point that equality and meritocracy are pure republican fantasy ... The stadium provides a sense of communal ownership for those who feel excluded. (1999, 82)

The clerical-bourgeoisie possesses a number of qualities making it 'superior' to its monarchal predecessor. For one thing, even after decades of dominating the people, it retains more organic links with society than the Shah's regime did at the end of its tenure. However, in many respects, its level of sophistication falls far short of its 'Western' and Argentinean counterparts. Recuperating the subversive elements of the carnivalesque is simply not within its purview. Eagleton's (quoted in Alabarces 1999, 82) cautionary description of carnival as a 'controlled rupture of hegemony' may have some relevance in a 'Western' context but in Iran the carnivalesque is nearly always on the side of emancipation and nearly always uncontrollable (cf. Ehrenreich 2007, 102-105).

Nowhere is this more evident than in women's relation to football. Unlike Argentinean female fans who 'speak the male language' when attending matches and do so without the 'prospect of creating autonomous space because of the strength of Argentinean male traditions' (Alabarces 1999, 82), Iranian women occasionally manage to use football to invert patriarchal mores. In a society where female sexuality and the reproduction of labour power are as heavily guarded as the tomb of Ayatollah Khomeini, any infraction is tantamount to full-blown rebellion. When the national team returned from Australia after qualifying for the 1998 World Cup,

> several thousand women, mostly young, invaded the Azadi ('Freedom') stadium where the national heroes were being welcomed, even though the media had called on its sisters to stay at home and watch it on TV. (Bromberger 1998, 5)

Their demand seemed innocuous enough: 'We want to celebrate too. We aren't ants!' (Bromberger 1998, 6). To reject the condition of the 'ant' (i.e., being small and insignificant) is in this context also a denunciation of the ant's mortal enemy, the 'cockroach', which in Iranian culture is a term of abuse for mullahs.

The 'grotesque' aspects of carnival are particularly worthy of attention. In a historical study of European carnivalesque, Gross mentions the prevalence of 'undesirable' types, such as 'vagabonds, gypsies, ne'er-do-wells, [and] prostitutes', or what some of us without a hint of irony or romanticism may prefer to call the 'undomesticated proletariat', as a vital cog in this defensive strategy. The ungovernability of this section of the working class in present day Iran has been a constant source of despair for the regime's 'moral police'. The mullahs' fear of this strata is linked to the latter's sexually charged forms of resistance against puritanical hypocrisy. This more sensuously adventurous section of the proletariat has been directly responsible for suspending official rules and etiquettes of behaviour during football protests and permitting voyeurism without embarrassment. In a culture where gaze-aversion is sanctioned in moralistic terms, the unashamed voyeur becomes a radical. Naficy (1999, 53) reminds us that in the Islamic system of looking 'the eyes are not passive organs like ears . . . eyes are active, even invasive organs, whose gaze is also construed to be inherently aggressive'. An extreme version of this notion was expressed by Ayatollah Ali Meshkini, 'Looking is rape by means of the eyes ... whether the vulva admits or rejects it, that is, whether actual intercourse takes place or not' (quoted in Naficy 1999, 54). It is, therefore, understandable how unashamed gazing becomes a threat to such a worldview.

Carnival, it will be remembered, is the celebration of the 'grotesque body' and 'lower bodily stratum' such as sexual promiscuity, alcohol consumption, fattening food and uncontrollable bodily movements. This type of dissent allows the raising of 'the threshold of shame and embarrassment' (Norbert Elias, quoted in Stallybrass and White 1986, 188). What I am claiming is that there is direct link between female football fandom and the corpus of secular, theatrical games known in Farsi as *bazihayé namayeshi*. These are festive occasions where women perform roles concerned with their everyday lives in an egalitarian setting and away from the disciplinary male-gaze. As Safa-Isfahani (1980, 36) describes, 'Their festive mood is marked by food, drink, special music, dancing, singing, costumes, makeup, bawdy language, joking, and horseplay ... the exclusion of males is especially emphasized in those dealing with erotic themes'. Female fans preparations for games and the creation of a homosocial space with bawdy chanting and dancing function similarly to performances of *bazihayé namayeshi* in challenging male-centred norms and values.

WOMEN FOOTBALLERS AND PUNITIVE RESTRICTIONS

Authorities nearly always put obstacles in the way of sportswomen. This is as true of 'regressive' Iran as 'progressive' USA, Japan and China. In China the phenomenon of 'the female blossoming and the male withering' is typical of the football 'community' (Jinxia and

Mangan 2001, 92). 'The serious participation of Chinese women in modern football began [only] in the early 1980s' (Jinxia and Mangan 2001, 93). Yet by the mid-1980s they dominated Asia and by the 1990s they were amongst the very best in the world. Despite these achievements, they were constantly overlooked in terms of budget allocation and training facilities,

> They were housed in a former warehouse. There were no electric fans in the summer and no hot water for showers. Owing to the shortage of dinner tables, those who arrived late for meals had to stand. In addition, there were so many mosquitoes that, at one meal, one player was bitten 27 times. The situation gave rise to the belief that women were being penalized for taking up so prominently a 'man's sport' - and perhaps being doubly penalized for doing so well at it! (Jinxia and Mangan 2001, 93)

In Japan women, as both players and fans, are 'managed' as part of a very deliberate marketing strategy. The J-League actively pursues the younger generation as consumers and ironically also as 'trend-setters', in the hope of enhancing the League's fashion image (Nogawa and Maeda 1999, 229). A very institutionalized form of 'carnival' was encouraged by authorities to change 'spectating behaviour from traditional passive style to a much more pro-active European style' (Nogawa and Maeda 1999, 229).

Significantly 'female spectators use patriarchal language at [away] matches much more freely than socially permitted in their daily settings', although most never engage in pitch invasions or violent behaviour (Nogawa and Maeda 1999, 229).

Iranian women seem to be more defiant in their displays than their Chinese or Japanese counterparts. After qualifying for the 1998 World Cup millions of people burst into the streets to party. Significantly,

> Young women were seen brazenly pulling off their black scarves, dancing with men and in some cases drinking alcohol in defiance of Islamic law. This street party went on for hours - and the authorities did not try to stop it. (Thomsen 1998, 4)

The ban on alcohol is perhaps the most effective way for Islam to distinguish its corporate identity from its main monotheistic rival -

Christianity. Given the severe penalties for transgressing this law, one could argue Iranian women's defiance of it, is more radical than similar behaviour by mediaeval European women during carnivals. Mary Roth (1997, 4) drawing on historical connections between intoxication and creativity suggests: 'Carnival is unthinkable without mood alteration, and no other component of the carnival mixture explains the quality of transformation better than drink and drugs'. Intoxication was also a catalyst of carnival behaviour in the Bacchanalia 'when wine [would] inflame their minds, and night and the mingling of males and females, youth with age, [would destroy] every sentiment of modesty ...' (quoted in McGinty 1978, 15-16).

What is more, drinking, even when not accompanied by literal intoxication, is conducive to further discursive transgression. As Martin Johnes has argued regarding soccer crowd disorder in South Wales,

> Verbal misconduct was viewed gravely by the game's authorities. It did not fit into their middle-class ethos of fair play and decorum, while the bad language often involved also offended ... swearing was common both in the conversation and jeers of the crowd ... occasionally prosecutions that resulted in heavy fines were brought against spectators and players who swore at games. [One] judge thought it 'scandalous' and 'monstrous' that such a thing could go on in a town like Merthyr with its educational establishments, schools and churches, particularly when it was overheard by women. (2000, 21)

During the Tehran leg of the Iran-Republic of Ireland World Cup qualifier in 2002, Iranian female fans were barred from attending the match on the grounds that the vulgar language now routinely used by male proletarians would corrupt their 'sensitive nature'. Some forty Irish women fans, however, were allowed to attend the match at Azadi stadium as their lack of Farsi protected them from 'cultural contamination'. Forced to wear a *hejab* they were consistently harassed by petty-minded Iranian police officers for the slightest infringement in dress-code (Byrne, 2002). Occasionally, women's defiance has forced the clergy on the defensive, although the intensity of repression seems dependent on wider class conflicts in society. Since 2011 women, already banned from attending matches, have also been thrown out of public screening rooms.

GENDER AND 'BIO-POWER'

Recent Iranian football riots (mid 1990s onwards) have been celebrations of life during which hierarchy and official culture have been temporarily suspended. Protestors not only sing and dance but, to borrow a term from Barbara Ehrenreich (2007), do so 'ecstatically'. Writing about Renaissance Europe, Craig Brandist (1996, 64) comments,

> ... the official culture was dismembered, its pomposity and inadequacy paraded in a ritual of popular scepticism. Carnality and corporeality were brought into unrestrained and familiar contact with the sacrosanct and dignified elements of ruling culture, leading to the emergence of grotesque combinations which deprives the official culture of its authority and fear-inspiring elegance.

The fear of the flesh is connected to the ruling elite's fear of losing dominance over the reproduction of labour power. It should be noted that even before the mullahs' rise to power at the end of the 1970s, the clergy enjoyed massive influence within the family and what Foucault called the realm of 'bio-power',

> [The family and the mosque] also acted as factors of segregation and social hierarchization ... guaranteeing relations of dominance and effects of hegemony. The adjustment of the accumulation of men to that of capital, the joining of the growth of human groups to the expansion of productive forces and the differential allocation of profit, were made possible in part by the exercise of bio-power ... The investment of the body, its valorisation, and the distributive management of its forces were at the time indispensable. (Foucault 1984, 141) [Added in order to concretise the link between family, mosque and bio-power.]

The clerical-bourgeoisie, traditionally more adept at extracting surplus value form the family rather than the factory, is now being threatened at its power base. More terrifying still for the bosses is the feedback loop that seems to have been established between workplace struggles over exploitation and safety with cultural and social struggles for freedom.

Those who see 'Islamic Fundamentalism', 'Islamism', 'political Islam' or whatever one chooses to call the resurgence of Islam initiated in the 1970s as a mere feudal aberration, steeped in 'catholic' rites, might raise an eyebrow at my claim that it also possesses a 'modern' impulse and a puritan asceticism. In fact, future historians may come to describe the Islamic Republic's ideology as a resurgence of fascism combining a 'protestant work ethic' with a 'catholic guilt ethic'. This distinction has become gender specific in contemporary Iran, in the sense that men's bodies are accorded classical status through 'muscular Islam' and the protestant work ethic, whereas women's bodies are emasculated through invisibility and the catholic guilt ethic. Since just like 'muscular Christianity' this Islamic doctrine envisions muscular growth, morality and masculinity to be interwoven (Wiegers 1998, 149), women, who are denied the right to muscular growth and outdoor activity, are de facto categorized as immoral.

WOMEN AS FOOTBALL PLAYERS

The role of Iranian women is not confined to fans, of course. In August 1998 for the first time since the 'Islamic Revolution' forty women 'took part in an amateur football training session at Tehran's Hejab Stadium' (Ghazi 1998, 1). They participate passionately in female indoor leagues and at a reasonably decent international standard. In 2008 Iran women's Futsal team won the West Asian Futsal Tournament. Three defeats to Ukraine in 2011 suggests there is room for improvement. Apart from football women are active in at least 24 other sports including,

> karate, judo and gymnastics ... Many women have been trained in recent years as referees and coaches - about 16,000 of them, in all sports ... Iran now has 56 international-level women trainers for volleyball and 6 for fencing ... and in recent months, women have been taking part in motor racing. (Ghazi 1998, 2)

The list of small victories is growing all the time. In 2006 Iranian footballers hosted a German club side BSV Aldersimspor- the first proper match the Iranian women had ever played against other footballers and in front of fans (Haeming, 2007). The return match due to be held in Berlin was banned by the 'moral police' since by then a new assault on Iranian feminists had been ordered from above.

These gains have been won by women in the teeth of clerical opposition, making them more significant than concessions granted from above. The struggle has fostered a combative collective identity that is jealously guarded by Iranian women (especially proletarian and petit-bourgeois women) who see themselves as the champions of freedom against Islamic tyranny. Cynthia Fabrizio Pelak (2002, 95) has shown in the context of the emergence of a women's collegiate ice hockey club in the mid-western US in the 1990s that,

> the club members are not political actors by virtue of their sharing a common structural location but rather through the creation of a collective identity in the course of struggling against discrimination at the ice rink.

Collective identity theorists argue that in order for subordinate groups to resist hegemony, 'they need to come to some common understanding of their experiences' (Pelak 2002, 95). Crucially three factors help to forge their collective identity: boundaries, consciousness and negotiations.

> Boundaries are defined as the social, psychological, and physical structures that highlight differences between subordinates and dominants; consciousness refers to the interpretative frameworks used by a challenging group to define and realize its interests; and negotiations are the symbolic and everyday actions that subordinate groups take up to resist and restructure existing systems of domination. (Pelak 2002, 95)

Regarding *boundaries* one could suggest that Iranian women (of all classes) crossed most social and psychological borders long ago. Yet many physical boundaries still persist, precisely because the clergy cannot afford to acknowledge defeat publicly. Decorum demands pretence, hence, the physical separation of women spectators from men in sporting arenas and their continued segregation on public transport. With respect to what Pelak calls *consciousness*, one could posit that Iranian women employ different interpretative frameworks to challenge their oppressors depending on their class position. Bourgeois and petit-bourgeois feminists usually limit themselves to formal, legalistic and educational *negotiations* whilst proletarian feminists occasionally aim higher within football as coaches and players.

However, the pettiness of patriarchs of both religious and secular variety is an ever-present source of frustration. The most recent controversy regarding Iranian women footballers relates to a Fifa ruling that their full-body strip and head scarf was in contravention of the rules. Iran was banned from playing in an Olympic 2012 qualifier against Jordan moments before they were to start the match. FIFA officials defended the decision by claiming 'the headscarf could pose a choking hazard' (Dehghanpisheh, 2011). Iranian authorities countered by claiming their new kit had taken into account earlier concerns expressed by Fifa and had received Sepp Blatter's personal seal of approval (*The Guardian*, 6 June 2011). The problem also relates to the description of the headwear as either a hair covering cap (allowable under the rules) or a hejab (a religious symbol impermissible according to Fifa protocols). No sooner was the Bahraini official responsible for the decision accused of political machinations by Iranian officials that yet another trivial issue had managed to become a diplomatic crisis.

IRANIAN SPORTSWOMEN AS 'DISABLED'

In a society where 'attacking female cyclists' by fascist gangs of the Ansar-e Hizbollah (literally, 'supporters of the party of God') is considered a legitimate negotiating opening bid (Petrossian 1996, 1), and invading the Muslim public space with the cacophony of pop music and rap is tantamount to a declaration of counter-hostilities (Pelham 2001, 1), leisure becomes a fierce site of social contestation. In such a hostile climate, even partisans of the regime such as the daughter of ex-President Rafsanjani find it difficult to push for women's participation in sports. Nevertheless, women players and referees defend their right to play and officiate in front of a mixed crowd: 'For the young people, qualifying for the World Cup is far more important than the presidential election ...Young people cannot reach their goals through politics, but the World Cup gives us some excitement. Football is a means of escape' (Elaheh Moladoast quoted in The Guardian, 6 June 2005).

The Islamic literature on women shows that clerics view women as 'disabled'. If Iranian women are considered 'disabled' by the ruling elite, then Iranian sportswomen are doubly so. Chappell et al.

(2001, 2) define disability as 'a construct of the social and economic structures of a society at a particular historical point'. To put it differently, the social model posited by Chappell et al. (2001)

> distinguishes between *impairment* (i.e. the loss or lack of some functioning part of the body) and *disability* (i.e. the meaning society attaches to the presence of impairment) ... People with impairments are disabled by a society that excludes, disadvantages and discriminates against them.

In this case both the impairment and the disability are rhetorically constructed through religious propaganda and imposed by a patriarchal regime in need of total subservience. Chappell et al. (2001, 2) show that 'great efforts have been put into dividing disabled people from each other as they are channelled into segregated services aimed at specific impairments'.

Comparing my case study with the role played by football in Britain's deaf community underlines the analogy. To counteract loss of hearing, deaf people use sign language. Through social networks such as football, deaf people maintain friendships. However,

> football within the deaf community has served as much more than a sporting or recreational pastime for the players; it has come to provide a means to travel, often long distances, to meet old friends within the widely dispersed community, and an opportunity to meet and make new contacts. (Atherton et al. 2001, 23)

Football is used in a similar vein by Iranian women to socialize, bond and disseminate cultural and sexual values at odds with patriarchy. They too employ 'sign language' and eye contact to communicate in code. Being involved in a women's football team provides 'a purpose and emotional sustenance' missing from alienated lives (Atherton et al. 2001, 28). It is subversive culture in the real sense of the word, promoted by gossiping and practiced through football.

DISCUSSION

Elsewhere I have recounted how the relationship between sport and the Islamic Republic has proceeded along three distinct but overlapping phases (Fozooni, in print):

1. circa. 1978 to early 1980s: this was a period characterised by chaos and mutual distrust when the emerging Islamists were too enmeshed in political manoeuvrings to conduct a sound sporting policy. Within the Islamic ruling class, once the populist-fascist wing ousted the liberal-social democratic faction, it felt secure enough to use sport instrumentally to promote its values.

2. circa. early 1980s to mid-1990s: however, these Islamic sporting values had to be constructed from scratch. The state required a period of truce with sport during which theologians provided sport administrators with a set of clear and enforceable codes based on the Koran and the hadith. Values such as sacrifice, discipline and unity were foregrounded to bolster the war effort with Iraq and *muscular Islam* became the dominant ideological expression of the state in sporting activities. In this period, gender segregation in sport became normalised and women were actively discouraged from 'masculine' sports such as football and martial arts.

3. circa. mid-1990s to present: this has been a period of contestation with every facet of Islamic sporting ideology being queried, critiqued and at times superseded by a population eager to claim its freedom. Women have played a crucial role in upping the ante in a high stake game of poker with the clergy.

Football gatherings in Iran are connected to 'a realm of erotic conspiracy and license' (cf. Castle 1983-1984, 156). The challenge is both symbolic and real. Through cross-dressing and engaging in suggestive behaviour, proletarians parody and 'demystify supposedly natural socioerotic categories' (1983-1984, 159). A new liberated language of gestures is being forged whose embryonic syntax includes spontaneous touching, shoving, embracing and gazing. Sporting occasions provide women a space where erotic consciousness can be expressed and enhanced through experimentation.

The attacks on intoxication, prostitution and homosexuality are in reality attempts to curb proletarian sexuality. When a leading cleric and ex-president, Rafsanjani, dismisses football rioters as 'effeminate' men and (by implication 'masculine' women) he is expressing the clergy 'fear of the flesh', as well as their absolute terror of losing control over the reproduction of labour power. The resistance of prostitutes and homosexuals to draconian Islamic measures ought to serve as a source of inspiration for the rest of the proletariat.

I would like to end this paper by returning to the example of the Pankhursts cited above and indulging in an exercise of imaginal ethnography. This exercise is of greater importance today after the great wave of struggles throughout the 'Middle East and North Africa' in 2011. Many taboos were broken by courageous participants of these events but there was also, I fear, a dearth of imaginal rupture with *normalised* capitalists values. At times it seemed some activists and spokespersons were reading from pre-rehearsed scripts written by their middle class liberal counterparts in Europe and the USA, without reflecting the more radical proletarian demiurge emanating from below. I am suggesting that history has provided us with the opportunity to bypass both *abnormal* and *normal* capitalist paths of development.

Radicals have always been aware of the dangers of false choices and pseudo-emancipation. By the time the British ruling class decided to extend the vote to women over thirty (February 1918), Sylvia Pankhurst had damned parliament as an institution manipulated by the capitalist class and as an anti-parliamentarian communist would not have anything to do with it. It is perfectly feasible, of course, that by the time the next wave of revolutionary struggle has toppled the Islamic theocracy, Iranian women too instead of rejoicing in their newly won freedom to play football, denounce football as a bourgeois institution unworthy of their continued support. Our imaginal ethnography may find them engaged in a game of 'three-sided football' on the streets of Tehran on the morrow of the revolution. As Michael Hodges (1999) has reported,

> Played on an hexagonal pitch between three sides, each defending one goal, the aim [of three-sided football] is not to score the most goals, but concede the least. Goals are conceded when the ball 'is thrust through a team's orifice', so dissolving 'the homoerotic/homophobic bipolarity of the two-sided game'. Put simply, three-sided football is, ideally, an exercise in co-operative behaviour, with one side persuading another to join in a campaign against the third - thus breaking down the very basis of capitalist organisation - and all before teatime.

Three-sided football is a game closer to the complexities of the Middle East than the orthodox two-sided version. Luther Blissett explains, 'In three-sided football, there's no *us* and *them*. It's a thrilling mind game, a sort of Middle East where alliances are continually changing and unpredictable. It's a game of deception. It's like intelligence activity' (Blissett, quoted in Cramer 1996).

Future struggles by Iranian women in the arena of football have a stark choice before them: to mindlessly imitate the contours of feminist development in the 'West' or to attempt to go beyond its limitations. Perhaps we can reach a stage when instead of merely demanding representative and participatory equality with sportsmen, women can undermine the very edifice of capitalist sport in favour of festive games.

ACKNOWLEDGEMENTS

An earlier version of this paper was published in *Cultural Studies*. My thanks to the anonymous reviewers at *Cultural Studies*.

REFERENCES

Abdo, G. (2003) Media and information: the case of Iran. *Social Research*, Fall, 70(3): 877-886.

Afary, J. (1996) Steering between Scylla and Charybdis: shifting gender roles in 20th century Iran. *National Women's Studies Association Journal*, spring [online] Available at: http://www.iranian.com/Dec96/Opinion/Women/Women.html (accessed 10 May 2006).

Alabarces, P. (1999) Post-modern times: identities and violence in Argentine football. In G. Armstrong and R. Giulianotti (eds.), *Football Culture and* Identities. London: Macmillan Press, 77-85.

Atherton, M., Turner, G. H. and Russell, D. (2001) More than a match: the role of football in Britain's deaf community. *Soccer and Society*, autumn, 2(3): 22-43.

Ayubi, N. N. (1995) Rethinking the public/private dichotomy: radical Islamism and civil society in the Middle East. *Contention*, 4(3), spring.

BBCPersian.com (2005) Basketball players pressure to remove copy-cat tattoos. [online Farsi article, published 10 November 2005] Available at: http://www.bbc.co.uk/persian/sport/story/2005/11/051110_ra-basket ball-tattoo.shtml (accessed 10 May 2006).

BBCPersian.com (2006a) Ahmadinejad: the best seats in stadiums must be allocated to women. [online Farsi article, published 24 April 2006] Available at: http://www.bbc.co.uk/persian/interactivity/debate/story/2006/04/060424 _h_women_stadium.stml (accessed 10 May 2006).

BBCPersian.com (2006b) Religious authorities oppose women's participation in football stadiums. [online Farsi article, published 26 April 2006] Available at: http://www.bbc.co.uk/persian/iran/story/2006/04/060426_mf_footbal.sht ml (accessed 10 May 2006).

Bickerton, E. (2006) Female fans play political football. *New Statesman*, 22 May 2006, pp. 16-17.

Brandist, C. (1996) The official and the popular in Gramsci and Bakhtin. *Theory, Culture & Society*, 13(2): 59-74.

Bromberger, C. (1998) Sport as a touchstone for social change: a third half for Iranian football. *Le Monde diplomatique* [online] Available at: http:// mondediplo.com/1998/04/04iran (accessed 3 April 2003).

Byrne, N. (2002) In Iran, It's Called Progress. *Middle East Quarterly*, summer, p. 38.

Castle, T. (1983-1984) Eros and liberty at the English masquerade, 1710-90. *Eighteenth-Century Studies*, 17(2): 156-176, winter.

Chappell, A. L., Goodley, D. & Lawthom, R. (2001) Making connections: the relevance of the social model of disability for people with learning difficulties. *British Journal of Learning Disabilities*, 29(2): 45, June. [online] Available at: http://www.blackwellpublishing.com (accessed 18 December 2003).

Chehabi, H. E. (2002) A political history of football in Iran. *Iranian Studies*, 35(4): 371-402, Fall.

Cramer, F. (1996) Three-sided football. Dahlemer Diwan on Radio Charlie 87.9, 9 June 1996, six minute feature with excerpts of a studio interview with Luther Blissett, broadcasted as part of a radio hour on 'literature and soccer' on the second day of the European Soccer Championship [online] Available at: http://www.LutherBlissett_net.htm (accessed 18 December 2003).

Dehghanpisheh, B. (2011) Soccer's wardrobe Malfunction. *World News*, 17 July 2011. available at http://www.thedailybeast.com/newsweek/2011/07/17/soccer-s-headscarf-scandal-in-iran.html (accessed 20 October 2011).

Eagleton, T. (1989) Bakhtin, Schopenhauer, Kundera. In K. Hirschkop and D. Shepherd (eds.), *Bakhtin and Cultural Theory*. Manchester: Manchester University Press, pp. 178-189.

Ehrenreich, B. (2007) *Dancing in the Streets: A History of Collective Joy*. London: Granta Books.

Foucault, M. (1984) *The History of Sexuality: Volume 1, An Introduction*. Harmondsworth: Penguin.

Fozooni, B. (2004) Religion, politics and class: conflict and contestation in the development of football in Iran. *Soccer & Society*, 5(3): 356-370, autumn.

Fozooni, B. (in print) Sport and the Islamic *Revolution* in Iran. *ABC-CLIO Sports Around the World: History, Culture, and Practice* (MENA Region).

Haeming, A. (2007) Iran cancels Women's Football Game in Berlin. *Spiegel Online International*, 6 January 2007, Available at http://www.spiegel.de/international/germany/0,1518,486086,00.html (accessed 20 October 2011).

Hodges, M. (1999) The anarchists' ball: 3-sided football [online] Available at: http://www.deepdisc.com/space1999/archive/18.html (accessed 18 December 2003).

Ghazi, S. (1998) Iranian women put on their running shoes [online] Available at: http://www.unesco.org/courier/1999_04/uk/dossier/txt12.htm (accessed 18 December 2003).

Johnes, M. (2000) Hooligans and barrackers: crowd disorder and soccer in South Wales, c.1906-1939. *Soccer & Society*, 1(2): 19-35, summer.

Knabb, K. (1977) The Realization and Suppression of Religion. [online] Available at: http://www.bopsecrets.org/PS/religion.htm (accessed 18 December 2003).

McGinty, P. (1978) *Interpretation and Dionysus: Method in the Study of a God*. The Hague: Mouton.

Mojab, S. (2001) Theorizing the politics of Islamic Feminism. *Feminist Review*, 69: 124-146, winter.

Naficy, H. (1999) Veiled vision/powerful presences: women in post-revolutionary Iranian cinema. In R. Issa and S. Whitaker (eds.), *Life and Art: The New Iranian Cinema*. London: National Film Theatre.

Nogawa, H. and Maeda, H. (1999) The Japanese dream: soccer culture towards the new millennium. In G. Armstrong and R. Giulianotti (eds.), *Football Culture and Identities*. London: Macmillan Press, pp. 223-233.

Pelak, C. F. (2002) Women's collective identity formation in sports: a case study from women's ice hockey. *Gender & Society*, 16(1): 93-114.

Panahi, J. (2006) *Offside!* [Farsi movie] Jafar Panahi Film Productions.

Pelham, N. (2001) *Tehran gripped by worst rioting since revolution*. 27 October [online] Available at: http://groups.yahoo.com/group/unmedia/message/9 (accessed 18 December 2003).

Petrossian, V. (1996) Iran: a little local difficulty with the Hizbollah. *Middle East Economic Digest*, 40(23): 22. [online] Available at: http://web4.infotrac.gategroup.com/itw (accessed 18 December 2003).

Pickard, J. (1982) *Sylvia Pankhurst -Suffragette and class fighter*. [online] Available at: http://www.marxist.com/women/sylvia_pankhurst.html (accessed 18 December 2003).

Roth, M. (1997) Carnival, creativity, and the sublimation of drunkenness. *Mosaic* (Winnipeg), 30(2): 1.

Rubin, G. (1975) The traffic in women: notes on the political economy of sex. In R. Reiter (ed.), *Toward an Anthropology of Women*. New York: Sage Publications, anthologized in Second Wave- A Feminist Reader.

Sabūri, H. (1996) *Varzesh Dar Islam* (Sport in Islam), [Farsi]. Office for Islamic Propagation, Seminary of Qom: Publication Centre.

Safa-Isfahani, K. (1980) Female-Centered World Views in Iranian Culture: Symbolic Representations of Sexuality in dramatic Games. *Signs*, 6(1): 33-53, Autumn.

Sedgwick, E. (1985) *Between Men: English Literature and Male Homosocial Desire*. New York: Columbia University Press.

Stallybrass, P. and White, A. (1986) *The Politics and Poetics of Transgression*. New York: Cornell University Press.

Tajbakhsh, K. (2003) Media in the Islamic world: introduction. *Social Research*, 70(3): 869-876, Fall.

The Freethinker (2011) Iranian footballers face a flogging after televised bottom-pinching incident. http://freethinker.co.uk/2011/11/05/iranian-footballers-face-a-flogging-after-televised-bottom-pinching-incident/ (accessed 6 November 2011).

The Guardian (2011) *Iran's women footballers banned from Olympics because of Islamic strip*. Published 6 June 2011. Available at: http://www.guardian.co.uk/football/2011/jun/06/iran-women-olympic-strip (accessed 20 October 2011).

The Guardian (2011) Turkey imposes 'women and children only' rule on badly behaved clubs. published 20 September 2011. Available at: http://www.guardian.co.uk/football/2011/sep/20/turkey-women-children-only-clubs (accessed 18 October 2011).

Thomsen, I. (1998) Political football. *Sports Illustrated*, 88(22): 66.

Wiegers, Y. (1998) Male bodybuilding: the social construction of a masculine identity. *Journal of Popular Culture*, 32(2): 147-161, Fall.

Magnus Hirschfeld's Contributions to Sexual Politics and the Nazi Backlash

Magnus Hirschfeld (1868-1935) is lauded as a pioneer in the field of sexology. Philosophically, Hirschfeld was a liberal who forged alliances with Social Democrats and Leninists in an effort to repeal heteronormative and misogynistic laws. He changed the way sexuality is discussed and challenged the description of sexual *transgression* as abnormal or insane. Following a short profile of Hirschfeld, I present his limitations and contributions in terms of the duality between *biomedical* and *biopsychosocial* paradigms. Usually traced to the work of George Engel, the biopsychosocial model prescribes that to be genuinely scientific, a model for medicine must include the psychosocial dimensions (personal, emotional, behavioural, family, community) *in addition to* the biological aspects. This is a humanistic science that claims to have superseded the limitations of biomedicine, reductionism, positivism and biological determinism (see Engel 1980; for a strong critique see Pilgrim 2002; also Epstein and Borrell-Carrio 2005).

By referencing the earliest film to depict homosexuals sympathetically, *Different from the Others* (Dir. Oswald 1919), I discuss Hirschfeld's role as propagandist for a humanistic acceptance of homosexuality. He spent a great deal of time and energy defending himself against sceptical colleagues and political foes. Misunderstood and derided in his lifetime by (some) liberals, social democrats, bolsheviks and fascists, he was grudgingly tolerated during the Weimar Republic by a reactionary left and targeted by the Nazis after 1933. And yet he remained popular with huge segments of the population, particularly the working class. He fled the Nazis and died in exile. I end by discussing his political philosophy and the Nazi backlash against his work.

A SEXOLOGY-FOCUSED PROFILE OF HIRSCHFELD

Hirschfeld (1868-1935) was born into a middle class Jewish family in Kolberg on the Baltic coast of Prussia (present-day Kolobrzeg in Poland). His father was a physician and reformer who, alongside other civic duties, succeeded in installing a salt-water bath in the town. Hirschfeld inherited a belief in nature cure and a social conscience from him (Wolff 1986, 23). At the mild end of nature cures, he recommended bicycling, swimming and outdoor activities, whilst at the extreme end he admired the fashionable Theosophy Movement of Annie Besant (ibid, 333). He combined a belief in nature cures and a socialised medicine throughout his career. Unfortunately, Hirschfeld also acquired his father's stern patriotism[23] and snobbism which his biographer, Charlotte Wolff, attributes to deep social insecurity (ibid. 23). He ended up supporting W/W I, despite his own pacifist leanings and the government's order dismissing homosexual officers from the army.

Hirschfeld studied medicine but was also keenly open to artistic influences. Looking back at his life he provides a critical assessment of science, 'The natural sciences have always left aside the most important aspect of life, which is love' (Hirschfeld, quoted in Wolff 1986, 27). At other times he would employ a narrow, rationalistic definition of science, 'soon the day will come when science will win victory over error, justice a victory over injustice, and human love a victory over human hatred and ignorance' (http://www.youtube.com/watch?v=JaZUh3VkPJg as part of the GLBT History Month 2009 event, accessed 18 August 2010).

He brought out his first pamphlet on sexuality (*Sappho and Socrates*, 1896) anonymously, since the subject matter (love and homosexuality) was deemed too risqué for a promising medical professional. In it he argues that homosexuality is 'natural' and therefore should not be punished. He was probably basing his argument here on Nietzsche who claimed that 'what is natural cannot be punished,' (Brennan and Hegarty 2007).

---

[23] The situation is more complicated than this since Hirschfeld was also keen to point out the self-deceptive nature of nationalism, 'Jews and Germans considered themselves to be the chosen people, and both were the most hated in the world' (Hirschfeld quoted in Wolff 1986, 29). As a liminal character, it would not surprise the reader to hear that he expressed German patriotism, pro-Zionism and internationalist tendencies without seeing the contradictions. To his credit, he foresaw the dangers of both Jewish nationalism and anti-Semitism and welcomed the unity of Arab-Jewish working classes. He also alluded to the similarities between anti-Semitism and homophobia on more than one occasion (ibid, 356).

~ 103 ~

His approach to sexology employs a mixture of psychology, sociology and biology. Contemporary advocates of the biopsychosocial approach would find much in both Hirschfeld worthy of consideration (cf. Toates 2010). In part as a reaction against psychoanalysis's fabricated cleverness, Hirschfeld was anxious to retain a biological *base* upon which the psychological *superstructure* could be erected.

He was a keen ethnographer who frequented places of 'bad' repute in Berlin and later on during his world tour. He was probably influenced by Iwan Bloch's work in ethnology. Hirschfeld was also influenced in this regard by the early sex researcher Paolo Mantegazza (1831-1910), who had carried out anthropological and ethnographic studies during his travels to Argentina and East India. Mantegazza as a eugenicist conducted experiments in sexual physiology (Sigusch 2008). Haeberle has referred to him as the 'first true sexologists in the modern sense' (Haeberle 1997).

As with most ethnographers he combined serious research with fun. He observed behaviour and discourse in homosexual bars, swimming pools, hotels and private houses and made an interesting separation between *Berufsmensch* (the person in their professional or open life) and *Geschlechtsmensch* (the person in their sexual life) - a separation that persists even today. He underscored a subtle insight into the unconscious nature of certain forms of homophobia where the separation between the two spheres is so great 'that the *day person* is morally outraged by the lifestyle of the *night-I* and strongly inveighs against it. It is not always simple hypocrisy ...' (Hirschfeld 1904, quoted in Brennan and Hegarty 2007, 15). The only 'vice' he was vociferously against seems to have been alcoholism and prostitution. He advised both workers and pregnant women against drinking and its inimical link to the spread of venereal diseases, especially syphilis. Rather naively, he was in favour of religious morality laying the precondition of a *hygienic life*, even though he was not a religious man himself.

He came to prominence as an expert medical witness in the Harden case – editor of *Die Zukunft* who had accused a number of Kaiser Wilhelm II's advisors of homosexuality. Hirschfeld's defence of homosexuality was at this stage based on biological determinism with him arguing that as an inborn condition homosexuality could not be punished. Ironically this instance of biological determinism was used to combat even more reactionary opinions about homosexuality as pathology. It is possible he was using the trial as a clumsy attempt at 'outing' with the aim of making homosexuality more acceptable (Bullough 2003, 65). The appeal process was damaging since it threw his expertise into doubt and, more significantly, lost him the support of the Kaiser. Shortly afterwards, under a vicious orchestrated press campaign, he came close to a nervous breakdown. The (liberal) academic youth proved a willing receptor of prejudice, attacking Hirschfeld during his public talks in Danzig and other German towns in a precursor of more violent attacks by proto-fascist militias during the Weimar Republic.

Travelling opened up new intellectual horizons for Hirschfeld. In Calcutta, for example, he came across the *Kama Sutra* and was impressed by the close connection between its teachings and his own work. Returning to his routine physician's life after his 'exotic' adventures proved tedious enough for him to seek alternatives. One natural escape route was research and writing, the other psychiatry. It was a matter of time before he would combine the two trends to produce his seminal Transvestites (*Die Transvestiten*, 1910). This work used a hybrid research method employing both quantitative surveys and qualitative first-person accounts of transvestites. Its cumulative effect is to subvert binaries such as: male/female, gay/straight, and sex/gender (Steakley 1999, 196).

In 1913 he gave a series of successful lectures in London which inspired the creation of the British Society for the Study of Sexual Psychology. He was also interested to learn more about the Suffragettes whilst in London and took note of the heavy-handed approach of the British state in dealing with dissent. The British wing of the sex movement seems to have been one or two steps behind Hirschfeld at all times. Somewhat atavistically, even in 1934 they were still echoing Havelock Ellis on the hopelessness of a satisfying sexual relationship for homosexuals. They went as far as calling for castration in some cases. Ralf Dose reminds us of 'the almost complete impossibility, well into the 1950s, of discussing homosexuality publicly in England' (Dose 2003; for a counter-argument see Cocks 2006).

Around the same period (1913-14) he presented a series of public lectures in Austria on 'Sexual Intermediaries' (*Zwischenstufenlehre*) which endeared him to the adherents of Carl Gustav Jung. It would be remembered that Jung identified the *animus* with intellectual and *anima* with intuition and feeling. This belief prepared Jungians for the notion of intermediaries. The perspective suggests we are all constituted of different proportions of *masculinity* and *femininity*, a dynamics that is subjected to constant change and evolution. To quote Hirschfeld, 'The number of actual and imaginable sexual varieties is almost unending; in each person there is a different mixture of manly and womanly substances, and as we cannot find two leaves alike on a tree, then it is highly unlikely that we will find two humans whose manly and womanly characteristics exactly match in kind and number.' (Hirschfeld 1910, quoted in Stryker and Whittle 2006, 37). This is, of course, a prefiguring of similar ideas in transgender and queer studies.

He worked as a physician for the Red Cross during W/W I. He called war an addictive psychosis and yet supported conscription (Wolff 1986, 164). He oversaw a number of prisoner exchanges and the title *Sanitätsrat* (State Councillor for Hygiene) was bestowed upon him. After the war and the establishment of a social democratic government, Hirschfeld's ideas took a more radical twist. He began to praise Marx, Engels, Bebel, Liebknecht and Lassalle and his patriotism was shelved for *internationalism*. It is difficult to ascertain with certainty whether this turn toward Marxism was genuine or opportunistic. However, his social democratic policies were presented with gusto and enthusiasm. They were also many decades ahead of their time. As Sanitätsrat he produced a document in 1919 which called for the 'The Nationalisation of the Health Service,' as well as education, pharmaceutical products and the judiciary. As Wolff makes clear this was more advanced than the parallel blueprint proposed by Beveridge in Britain (ibid, 170-171).

In the same year he acquired a beautiful building courtesy of the Weimar Republic which he energetically transformed into the first Institute for Sexual Science in the world. Foreign dignitaries were taken on tours together with members of the general public. He informed a Russian ministerial delegate that the legalisation of homosexuality had had no regrettable consequences in Germany. His 1926 visit to the USSR did not lead to a denunciation of Leninism or even (the emerging) Stalinism. Although he was complimentary toward Alexandra Kollontai and Sergei Eisenstein, he did not seem to have possessed the political nous to diagnose the regime as capitalist. The magnificent reception he received in the Soviet Union as a pioneer of sexology may have clouded his judgment. To the end of his life, he retained romantic notions about the emancipatory character of the USSR.

Bolsheviks were not his only left wing admirers. Even genuine revolutionaries such as Sylvia Pankhurst and Emma Goldman were supportive of Hirschfeld's work, although as with all radicals, they retained their entitlement to remain *critically* supportive. For instance, when a text appeared in Yearbook XXIII by Freiherr von Letsow claiming that the great Paris Commune leader, Louise Michel, was a lesbian, Emma Goldman prefaced her criticisms by saying, 'Dear Dr Hirschfeld: I have been acquainted with your great work on sexual psychology for a number of years. I have always deeply admired your courageous intervention.' However, she goes on to insist, 'But there exists amongst very many homosexuals a predominant intellectual outlook which I must seriously challenge. I am speaking of the practise of claiming every possible prominent personality as one of their own, attributing their own feelings and character traits to these people' (Goldman 1923, quoted in Maclellan 2004, 112-114).

Around the same time he felt secure enough to acknowledge his homosexuality, at least to friends and sympathisers. The Institute was used by all manners of people and political tendencies, including a great many proto-Nazis who were under treatment for their sexual problems. Ironically, even during these years of relative tolerance, Hirschfeld had to content not only with right-wing outsider attacks but also insider intimidation from his own colleagues- scientists such as Albert Moll, who threatened to expose his homosexuality, or as he put it, Hirschfeld's 'problematic nature' (Haeberle 1981, 272).

His resignation from the Institute and the transfer of management to the government provided an opportunity for further travel. Hirschfeld fulfilled his long ambition of visiting China, Japan, Palestine, India and Egypt. When in 1932 after more than a year of travelling he decided to go back to Germany the political climate had shifted dangerously. His friend, Karl Giese, met him in Athens and warned him in no uncertain terms about returning to Berlin. The seizure of power by the Nazis in 1933 saw an increase in surveillance, harassment and finally arrest and prosecution of left-wing researchers. During the early days, the Institute of Sexual Science was visited several times by the Gestapo who wanted to seize questionnaires, interview transcripts and medical files pertaining to the sexual proclivities of the German elite, including Nazi Party members. Karl Giese and other members of the Institute managed to remove many of the documents abroad for safe keeping but not before a substantial part was seized by the Gestapo for the purpose of blackmail. As Nazi arrogance grew, so did the bonfire of books and literature which their bigoted minds deemed 'decadent.'

Invaluable paraphernalia and cultural artifacts were destroyed in these attacks.

Thereafter, it would be more accurate to describe Hirschfeld not as a cosmopolitan *flâneur* but an exiled scientist forced to roam the world in order to avoid Nazis. He planned to return to the United States, however, his plans for an ambitious U.S. lecture tour came to nothing. Instead he travelled to Austria and Czechoslovakia and finally in 1933 settled in France. Two years later he died of a stroke. His body was cremated and his ashes are interred at the Cauçade cemetery in Nice.

One of his creations, the World League for Sexual Reform (WLSR) fragmented after his death in 1935 along liberal and radical lines. Its ten demands included equality for women, birth control, prevention of prostitution and venereal disease (Dose 2003, 7). By this time it claimed 190,000 organisational members worldwide. One of its leaders, Leunbach, identified the League's failures as 'its unwillingness to join the workers' movement, to integrate the struggle for sex reform into the struggle against fascism and for socialism' (Weeks 1996, 186). The other main leader, Haire, adopted an *apolitical* stance which in practice meant distancing the League from the workers' movement. It may even be the case that the short-lived Spanish section of the WLSR was under the influence of Wilhelm Reich and the anarchists (Dose 2003, 3). There was a revival of some aspects of the WLSR in West Germany in the 1950s but devoid of its sex-pol elements. Sex educators of this timeframe limited themselves to providing purely technical and informational manuals in support of family planning.

HIRSCHFELD'S CONTRIBUTION TO SEXOLOGY

Hirschfeld was granted an audience in 1896 with the justice secretary regarding repeal of anti-homosexual laws. The minister recommended a two stage strategy for abolishing such laws: first, educate the public (by which he probably meant the heterosexual bourgeoisie), and petition again. A year later Hirschfeld became one of the founding fathers of the Association for the Scientific Humanitarian Committee (SHC), principally to fight Paragraph 175- a law which persecuted and imprisoned homosexuals as well as making homosexuals victims of blackmail. Paragraph 175 of the Penal Code was the law against 'unnatural vice between men.' In

1914 the Reichstag Commission narrowly rejected Hirschfeld's Petition to repeal the law. The law was toughened up by Nazis, liberalised in both west and east Germany after W/W II to some extent (but significantly not abolished), and finally repealed in 1994. The history of this law serves once more to foreground uncomfortable philosophical and moral commonalities between liberalism, social democracy and fascism. In general, Paragraph 175 was interpreted by the executive with varying degrees of harshness based on socio-economic circumstances, the balance of class forces, and the sensibilities of powerful figures in authority. For example, in 1912, 'of 100,000 homosexual men who had come before the courts, only 1.5 per cent had been punished. And at about the same time the Chief of Police had shown amazing tolerance by the standards of the time for three *hermaphrodites* who wore women's clothes' (Wolff 1986, 125).

The purview of SHC gradually expanded to include other demands such as the fight against Paragraph 218 (the law against abortion). Petitions were organised and sent to the Reichstag and eminent social democrats like August Bebel were persuaded to speak on its behalf. Hirschfeld understood the vital role *community medicine* can make in improving people's living standards and set about establishing cheap preventive measures to this effect. Although the 'Committee itself never had more than 1500 supporters', it played a pivotal role in campaigning against discrimination (Johansson n.d.). He probably would have found the separatist wing of contemporary gay and lesbian movement in many countries at odds with his aim of internationalising and '[integrating] the homosexual movement into other reform movements' (Dose 2003, 8). Hirschfeld passed on the chairmanship of SHC to his friend and fellow gay activist, Kurt Hiller, in 1929. Hiller was a pacifist social democrat with an original mind. He elaborated Hirschfeld and argued in a vein similar to both Foucault and critics of the diagnostic labelling approach that it was Article 175 and not homosexuality that made people 'mentally ill' (Melching 1990, 79). He also stated the liberal case for sexual pleasure with aplomb, 'I believe that the freedom of a people comes down to the freedom of every individual to do what gives him pleasure (as long as it annoys no one else)' (Hiller 1930, quoted in Melching 1990, 82).

Hirschfield developed, on a more scientific level, the notion of an intermediate sex which was popularised earlier by Karl Ulrichs and Edward Carpenter. He was also one of the first to integrate the intermediate sex with the latest discoveries in hormone research (Weeks 1996, 104). He borrowed from animal research into castration and testes transplantation by Steinach to validate his writings. Surveys, questionnaires, case studies and interviews provided him with ample data to forge ahead with what we might today consider an overdeveloped classificatory zeal. For instance, he classified male homosexuals according to the direction of their desire into three groups, '*ephebophiles* who are attracted to youths from puberty up to the early twenties; *androphiles*, who love persons between the early twenties and fifty; and gerontophiles, who love older men, up to senile old age' (Hirschfeld 1838/1956, 236). This predilection for classification went as far as distinguishing between homosexuals according to their nervous system! It is only fair to point out that medicinal and psychiatric classification were all the rage amongst scientists at the beginning of the twentieth century, influenced by a general trend within capitalism for ever greater social and technical division of labour as well as the impact of parallel fields such as evolutionary biology.

He fully understood the importance of presentation. *Transvestites* (1910), for instance, was published with illustrations by Max Tilke in order to better capture the zeitgeist. Short aphorisms were another method of leaving a lasting mark, 'Transvestism is not a veil but a disclosure of one's true sex' (Hirschfeld quoted in Wolff 1986, 211). It is also worth noting that Hirschfeld's main biographer has accused him of ignoring his own quantitative survey which demonstrated 35% of transvestites were homosexuals and a further 15% bisexual (Wolff 1986, 108). Although he took onboard a great deal of Freud's work regarding psycho-sexual development, he came to disagree with Freudians who saw transvestites as a variety of homosexuals, preferring instead to focus on commonalities between transvestites and androgens. Hirschfeld borrowed freely from Freud's ideas on the 'erogenous zones' and 'component impulses', although 'we [Hirschfeld] on our part wish to leave entirely open the question whether or not this infantile sexuality is a true sexuality...' (Hirschfeld 1938/1956, 50). Regarding the relationship between children and parents again Hirschfeld conceded the possibility of the 'true Oedipal situation' in exceptional cases although he felt it is not necessary to go as far as Freud in generalising the Oedipal and Electra complexes (ibid, 53).

According to Meyenburg and Sigusch 'from 1899 to 1923 Magnus Hirschfeld edited a total of 23 volumes of the [*Yearbook for*

Sexual Intermediate States], which was mainly dedicated to the study of homosexuality...' (Meyenburg and Sigusch 1977, 198). Amongst other things, Hirschfield's journal became a confessional for lapse heteronormatives like Krafft-Ebing who began to make grudging concessions to homosexuality, which although still considered a form of 'degeneration' was now deemed 'compatible with intellectual excellence and highly developed spiritual faculties' (Mosse 1985, 38). It is somewhat ironic that Hirschfeld had so much respect for a reactionary homophobe like Krafft- Ebing (for a good critique see Fout 1992, 403).

Another convert was Wilhelm Oswald who confessed that as a Christian he had been prejudiced against homosexuals but after reading *The Homosexuality of Men and Women* (Hirschfeld 1914), understood the need for re-evaluation. The book represents a more nuanced understanding of sexual orientation beyond Hirschfeld's initial crude notion of the 'third sex' and is based on a staggering number of interviews with gays and lesbians (10,000 in all). Additionally, the 23 volumes of the *Yearbook* gathered some of the highest scientific attempt to grapple with the complexities of sexual activities from a variety of perspectives with Freud and Karl Abraham as contributors. Sadly Hirschfeld would from time to time undermine his own good work by sanitising critical essays. Hans Blühler's critique of Hirschfeld's theory of sexual intermediaries is a case in point, although Hirschfeld was shrewd enough not to misrepresent weightier contributors.

Freud cautiously accepted Hirschfeld's notion of 'sexual intermediaries' but considered these to be only one of two categories of homosexuals- the other being 'obsessional neurotics' (Wolff 1986, 65). Freud's *Three Essays on the Theory of Sexuality* (1905), where he questions the innateness of heterosexuality, was influenced by the *Yearbook*. Despite Freud's conservatism, the mutual respect between him and Hirschfeld resulted in the latter becoming a co-founder of the Berlin Psychoanalytic Association (either 1907 or 1908). However, when he resigned his position, Freud was dismayed and henceforth whispered against this 'flabby, unappetising fellow' (Wolff 1986, 101).

Hirschfeld encouraged linkage between lesbians and the wider women's movement. He provided examples of famous, successful women such as Queen Christiana of Sweden in an echo of earlier positive profiling techniques used to enhance the reputation of gay men. Under the influence of the great psychiatrist August Forel, who is considered one of the pioneers of group therapy, he made the mistake of assuming that lesbians were 'masculinised women.' He claimed that bi-sexuality 'is more pronounced in women than in men,' without valid evidence.[24] The causes of homosexuality are the same in women as men, Hirschfeld believed. However, cultural and social peculiarities play a role in complicating the scene. For instance, he was of the opinion that 'the inclination of prostitutes to homosexual practices ... is usually acquired through satiety with normal intercourse. This is confirmed [he believed] by the fact that the percentage of homosexual prostitutes under 25 to 30 is smaller than at later ages'(Hirschfeld 1938/1956, 282).

In 1919 he set up the Institute for Sexual Research, an ambitious research enterprise thirty years ahead of Kinsey's American simulacrum. Here sexology was to be studied through biology, pathology, forensic medicine, sociology, psychology as well as ethnology. Although conservative by Wilhelm Reich's standards, the Institute planned to study issues like free love alongside problems of marriage, abstinence and prostitution. Hirschfeld was also keen to develop the pedagogic elements of his work through the Institute. Public lectures with extensive Q & A sessions were organised on a regular basis. Many of the physicians and administrators working alongside him at the Institute were Communists although in this phase of his life, Hirschfeld remained faithful to the tenets of social democratic reform. One such radical was Richard Linsert (1899-1933) who as secretary of the SHC even collaborated with Hirschfeld in writing books on birth control.

A key contribution of Hirschfeld was his study of sexual mores during the course of World War I (Hirschfeld 1941/2006). This is part historical documentation, part scientific investigation of the dramatic transformation in people's perspective on sex and love during four cataclysmic years that reshaped Europe. Significantly, he advertised in leading newspapers a request for soldiers to send him 'whatever material they had relative to the history of morals and war' (Hirschfeld 1941/2006, vii). The book starts with an explanation of how the war released sexual restraints, spread venereal diseases and

---

[24] See Hirschfeld, 1938/1956, 281. This is in fact the compiler Norman Haire expressing what he believes to be Hirschfeld's position. The style of the book makes it difficult at times to decide when Haire ends and Hirschfeld begins.

eroticised nurses! Some of the descriptions of the crowds on the eve of battle are sadly reminiscent of Gustav Le Bon, although Hirschfeld takes care to qualify most of his more rhetorical utterances. Regarding the war fever that overtook Europe, Hirschfeld writes, 'The masses poured through the streets jubilantly, aroused to a blazing hatred, an enormous beast ready to hurl itself upon the enemy...' (Hirschfeld 1941/2006, 24).

The model employed throughout the book is a biopsychosocial one with Hirschfeld attempting to contextualise the sexual impulse for the war within economic and social conditions. However, occasionally as for instance in discussing the eroticisation of female nurses during the war he reduces the biopsychosocial model onto the biomedical terrain of libido sublimation. In short, he accuses nurses of taking sexual pleasure out of healing the wounded (Hirschfeld 1941/2006, 56). The book continues with a series of hit and misses ranging from a discussion of brothel-regulation by the army to an analysis of sadism and rape in war. No subject is taboo and no phenomenon too complex for Hirschfeld. He even tries to unearth the reasons behind the increase in genital mutilation and castration of enemy troops during war (ibid, 303). Of course, one can be fastidiously critical of these pioneering attempts to grapple with the relationship between war and sex but what I find daring within these pages are first, Hirschfeld's insistence in cruising scholarly no-go areas, and second, his ability to carry out his investigation 'with no prejudice in behalf of any of the warring groups' (Hirschfeld 1941/2006, vii).

Hirschfeld was a cosmopolitan or in his own words, a Panhumanist (Hirschfeld 1938, 115). He predicted that the next world war will have a racial element and that the only thing capable of preventing it is Panhumanism, 'When that storm bursts, in extent and in frightfulness it may outdo the World War of 1914-1918. There is only one way of preventing the outbreak. Not Pan-Europa can hinder it, nor Pan-America, nor the League of Nations, nor the Pact of Four, nor any such half-measure; nothing can avert it but Panhumanism ... We must hitch our wagon to a star' (ibid,).

In some ways his ideals are remarkably close to contemporary multi-culturalism. Thankfully his respect for other cultures did not involve blind spots and selective self-censorship as practised by today's cultural relativists. When, for instance, he came across the practice of circumcision amongst Jews or Muslims he condemned it vociferously. He believed circumcision for boys was 'not done for hygiene but for sacrificial reasons' (Wolff 1986, 347). It was even worse for girls who were terrorised by the procedure. In Egypt, he contrasted the ancient power of women with the modern suppression of their rights.

One of his last works was a 1934 denunciation of Nazi law on forced sterilization which initially targeted the 'mentally or morally inferior' and was soon expanded to include anyone who 'sinned against the Aryan race' (ibid, 405). His outstanding contribution in this field is a book entitled *Racism* (1933-34/1938). This is not the place for an analysis of this work but it is noteworthy that he critiques nationalism and racism in Germany and the rest of the world with ideas remarkably similar to discourse analysis and social constructionism. Using etymological, historical and cultural evidence he demonstrates the fictive nature of concepts such as 'race'. The 'blood myth', as well as skin colour as criteria of human worth are both subjected to critique. The 'evil practice of attaching national names to sexual peculiarities' (e.g., syphilis as 'the French pox' or homosexuality as 'le vice Allemand') is also dismissed as 'quite unjustified' but he cautions 'the error is hard to uproot' (Hirschfeld 1933-34/1938, 149-150).

HIRSCHFELD IN *DIFFERENT FROM THE OTHERS:*
PARAGRAPH 175

The authoritarian 20th century march of German filmmaking did not begin with the Nazis but with social democracy during the 1920s. It was the latter that denounced comedy as a lower form of art and sexuality as animalistic. Significantly, Taylorism and Fordism were introduced into the German filmmaking industry only after W/W I but their deskilling propensities took many years to filter through. This meant that film and theatre workers continued to be highly creative throughout the 1920s and 30s. Most German films of this period were constructed by or under the supervision of the Universum Film Aktiengesellschaft (UFA) which was established in 1917 by the Ministry of War. UFA survived under the social democrats and served as producer for the iconic *The Cabinet of Dr Caligari* (Dir. Wiene, 1920) and *Metropolis* (Dir. Lang, 1927). The Nazis took over UFA and used it brazenly for the production of anti-working class, anti-Semitic and patriarchal propaganda.

After the conclusion of World War I, the social struggle in Germany won a few concessions from the Weimar Republic, chief amongst them what proved to be a temporary abolition of censorship. According to Micheler, 'Approximately twenty periodicals for same sex desiring men and women appeared between 19119 and 1933'. However, 'these periodicals were subjected to censorship throughout the Weimar Republic, and some were placed on the index of banned books, but despite these repressive measures, most were published regularly, without interruption' (Micheler 2002, 102). This was a brief window of opportunity and radical filmmakers took to their new liberties with gusto. Expressionism and Futurism are the best known genres associated with this period but film criticism also emerged as a product of a more sophisticated engagement with film. According to Monaco, two thirds of the films made between 1919-1929 deal with the theme of. Others were focused on foreign pollution, blood, and alienation. It is in this context that the first ever films about homosexuality were produced and Hirschfeld supported this trend either through consultation or direct participation betrayal (Kaes, 1995; Leiser, 1974; and, Monaco, 1976).

Different from the Others: Paragraph 175 (Dir. Oswald, 1919, b & W, silent with inter-titles) is often cited as the first film to deal explicitly with the subject of homosexuality. In comparison *Pandora's Box* which featured a groundbreaking lesbian relationship was produced in 1928 (Dir. Georg Wilhelm Pabst). It focuses on how Paragraph 175 promotes extortion but it also tackles wider anti-homosexual discrimination. The director Richard Oswald (1880-1963) worked closely with Hirschfeld and other sexologists to produce a series of sex-ed works which dealt with issues important to SHC, namely prostitution, abortion and venereal disease. In his scholarly study of the film, Steakley claims the plotline was also by Hirschfeld (Steakley 1999). Oswald had previously produced a series of important films including an anti-war movie and a medical melodrama about syphilis (Steakley 1999, 189). *Different from the Others* survives as a fragment with photographs replacing the lost scenes. The only partial version of *Different from the Others* that remains was discovered in Ukraine.

At the centre of the film is the love affair between Paul Körner, a successful violin virtuoso and his student, Kurt Sivers, both from a bourgeois milieu. The movie begins with news of a series of apparently random, motiveless acts of suicide by people from all walks of life- a factory owner, a judge and a student. Paul Körner sees a common thread, Paragrapgh 175. Contemporary homosexuals are linked to a historical procession of persecuted individuals in his mind, including Tchaikovsky, Leonardo da Vinci, Oscar Wilde and King Ludwig II of Bavaria. The next sequence sees an infatuated Kurt Sivers plead with Körner to take him on as an apprentice. The acting is not as overdramatized as the prevalent Expressionist style of performance but rather suggestive and charged with erotic tension. Kurt's father, unaware of the attraction between his son and the musician, pressurises Kurt to take up a practical profession. To complicate matters, Körner's family are also attempting to arrange a marriage for him. Instead of explaining himself, Körner sends his parents to a sexologist. Hirschfeld plays himself in the movie and has these memorable lines, 'You mustn't think poorly of your son because he is a homosexual. He is not at all to blame for his orientation. It is neither a vice nor a crime, indeed, not even an illness, but instead a variation, one of the borderline cases that occur frequently in nature. Your son suffers not from his condition, but rather from the false judgment of it.'[25]

The film then takes a darker turn when Körner and Sivers are blackmailed by a shady character. The power that the blackmailer exercises over Körner is immediate and absolute, brazenly visiting Körner at his home and demanding money. The theme of homosexuality and blackmail are also studied in Basil Dearden's *Victim* (1961), starring Dirk Bogarde. Made 42 years after *Different from the Others* this was the first film in the English language where the word 'homosexual' is used. This fact alone is suggestive of the pioneering status of Hirschfeld's contribution. The blackmailer's performance is studded with moments of schadenfreude at the psychological distress of his victim that homophobic audience members may have found pleasurable. He is humiliating and blackmailing Körner simultaneously. Ironically the blackmailer

---

[25] Watch the film in three parts at <http://www.youtube.com/watch?v=oxW-6d3abhc> (accessed 12 July 2010). Hirschfeld is also the subject of a film by Rosa Von Praunheim called *The Einstein of Sex* (Der Einstein Des Sex, 1999) a brief introduction to which can be found at <http://www.youtube.com/watch?v=wYk3DEepnRE> (accessed 20 August 2010). In the clip he is depicted as a sensitive and gifted 10-year old whose artistic talents are nurtured by a caring father.

himself is depicted in a homosexual bar where gay and lesbian lovers are dancing joyously in the background. At this stage some viewers may interpret his presence as an allusion to latent homosexual tendencies. It is significant that this dancing scene precipitated a riot in one Berlin cinema in 1919 (Steakley 1999, 195).

When Körner decides to resist the blackmailer, the latter breaks into his home in search of incriminating evidence. However, he is caught in the act by Körner and Sivers and an unintentionally comical fight ensues, after which Sivers disappears ending up as a troubadour musicians, playing pubs to make a living.

A flashback begins to fill in some of the missing pieces: Körner in his youth at a dormitory consoling a friend is 'caught in the act' by the house-master and punished. He is expelled from the school. Later at university he tries to keep to himself but is pressurised into performing his role as a heterosexual man at a local brothel. He is shown in a scene surrounded by female sex-workers who are trying to seduce him without success. On seeing the exchange the Madame utters the memorable line, 'If that boy's completely normal, then I'm a virgin.'

After another flashback that shows a younger Körner discovering his homosexuality, the film shows him in search of a 'cure' for his 'condition.' He initially tries hypnosis which proves unsuccessful. If this is a dig at psychoanalysis it is not heavily underscored. Körner then seeks advice from Hirschfeld who tells him, 'Love for one's own sex can be just as pure and noble as that for the opposite sex. This orientation is to be found among many respectable people in all levels of society.' Hirschfeld further assures him that, 'Only ignorance and bigotry can condemn those who feel differently. Don't despair! As a homosexual, you can still make valuable contributions to humanity.' The session is reminiscent of Rogerain person-centred counselling rather than a classical psychoanalytic encounter.

A movie which from our contemporary perspective was moving along very predictable lines, develops a twist at this junction when following yet another flashback it is revealed that Körner's first attempt at a sexual liaison was with the very individual who is blackmailing him now. The previous depiction of the blackmailer in a gay bar and his 'lewd' and suggestive gestures toward 'handsome lad' Sivers begin to make sense. The blackmailer is revealed to the audience as a money grabbing male-prostitute who even at this first encounter threatens to turn in Körner for violation of paragraph 175. This scene may even be read as an attempt to portray two kinds of homosexual: the respectable and dignified bourgeois as played by Körner and the working class rascal as portrayed by the blackmailer.

The didactic nature of the film continues with a public lecture by Hirschfeld who informs his enthralled audience that, 'Nature is boundless in its creations. Between all opposites there are transitions, and this is also true of the sexes. Thus, apart from man and woman, there are also men with womanly physical and psychological traits, as well as women with all sorts of male characteristics.' Slides, mostly of transvestites, are shown to the audience with all the authority of current academics giving a PowerPoint presentation. The only nudity depicted in the entire film is in this lecture sequence. Hirschfeld acknowledges that some homosexual men do not show any feminine traits. The talk then makes an important linkage between the persecution of homosexuals and the persecution of heretics and witches. The French Revolution and Napoleonic Code are credited with freeing homosexuals from persecution in many countries. Hirschfeld's talk ends with these memorable sentiments, 'May justice soon prevail over this grave injustice, science conquer superstition, love achieve victory over hatred!'

The final sequence shows the blackmailer and Körner side by side in the dock, the first on blackmailing charges and Körner for violating paragraph 175. Hirschfeld appears as an expert witness in the court. The blackmailer is imprisoned for three years whilst Körner after having his 'honour' restored is given a minimum sentence of one-week in prison, since 'as long as paragraph 175 exists [the court] is not entitled to grant acquittal.' However, outside the court the damage to Körner's reputation is more severe. He is stigmatised and shunned by 'polite society.' His concerts are cancelled. In despair, he commits suicide. On hearing the news of the tragedy, Sivers also attempts to end his life but is stopped by Hirschfeld who urges him to honour his friend's memory by fighting anti-homosexual prejudice instead. Paragraph 175 is symbolically crossed out in the last frame of the movie.

The film was a success, playing to full houses and was even exported to Holland and Austria. Hirschfeld saw his filmic role as an extension of his earlier educational work and many people admired the film and communicated their gratitude to Hirschfeld personally but he was also the target of vicious attacks by clerics, politicians and proto-fascists. There was even an attempt on his life. The government did little to prevent anti-Semitic outbursts against Hirschfeld and in 1920 censorship was re-established. Steakley has noted that these censorship standards 'were so harsh that they required no revision under the Nazi regime' (Steakley 1999, 191). *Different from the Others* was banned for endangering 'public order and security,' as well as seducing impressionable audience members. Three prominent scientists played a pivotal role in its censorship: Kraepelin (who regarded homosexuality as a disease adopted through 'seduction'), Placzek (whose conservative sensibilities had been offended), and Albert Moll (who detested Hirschfeld and the popularisation of science through films). As Lesley Hall explains many contemporary scientists and sexologists still find this 'popularisation of science' vulgar (Hall 2004, 48).

In addition, Kraepelin and Moll were advocates of hypnosis for 'curing' homosexuality, a practice portrayed in the film as futile. Moll had broken with Hirschfeld in 1903 after the latter reported that 2.2 of respondents of his survey were homosexuals. Moll considered this as exaggerated statistics (Bullough 2003, 64). In an amazing passage replete with prejudice and ignorance Moll even criticises the film for *not* depicting sexual acts, bizarrely he was dismayed that *Different from the Others* did not show 'mutual onanism, *coitus inter femora*, the widespread practice of introducing the member into the mouth!' (Steakley 1999, 193). Reminiscent of contemporary religious fundamentalist arguments, it is an indication of the tautological nonsense Hirschfeld had to put up with. A few years later even long standing research journals were classed as 'smut and kitsch' by the Weimar government. Prints of the film were burnt by Nazis.

HIRSCHFELD'S LIMITATIONS AND ERRORS

In many ways Hirschfeld's imagination remained encapsulated within an idealised nuclear family. For him, only a 'normal' bourgeois marriage created the preconditions of childhood bliss. Despite his genuine concern for the poor and underprivileged he would occasionally display disdain for the masses. On a visit to the USSR in 1926 insightful comments about the causes of prostitution sit uneasily alongside derogatory comments about the 'common man,' who is deemed corrupt and opportunistic by nature. He even claimed without empirical corroboration that sexual molestation of children was more common in the lower classes (Wolff 1986, 281). Bourgeois humanism was indeed Hirschfeld's refuge from the realities of class antagonism, and class identity he dismissed as yet another form of selfishness.

His early attempts at sexual classification were crude but it would be unfair to be too critical here since he lived in an era when scientific endeavour was fast becoming subjected to both a social and technical division of labour. Yet he insisted on bucking the trend by painting his ideas on the widest of canvasses, and that meant combining knowledge from fields he had not fully mastered. In one instance, his lack of understanding of genetics and endocrinology let him down rather badly. As Wolff has pointed out, it is 'nonsensical to claim that the *female sexual residues* disappear in homosexual men, and that in women who love women the clitoris is atrophied' (Wolff 1986, 35). He was also insistent that psychosexual orientations were presented in specific 'brain centres,' a position that might endear him to current advocates of brain localisation. His views on the endocrine glands as the key to sexual orientation would find little support amongst researchers in the field today. Even the homophobe researcher, Albert Moll,[26] made a few astute observations regarding Hirschfeld's more outlandish notions. For example, Hirschfeld's diagnosis of homosexuality in childhood based on physical appearance or demeanour was justifiably ridiculed. In the early 1900s Hirschfeld also conflated transvestism with trans-sexualism (Hill 2005, 318).

Hirschfeld whose support for gays, lesbians, transvestites was unconditional, condemned 'the androgyne for its supposed lack of harmony' (Mosse 1985, 104). Significantly, even his ideas of sexual equality would sound antiquated to our ears. For example, 'he compared homosexuality with a developmental defect, such as hare-lip or club foot' (Wolff 1986, 37). He erroneously insisted that homosexuals were different from 'normals' in certain physical traits. He even expressed fear that 'transvestites, like homosexuals, ran the risk of producing degenerate offspring, but he added that he could not be sure of this eugenic danger in the former' (Wolff 1986, 109). Elsewhere (e.g., *Der Urnische Mensch*, 1903) he suggested that homosexuals tended to enjoy helping and serving rather than giving orders, which made them born peacemakers.

---

[26] According to Moll homosexuals were despicable, horrible creatures, 'inclined to cheat, and ruthless in the pursuit of the gratification of criminal tendencies' (Wolff 1986, 244).

Hirschfeld's humanitarianism was from the outset tinged with an overbearing prescriptivism that meandered its way in and out of Malthusian and eugenic currents. It is highly ironic that in 1911 a neo-Malthusian conference became the unlikely venue for a rapprochement between two 'progressives'- Hirschfeld and the feminist, Stöcker. Helene Stöcker (1869-1943) was a German feminist who helped found the League for the Protection of Mothers and called for the legalisation of abortion and sexual education.

He also seems to have formed erroneous ideas related to causes of criminality under the influence of the Italian Cesare Lombroso (1835-1909). Lombroso was the founder of the Italian School of Positivist Criminology and believed in the inherited nature of crime. His theories were nurtured by ideas prevalent at the time in the form of Social Darwinism, eugenics and physiognomy. And modelled on the much admired Forel, Hirschfeld produced a list of 'degenerative symptoms' such as small eyes, squinting, too big ears, stammer, etc., which would be considered extremely naïve today. He was also convinced that left-handedness appears twice as often amongst homosexuals than heterosexuals. Narrower shoulders, broader hips, ability to whistle and a penchant for certain scents were all criteria by which homosexuals could be identified (Brennan and Hegarty 2007, 20). This predilection for positivism and empiricism occurred whenever he abandoned the biopsychosocial paradigm in favour of the biomedical one.

Whenever the tensions within the biopsychosocial model are collapsed in favour of one element, ontological and epistemological errors tend to creep in. Hirschfeld was sufficiently critical to reject some of the wider claims of women's inferiority based on phrenology. However, he was not critical enough to supersede the more established biologically determined narratives prevalent in his time. For instance, he is on record as supporting the gendered version of the intellect-emotion dualism, 'Woman is more receptive in her love and mental life than man ... But she has not the same gift of abstract thought, nor for real creative activity. Her capacity to produce is focused on relatively simple mental functions' (Hirschfeld quoted in Wolff 1986, 87).

Alongside conceptual and theoretical errors, one finds in Hirschfeld the occasion lapse in judgment. Hirschfeld is accused by Warren Johansson of being a blackmailer himself. He writes, 'There is evidence that the accusations printed in the Berlin *Vorwärts,* the Social Democratic daily, which led to the suicide of the industrialist

Alfred Krupp came from Hirschfeld himself, after he had unsuccessfully tried to extort the sum of 100,000 marks from him with the assistance of a young engineer' (Warren Johansson, 'Hirschfeld, Magnus,' *Encyclopedia of Homosexuality*, 538). I am in no way qualified to ascertain the truth or falsehood of this accusation. However, I do find Johansson's summing up of Hirschfeld rather dismissive and ungenerous.

Another story suggest, in order to pay the cumbersome cost of the Institute for Sexual Science he ventured into the preparation and sale of hormonal remedy for sexual impotence, the famous 'Titus Perlen.' The enterprise damaged Hirschfeld's reputation without making much profit. On the other hand, the Institute had a strict policy of not charging fees to patients who were poor. Contemporary qualitative researchers would find Hirschfeld's misinterpretation of the narratives he accumulated troublesome. When evidence did not fit pre-existing theory, Hirschfeld would sometimes simply ignore it (Hill 2005, 325). So keen was he to differentiate between transvestites and sadomasochists, for instance, that any evidence of overlap was dismissed. As Hill has observed regarding *Die Transvestiten* (1910), 'Hirschfeld's theory predicts a plurality of categories, yet he wrote a book that erected boundaries between identities, borders that, with close analysis, disappear' (ibid, 330).

DISCUSSION

Political complications

Since Humanism degenerated into Humanitarianism, the term no longer conveys the positive connotations once attached to it. It is, therefore, with some trepidation that I describe Hirschfeld as a humanist of the first order. This is evident in the way he interacted with his 'patients' not as cases but as friends. Most contemporary practitioners would be appalled by such lack of professional distance. His humanism is also evident in the positive response he received from working class audiences the world over. Hirschfeld's high regard for Émile Zola, as the champion of victims of injustice, is key to understanding his determination to fight for gay rights. In addition, his travels introduced him to new environments, allowed him to engage in cross-cultural thinking and forged him into a fierce critic of colonialism. Hirschfeld became a keen amateur ethnologist and instinctively saw the advantages of inter-cultural comparisons in undermining normalising tendencies.

Throughout his career, he had to struggle against not only homophobes and but also reactionary trends within the homosexual *community*. For example, Adolf Bland, the editor of the very first journal of sexuality in Germany (*Der Eigene*, The Personalist), used racism to gain respectability for homosexuality. The journal which photographed naked boys and men against the German landscape, in much the same way Leni Riefenstahl would later employ such imagery in pursuit of Nazi propaganda goals, praised a distorted Nietzschean 'Superman' for its manliness and toyed with anti-Semitism (Mosse 1985, 42). Another reactionary was the homosexual activist, Friedrich Radszuweit, who used anti-Semitic jibes to criticise Hirschfeld and to curry favour with the nascent Fascists. He also welcomed the banning of Hirschfeld's films (Steakley 1999, 194). As a rival for the leadership of the gay rights movement, Radszuweit had a great deal to gain by undermining Hirschfeld.

Then there was Ernst Röhm, the leader of the SA, who was an open homosexual and tentatively 'proud of it.' This pride has been linked to the nationalist principles of the *Männerbund*, a masculinist movement in Germany celebrating male comradeship (van de Wiel, 2007).[27] The existence of homosexuals amongst Nazis must not be exaggerated into a functional or psychological organic linkage. It certainly did not prevent the persecution of Hirschfeld. In conjunction with assaulting him and burning his books, the Nazis also demolished a monument the town of Kolberg had erected in honour of his popular father, Hermann Hirschfeld. The patriotism promoted by social democrats, liberals and even German Leninists during the Weimar Republic (1918-1933) became fertile ground for the extreme nationalism of the Nazis during their reign (1933-1945). As Mosse (1985) has expertly shown this new wave of nationalism was ushered in under the flag of 'bourgeois respectability.' It was the Social Democratic Party that denounced Röhm as a homosexual in 1931 not the SS (Micheler 2002, 108).

---

[27] R. Van der Wiel, 'Invisible Lines.' According to Van der Wiel, an anonymous homosexual SA member wrote to Hirschfeld in 1932. His letter attempts to create a divergence between the weak (effeminate) and strong (masculine) homosexual.

The attacks on Hirschfeld had begun as early as 1907 when he was portrayed as a freak by the liberal *Die Vossische Zeitung* whilst the right wing *Germania* declared after his appearance as an expert legal witness in a court case that, 'We must make an end of people like Dr Hirschfeld' (Wolff 1986, 73). A Reichstag member was quoted as saying, 'Homosexuals have the morals of dogs' and leaflets distributed outside Hirschfeld's house read, 'Dr Hirschfeld – a Public Danger. The Jews are Our Undoing' (ibid, 74). Although he did receive some vocal and financial support from the Weimar Republic, this remained grudging and intermittent. A great deal is made of Hirschfeld's own social democratic leanings and the respect with which the Weimar Republic treated him. And yet as his friend and collaborator, Max Hodann, reminds us, 'The academic gates were closed to Hirschfeld, and even after the fall of the Hohenzollern Empire in 1918 the Weimar Republic had no chair anywhere for the tireless investigator' (Hodann 1937, quoted in Haeberle 1981, 271). A minority of state officials in the executive and judiciary were sympathetic but the legislative was rarely open to his advances.

The overall critical current against Hirschfeld took a predictable pattern with liberals or social democrats initiating the denouncements and proto-fascists escalating it. Emile Kraepelin, one of the 'founding fathers' of psychiatry, was a key figure in this bridging process. He wished to initiate a struggle against 'sexual confusion' and 'primarily against masturbation' by, amongst other means, the 'toughening of the will through gymnastics' (Kraepelin 1918, quoted in Mildenberger 2007, 322). Kraepelin called for a ban on 'every form of information about homosexual intercourse that did not condemn it' (ibid). One of his students, Ernst Rüdin, denounced Hirschfeld's work as unscientific and 'even said that homosexuals always damage their *race*, whether by refusing to reproduce or, if they did, by passing on their sexual disposition to their children' (ibid, 323). Kraepelin followed this up by claiming that homosexuals were a serious danger to the German people. After 1933, his legacy was taken up by the Nazis without open acknowledgement. In 1933 Paragraph 175 was expanded to include all forms of male homosexual contact and the first homosexuals, together with transvestites and pimps were sent to concentration camps. The 1936 Berlin Olympics witnessed a temporary and partial lull in persecutions as part of Hitler's charm offensive. Immediately after the games were over, however, persecutions escalated although those rich or famous enough would sometimes manage to avoid the camps.

The Biopsychosocial model

In a summing up of Hirschfeld it has been suggested that 'he tapped at the door of science but could not get it to open' (Wolff 1986, 129). I believe it would be more accurate to say Hirschfeld vacillated between a narrow and an expansive definition of science. The narrow definition was based on a positivist and empiricist epistemology and a quantitative methodology which prefigured the errors of contemporary essentialism. This mode of investigation is a forerunner of the current dominant biomedical paradigm and perceives the categories and values of 'science' ahistorically. Regrettably whenever he tried to expand the boundaries of this biomedical approach he failed to reach the rigour and richness of historically materialist critical research- a crude version of biopsychosocial model was the best he could conjure up.

The modern version of the biopsychosocial model is usually accredited to George Engel's attempt to respond to reductionist and dehumanising tendencies within biomedicine. Engel's imaginary patient asks, 'Do my doctors know who I am, who I have been, who I still want to be? Do they understand what I am going through, my suffering, my pain, my distress?' (Engel 1988). The key to understanding patients is to listen intently and be genuinely curious about them during interviews. These are precisely qualities that Hirschfeld tried to foster in practitioners by privileging dialogue over the kind of monologue which is normally preferred in both classical psychoanalysis and medicine.

He would have been completely comfortable working within a paradigm described by recent practitioners in these terms, 'The biopsychosocial model is both a philosophy of clinical care and a practical clinical guide. Philosophically, it is a way of understanding how suffering, disease and illness are affected by multiple levels of organization, from the societal to the molecular. At the practical level, it is a way of understanding the patient's subjective experience as an essential contributor to accurate diagnosis, health outcomes, and human care' (Borrell-Carrio et al. 2004, 576).

The biopsychosocial model is also in tune with other aspects of Hirschfeld's practice. He practiced, whenever possible, *formulation* rather than *diagnosis*.[28] At a time when the temptation to retain as

---

[28] A recent example of formulating sexual problems instead of diagnosing them is to be found in Fagan, 2007.

much power for the physician must have been overwhelming, Hirschfeld was willing to share power with patients. He was even happy to share his feelings during treatment, in order to ensure a more equitable relationship with patients. This patient-centeredness 'has been shown to improve outcome' in treatment (See Biderman et al. 2005; Engel 1977). Moreover, just in line with Hirschfeld, the model attempts to understand societal factors causing illness in order to suggest preventive measures.[29] There have even been feminist attempts to use the biopsychosocial model of 'sexual desire' to undermine what is seen as the male-centeredness of the biomedical interpretation (Wood et al. 2006).

Serious objections have been raised regarding the biopsychosocial model by, amongst others, David Pilgrim (2002). He traces the model to the pioneering work of the Swiss psychiatrist, Adolf Meyer (1866-1950), who insisted on understanding patients through consideration of detailed case histories. His *ergasiology* (researching and noting all biological, psychological and social factors pertinent to the case) and empowerment through *community medicine* and meaningful activity became influential ideas within psychiatry. Another influence is the general field of systems theory as originally expounded by Ludwig von Bertalanffy and Paul Weiss (Pilgrim 2002, 585). The insistence on patient's personal history was at odds with the Kraepelinian method of diagnosis. It is this legacy that was taken up by Hirschfeld in the nineteenth century and expanded by George Engel in the twentieth century. Pilgrim also sees the modern version of the model as a reaction against the criticism levelled at psychiatry by the 'anti-psychiatry' movement of the 1960s and 70s.

Now that neuropsychiatry seems to be gaining ground, the biopsychosocial model is losing its earlier gains. Even though the term biopsychosocial is a modern invention, the interactionist impulse that drives it can be traced to the late nineteenth and early twentieth centuries, where it intertwines with the sexological research of Hirschfeld. In general, his breakthroughs were achieved within a biopsychosocial mode of inquiry and his errors committed within a biomedical one.

---

[29] Charles P. Samenow (2010) has applied the biopsychosocial model to 'hypersexual disorders/sexual addiction' with impressive results.

REFERENCES

Biderman, A., Yeheskel, A. and Herman, J. (2005) The Biopsychosocial Model- Have We Made Any Progress Since 1977? *Families, Systems & Health*, 23(4): 379-386.

Borrell-Carrio, F., Suchman, A. L. and Epstein, R. M. (2004) The biopsychosocial model 25 years later: Principles, practice and scientific inquiry. *Annals of Family Medicine*, 2: 576-682.

Brennan, T. and Hegarty, P. (2007) Who Was Magnus Hirschfeld and Why Do We Need to Know? *History & Philosophy of Psychology*, 9(1): 12-28.

Bullough, V. L. (2003) Biographical Notes: Magnus Hirschfeld, an Often Overlooked Pioneer. *Sexuality & Culture*, 7(1): 62-72.

Cocks, H. G. (2006) Making the Sodomite Speak: Voices of the Accused in English Sodomy Trials, c. 1800-98. *Gender & History*, 18(1): 87-107.

Dose, Ralf (2003) The World League for Sexual Reform: Some Possible Approaches. *Journal of the History of Sexuality*, January, 12(1): 1-15.

Engel, G. L. (1977) The need for a new medical model: A challenge for biomedicine. *Science*, April, 196: 129-136.

Engel, G. L. (1980) The clinical application of the biopsychosocial model. *American Journal of Psychiatry*, 137: 535-44.

Engel, G. L. (1988) How much longer must medicine's science be bound by a seventeenth century world view? In K. J. White (ed.) *The task of medicine,* 113-136. Menlo Park CA: The Henry J. Kaiser Foundation.

Epstein, R. M. and Borrell-Carrio, F. (2005) The biopsychosocial model: exploring six impossible things. *Families, Systems & Health*, 23(4): 426-431.

Fagan, P. (2007) Sex Therapy and Research: A View from Health Services Research. *Journal of Sex & Marital Therapy*, 33: 427-432.

Fout, J. C. (1992) Sexual Politics in Wilhelmine Germany. *Journal of History of Sexuality*, 2(3): 388-421.

Freud, S. (1905/1991) *On Sexuality: Three Essays on the Theory of Sexuality and Other Works*. Penguin Books Ltd.

Haeberle, E. J. (1981) Swastika, Pink Triangle and Yellow Star-The Destruction of Sexology and the Persecution of Homosexuals in Nazi Germany. *The Journal of Sexual Research*, 17(3): 270-287.

Haeberle, E. J. (1997) Sexology: from Italy to Europe and the World. Archive paper in *Archive for Sexology* website, http://www2.huberlin.de/sexology/GESUND/ARCHIV/PAPER2.HTM (accessed 8 June 2010).

Hall, L. (2004) Hauling Down the Double Standard: Feminism, Social Purity and Sexual Science in Late Nineteenth-Century Britain. *Gender & History*, April, 16(1): 36-56.

Hill, D. B. (2005) Sexuality and Gender in Hirschfeld's *Die Tranvestiten*: A Case of the *Elusive Evidence of the ordinary*. *Journal of the History of the Sexuality*, July, 14(3): 316-332.

Hirschfeld, M.(1896) [Ramien, T.] *Sappho und Sokrates. Oder Wie erklärt sich die Liebe der Männer und Frauen zu Personen des eigenen Geschlechts? Leipzig: Verlag Max Spohr. [Sappho and Socrates. Or How Can One Explain the Love of Men and Women for People of Their Own Sex?]*

Hirschfeld, M. (1903) *Der Urnische Mensch.* Max Spohr, Leipzig.

Hirschfeld, M. (1910/1991) *Transvestites: The erotic drive to cross dress* (M. A. Lombardi-Nash, Trans.). Buffalo, NY: Prometheus Books.

Hirschfeld, M. (1904) *The Homosexuality of Men and Women* (M. A. Lombardi-Nash, Trans.). Buffalo, NY: Prometheus Books.

Hirschfeld, M. (1933-34/1938) *Racism* (Translated and edited by Eden and Cedar Paul). London: Victor Gollancz Ltd.

Hirschfeld, M. (1938/1956) *Sexual Anomalies and Perversions: Physical and Psychological Development, Diagnosis and Treatment* (Compiled by Norman Haire). London: Encyclopaedic Press.

Hirschfeld, M. (1941/2006) *The Sexual History of the World War.* Honolulu, Hawaii: University Press of the Pacific.

Johansson, W. (n.d.) Hirschfeld, Magnus. *Encyclopedia of Homosexuality*, http://www2.hu-berlin.de/sexology/BIB/EOH/index.htm (accessed 28 August 2010).

Kaes, A. (1995) German Cultural History and the Study of Film: Ten Theses and a Postscript. *New German Critique*, spring/summer, 65: 47-58.

Leiser, E. (1974) *Nazi Cinema* (Gertrud Mander, Trans.). London: Secker and Warburg.

Maclellan, N. (2004) *Louis Michel: Anarchist and revolutionary feminist, jailed and exiled for leading the 1871 popular uprising in Paris.* Melbourne, New York: Ocean Press.

Melching, W. (1990) *A New Morality*: Left-Wing Intellectuals on Sexuality in Weimar Republic. *Journal of Contemporary History*, January, 25(1): 69-85.

Meyenburg, B. and Sigusch, V. (1977) Sexology in West Germany. *The Journal of Sex Research*, 13(3): 197-209.

Micheler, S. (2002) Homophobic Propaganda and the Denunciation of Same-Sex-Desiring Men under National Socialism. *Journal of the History of Sexuality,* January/April, 11(1 and 2): 95-130.

Mildenberger, F. (2007) Kraepelin and the *urnings*: male homosexuality in psychiatric discourse. *History of Psychiatry*, 18(3): 321-335.

Monaco, P. (1976) *Cinema & Society: France and Germany during the twenties.* New York, Oxford, Amsterdam: Elsevier.

Mosse, G. L. (1985) *Nationalism and Sexuality: Middle Class Morality and Sexual Norms in Modern Europe.* Madison, Wisconsin: The University of Wisconsin Press.

Pilgrim, D. (2002) The biopsychosocial model in Anglo-American psychiatry: Past, present and future. *Journal of Mental Health*, December, 11(6): 585-594.

Samenow, C. P. (2010) A Biopsychosocial Model of Hypersexual Disorder/Sexual Addiction. *Sexual Addiction & Compulsivity*, 17(2): 69-81.

Sigusch, V. (2008) The Birth of Sexual Medicine: Paolo Mantegazza as Pioneer of Sexual Medicine in the 19th Century. *The Journal of Sexual Medicine*, 5(1): 217-222.

Steakley, J. D. (1999) Cinema and censorship in the Weimar Republic: The case of Anders als die Andern. *Film History*, 11(2): 181-203.

Stryker, S. and Whittle, S. (eds.) (2006) *The transgender studies reader.* New York: Routledge.

Toates, F. (2010) Understanding drug treatment: a biopsychosocial approach. In Meg Barker, Andreas Vossler and Darren Langdridge (eds.) *Understanding counselling and psychotherapy,* pp. 45- 75. London and Milton Keynes: Sage Publications Inc. and The Open University.

van de Wiel, R. (2007) Invisible Lines: Homosexuality, Fascism, and Psychoanalysis. http://www.raymondvandewiel.org/index1.html (accessed 12 November 2010).

Weeks, J. (1996) *Sex, Politics & Society: The regulation of sexuality since 1800* (Second edition). London and New York: Longman.

Wolff, C. (1986) *Magnus Hirschfeld: A Portrait of a Pioneer in Sexology.* London, Melbourne, New York: Quartet Books.

Wood, J. M., Koch, P. B. and Mansfield, P. K. (2006) Women's Sexual Desire: A Feminist Critique. *The Journal of Sex Research*, August, 43(3): 236-244.

The Politics and Parables of Encyclopaedias

Here I assess the political credibility of three encyclopaedias (*Encyclopaedia Britannica*, *Encyclopaedia of Marxism* and *Wikipedia*) in relation to three chosen topics (Friedrich Engels's historical biography; the political philosophy of fascism; and, the discipline of social psychology). I am interested in discerning how these subjects are represented and critically evaluated within each encyclopaedia. What epistemological foundations are at work? What narrative mechanisms are employed? What type of information is privileged and what is marginalised? What kind of criticality is permitted? And, most importantly, how effective are the descriptions in terms of demystifying capitalist social relations and empowering the working class? My provisional findings suggest the political narratives of *Encyclopedia Britannica* are the least intellectually credible of the three. Whilst all three possess weaknesses, a combination of *Encyclopaedia of Marxism* and *Wikipedia* should provide a thorough and, by and large, trustworthy starting point for *any* researcher investigating social issues from a political perspective.

INTRODUCTION

This chapter came about as a result of three non-related occurrences during the course of my academic teaching in 2010: the first was an innocuous question from a student who wished to know where I stood in relation to the use of *Wikipedia* as reference; a few weeks later, I stumbled upon a written comment in the margin of a student essay by a fellow academic denouncing *Wikipedia* in scornful terms, '... really problematic, never, never use Wikipedia in any academic essay'; and, finally, a request by a colleague from Loughborough University to contribute an entry for a sports encyclopaedia (Fozooni, in print), and the protracted editorial negotiations over content and style that ensued. The cumulative impact of these three episodes compelled me to launch a belated investigation into the politics and story-telling mechanisms of 'knowledge trees'.

My initial reading had yielded a series of dualities that I found helpful for circumnavigating the often-hazardous terrain of compendium wars. The distinction between printed and online encyclopaedias, the antagonism between political and objective reference books, individual and collective authorship, and the difference between modernist and postmodernist epistemologies were all subjects that required careful investigation. To facilitate this, I selected three works: the printed version of *Encyclopedia Britannica* (henceforth, *EB*) was chosen as representative of academically reputable referencing; the online version of the *Encyclopedia of Marxism (EM)* as exemplar of no-holds-barred political referencing; and, lastly, *Wikipedia (WP)*, the postmodernist, academically derided, project of collective knowledge-making.

The chapter begins with a history of encyclopaedias. I justify my focus on the political credibility of encyclopaedias in contrast to most previous researchers who tend to dwell on issues of accuracy and academic respectability (Giles 2005; Nature 2006). I then analyse three distinct entries: the historical biography of Friedrich Engels; the political interpretation of fascism as a movement and ideology; and, the genesis and development of Social Psychology as a distinct discipline within the social sciences. The final part evaluates the strengths and weaknesses of encyclopaedias in dealing with complex political issues and draws some general conclusions.

ENCYCLOPAEDIAS, EPISTEMOLOGIES AND POLITICAL POWER

Encyclopaedic sorting, classifying, pruning, defining and describing are tasks with a dual-purpose. The stated aim of these activities is to clarify and comprehend the world we live in and to enhance our collective knowledge incrementally through the accumulation of 'objective units of facts'. However, pigeon-holing is at the same time an exercise in ideological power. The traditional encyclopaedists exercised this power by either ignoring a subject, or relegating it to the *trivium* (which in medieval universities consisted of grammar, logic and rhetoric) rather than the more prestigious *quadrivium* (arithmetic, geometry, music and astronomy), or by interpreting it in a way that foreclosed alternative explanations.

In his *Discours préliminaire* (1751), the French thinker d'Alembert would heap faint praise on the proto-empiricism of Bacon, whilst subordinating Bacon's trees of knowledge (the revealed and natural branches of theology) to Reason. The political implications of this re-classification were lost on no one. It seemed to many God himself was being interrogated. But as if to underscore the boldness of the break, the last section of *Discours préliminare* presented Bacon as the great but flawed progenitor of philosophy. Here d'Alembert narrates 'history as the triumph of civilization and civilization as the work of men of letters' (Darnton 1988, 199). Thus Bacon's residual scholasticism was burst asunder by 'Descartes the doubter', and 'Newton the modest' provided the perfect model of inquiry by restricting 'philosophy to the study of observed phenomena' (Darnton 1988, 200).

This unilinear narrative of progress is also a tale of moral uplift, with heroes and villains meeting on battlefields to storm rival citadels. The philosopher-warriors of the Enlightenment enjoyed a cult status as exalted as anything the contemporary era has to offer Wiki-warriors. Perhaps one could also speculate that both sets of elites had disdain for the unwashed masses equal to their faith in the emancipatory virtues of truth. Here is d'Alembert displaying his class prejudices: 'Doubtless the common people is a stupid animal which lets itself be led into the shadows when nothing better is offered to it. But offer it the truth; if this truth is simple ... it will definitely seize on it and will want none other' (d'Alembert 1770, quoted in Hyland et al., 2003, 49).

Diderot's *Pensée philosophiques* (1746) 'was burned by order of the Paris parliament because, among other things, of its atheism' (Báez 2008, 159). When d'Alembert and Diderot teamed up to produce the *Encyclopédia* (1751-1771), they further shifted the balance of power toward secularism at the expense of the sacred unknown. The printing of 1759 was suspended by authorities as it was deemed too scandalous (Báez 2008, 159). As Darnton makes clear the 'Encyclopedists conveyed a message merely by positing things ... [and] ... by subjecting religion to philosophy, they effectively dechristianized it' (Darnton 1988, 194). They also supplemented Bacon's *inductivism* (observation leading to theories) through the use of *deductivism* (logical arguments from a set of premises) (Wernick 2006, 33). What the sociologist Comte would later call *encyclopédisme* (a project of secular-scientific synthesis ranging from the 17th century to the 19th) was imbued with a political and moral mission. Bacon's motives were material progress and social peace. The *philosophes* desired on top of that to 'place the polity itself on a rational basis', whilst Comte wished to complete the arc in order to facilitate the preconditions of the new industrial order (Wernick 2006, 28-29).

In retrospect, the naive men of letter narrative of d'Alembert can be restated as semi-conscious capitalist triumphalism, a triumphalism representing a series of epistemological attempts to bring bourgeois order to disorder: Bacon's scholastic proto-empiricism and its link to primitive capital accumulation; Locke's more consistent empiricism laying the grounds for (neo-)liberalism (Caffentzis 2008) as well as cognitive psychology and behaviourism (Billig 2008); Diderot and d'Alembert's bourgeois individualism which walked a tightrope between religious obscuranticism of the church and proletarian rebelliousness; and Comet's *Scheisspositivismus* (Marx) inaugurating the industrial phase of capitalist development. In fact, Comte openly acknowledged his debt to counter-revolutionary thinkers like de Maistre who called for the restoration of a hierarchal monarchal state to recuperate the gains of the French Revolution. The link between various epistemologies and power becomes clearer with age.

The narrative so far has aimed to sensitise the reader to the dualities present in the construction of encyclopaedias. Most contemporary encyclopaedias present themselves as objective, factual, permanent and certain, the *summa* of consensual expert opinion. In reality, however, I will be arguing that the preparation, production and reception of these texts are thoroughly imbued with subjective, political, contingent, and moral intent. Their value for the status quo is to maintain the power and wealth of a minority elite by policing knowledge.

Ironically this mythical mind-map is strategically deployed in the construction of another fiction- that of the 'nation' - which as Anderson (1990) has demonstrated must be imagined as a community and reinforced through *banal* actions on a daily basis (Billig 1995). Nadine Kavanagh (2010) has described how the *Australian Encyclopaedia* (1925-26) was instrumental in the construction of national identity. This project quite deliberately skirted round any subject deemed negative or problematic:

> A simple strategy for glossing over Australia's undesired past therefore was to exclude all references to convicts or to call them *early settlers* or *pioneers* ... [this strategy however] did not address the widespread anxiety that Australia's convict ancestry just like its *degenerating* hot climate, made Australians inferior to their brothers and sisters in Britain (Kavanagh 2010, 244).

When a discussion of convictism was unavoidable, the cross-referencing system was deftly employed to reduce the definition of convict to one particular type: the political prisoner (Kavanagh 2010, 245). Avoiding undesirable convicts and the native Other were preconditions for the creation of a mythic sense of national identity revolving around 'white Australia'.

THE POLITICS OF ENCYCLOPAEDIA BRITANNICA *(EB)*

Encyclopaedia Britannica was preceded by Chamber's *Cyclopaedia* (1728) and the *Biographia Britannica* (1747-1766). Most Enlightenment encyclopaedias were written in the vernacular rather than in Latin (Hartelius 2010, 508). The publication of *EB* in 1768 was likewise a conscious political act. Born amidst the Scottish Enlightenment, *EB* was a conservative, pro-monarchist reaction against the perceived radicalism of the French *Encyclopédie*. This may explain why 'in the biographical entries, there is far less emphasis on criticism' (Tankard 2009, 58). The chief editor of the 3rd edition, George Gleig, is rather forthright about *EB*'s political mission: 'The French *Encyclopédie* had been accused, and justly accused, of having disseminated far and wide the seeds of anarchy and atheism. If the *Encyclopædia Britannica* shall in any degree counteract the tendency of that pestiferous work, even these two volumes will not be wholly unworthy of your Majesty's attention' (Gleig in Wikipedia, 'History of the Encyclopædia Britannica'). Perhaps this was damage limitation exercise mixed in with genuine pro-crown sympathy, since George III had earlier ordered offending illustrations 'depicting female pelvises and foetuses in the midwifery article ... ripped from every copy [of *EB*'s 1st edition]' (ibid.).

The tradition of dedicating *EB* to the reigning monarch persists to this day despite the fact that ownership was transferred from Scottish to American proprietors in 1901 and later still to a Swiss billionaire. However, it is now jointly dedicated to the British monarch and United States president, with the words 'Dedicated by Permission to the Heads of the Two English-Speaking Peoples ...' The *Americanisation* of *EB* was considered an act of impertinence by some British scholars who continue to criticise the emphasis on parochial American concerns. This despite the fact that an institution as British as *The Times* sanctioned the sale. This relationship between

EB and *The Times* was a source of amusement to *EB*'s critics: '*The Times* is behind the *Encyclopædia Britannica* and the *Encyclopædia Britannica* is behind the times' (ibid.).

In keeping with tradition, the 1st edition of *EB* did not include biographies of living people. When it was decided to include biographies, William Smellie resigned the editorship in protest. What was inventive about *EB* was the combination of alphabetic and thematic organisation. An alphabetic organisation, although a very egalitarian method of organisation because it reduced subjects to the same ontological level, was considered 'dismembering the sciences'. Although commercially successful, *EB* was derided by scholars for a few decades (Tankard 2009, 42), in a vein very similar to attacks on *WP* today. Smellie had to apologise for *EB*'s shortcomings in the same defensive manner current *WP* editors justify inadequacies, 'With regard to errors in general, whether falling under the denomination of mental, typographical or accidental, we are conscious of being able to point out a greater number than any critic whatever. Men who are acquainted with the innumerable difficulties of attending the execution of a work of such an extensive nature will make proper allowances' (ibid.).

Indeed some of the errors in early editions of *EB* were far more preposterous than any that can be attributed to in *EM* or *WP*. The 2nd edition fixed the origins of earth as 23 October 4004 B.C. and the 3rd edition imprudently rejects Newton's theory of gravity (ibid.). Gradually most of these errors were corrected. Contributions from leading scholars only began in 1815-24. Unlike *EM* and *WP* which disallow original research, some of these *EB* contributions were genuinely original such as Thomas Young's translation of the hieroglyphics on the Rosetta Stone (5th edition). By the 20th century the likes of Freud, Trotsky and Einstein were further enhancing *EB*'s reputation as a site of academic excellence, although the overall style had become less scholarly and more popular (http://corporate.britannica.com/company_info.html).

The 11th edition (1910-11) included an article by Baden-Powell on kite-flying which is interesting in view of the criticisms levelled at *WP* for containing 'banal subjects'. At this stage *EB* employed 35 female contributors out of 1500 (2.3%). Marie Curie (despite having won Noble Prizes in Chemistry and Physics) did not merit an entry although she is briefly mentioned under her husband Pierre Curie. I encountered a similar problem when looking up Sylvia Pankhurst. Sylvia is not deemed important enough to have a separate entry although she is briefly mentioned under her mother, Emmeline Pankhurst. This is despite the fact that Sylvia Pankhurst's politics are far more radical and relevant to our times than the bourgeois contributions of her mother or sisters (Fozooni 2007).

The 14th edition deleted information 'unflattering to the catholic church' (Wikipedia, 'History of the Encyclopædia Britannica'). The Great Depression caused a dangerous slump in sales. In 1933 it was decided to continuously update *EB* on a schedule in order to keep it timely and maintain profit margins. Spin-offs were produced for children, historians and cartographers in order to maximise niche markets. However, it has been estimated that less than 40% of *EB* has changed from 1985 to 2007 and the size (at approximately 40 million words) has remained nearly constant since 1954.

Roughly 25% of both the *Macropædia* (long essay section) and *Micropædia* (shorter entries) are devoted to geography, with biographies, science and social science occupying the following categories. *EB* has found it difficult to keep the *Macropædia* and *Micropædia* contributions consistent. *EB* has been marketed as the most 'non-western' of western encyclopaedias, although it is no stranger to overt promotion of racist and sexist views. Virginia Woolf called its art and literature entries 'bourgeois' and *EB*'s 11th edition promoted the Ku Klux Klan as protectors of the white race against the negro threat. This was mild compared to views expressed in 1898: 'No negro has ever been distinguished as a man of science, a poet or an artist ... By the nearly unanimous consent of anthropologists this type occupies ... the lowest position in the evolutionary scale ... the inherent mental inferiority [is] even more marked than their physical differences, (Encyclopaedia Britannica 1898, 316-318).

ENCYCLOPAEDIA OF MARXISM *(EM)* AIMS TO SHAPE LEFTIST DEBATE

The organisation of the Marxist Internet Archive (*MIA*) is confusing. Its web-page at http://www.marxists.org/admin/sitemap/index.htm is subdivided into categories that seem to overlap considerably. The 5 categories represented are: Selected Marxist Writers (e.g., Marx & Engels, Kautsky, Trotsky, Paul Mattick); Library (e.g., First International, Fabians, Paris Commune); History Archive (The Black Panther Party, Argentina, Capitalism), Subject Archive (Alienation,

Ethics, May Day); and finally what I will be concentrating on, the *Encyclopedia of Marxism* (alphabetically arranged relevant subjects).

EM is in many ways the exact opposite of *EB*, since it lays no claim to naïve objectivity. *EM* is an openly political reference guide to Marxism which operates as a volunteer based non-profit organisation. Within this self-imposed political remit, it also claims to be an 'open Encyclopedia': 'Our aim has been to present how a word has been used by Marxists, and to reflect the range of views found amongst Marxists of various hues, especially the views of the founders ...' (http://www.marxists.org/glossary/about/index.htm). Much of the material is scanned from old Progress Publishers books (Empson 2005).

Since 2002, *EM* has been attributing an article to the individual who wrote it, although the majority of entries remain the collective work of the editorial board. This board consists, as far as I can tell, of Leninists (mostly Leninist-Trotskyites). The secretary of *EM* is Andy Blunden, an Australian Trotskyite and an ex-member of the Workers Revolutionary Party whose leader was the infamous Gerry Healy.

The relationship between *EM* and *MIA* resembles the division of labor between *Micropœdia* and *Macropœdia* in *EB*. *EM* is mostly biographies and glossary of terms and *MIA* is a more comprehensive archival support. *MIA* relies on the voluntary work of many sympathisers (around 62 active volunteers in 2007 most of whom, it is claimed, are not academics) to research, transcribe, translate, proof-read, index and update its entries. Thanks to these volunteers material are translated into an impressive number of languages (45 different languages by the end of 2007). *MIA* has a charter with seven fundamental tenets including a promise to remain free and politically independent and to provide simple archival information (http://www.marxists.org/admin/intro/index.htm).

Very early on the editors had to address the thorny problem of 'distasteful views' such as racist or sexist ideas being expressed by some Marxist writers. It was decided to archive these works without filtering them (ibid.). *EM* has an uneasy relationship with 'bourgeois law'. Another leading member explains, 'We believe that neither the prohibition incurred by any cost nor any right of intellectual ownership should restrict Marxist education' (Basgen quoted in Empson 2005). On the one hand *MIA* exists in a capitalist world, and uses technologies subjected to legal procedures based on private intellectual property and on the other hand it wishes to be a prefiguring of a post-capitalist world where private property and bourgeois law have been superseded. *EM* is now licensed under the Creative Commons License. However, good intentions has not prevented a conflict developing between the original archivist of *MIA* (internet nickname: Zodiac) and volunteers for control of content and direction. According to Wikipedia, 'As the scope of the archive expanded, Zodiac feared that the opening toward diverse currents of Marxism was a *slippery slope* toward sectarianism' (Wikipedia, 'Marxist Internet Archive').

In 2007 a series of cyber-attacks were organised against *MIA*, allegedly from China. A leading member of the *MIA*'s steering committee, Brian Basgen, explained the 'irony' of a communist state attacking a communist archive: 't is ironic for people who don't know what is going on in China ... The Chinese so-called Communist government has nothing to do with communism. It has been going toward capitalism for a long time' (Cohen *The New York Times* 2007). The *MIA* (being a largely Trotskyite-oriented archive) does not even consider Mao himself to have been a 'true Marxist'. According to Cohen, '[Mao] is considered a *reference writer*, along with other authors like Adam Smith, Stalin and Jean-Jacques Rousseau'. To be included as a 'true Marxist' writer, the individual must fulfil the basic criteria of serving to 'liberate working people' (Cohen 2007).

EM/MIA thus constitute a Trotskyite project with the following self-proclaimed rationale, '[In 1990] ... Marxism needed a cocoon, an archive—to measure its validity in totality, and to give it rebirth amid the shattering of the Soviet style Marxism-Leninism ... We didn't have answers; we had information ... We weren't doing this just to understand the world, but also to create a new level of consciousness in people the world over' (See Marxist Internet Archive at http://www.marxists.org/admin/intro/history/index.htm).

WIKIPEDIA *(WP)* AS POSTMODERNIST 'COMMUNITY'

Vugt (2010, 64) believes that the spirit of the *Encyclopédia* has returned in the shape of Wikipedia. *Sapere aude* (dare to know, Kant's motto for Enlightenment) has transformed into *WP*'s *Dare to edit*. Even the *Encyclopédia*'s system of cross-referencing is seen in this light as a precursor of the modern hypertext. However, if the *Encyclopédia* kept 'the hierarchy between authority and the reader in place', *WP* actively encourages a new type of collaboration based on equality and horizontalisation (ibid., 66). Jandric (2010, 48) even claims that 'Wikipedia creates a virtual anarchist society'. The distinction between *writerly* and *readerly* texts, popularised by Barthes, is very relevant here (Barthes 1974). *EB* is a readerly text which safeguards the authority of the author as the final signifier and leaves little room for alternative interpretations. In contrast, *WP* and to a lesser extent *EM* actively encourage the reader to join in the process of editing the text into an open-ended network of multiple interpretations. In a discursive twist to this Barthesian analysis of authorship, Foucault was to prefigure projects such as *WP* in these terms: 'We can easily imagine a culture where discourse would circulate without any need for an author. Discourses, whatever their status, form, or value [...] would unfold in a pervasive anonymity' (Foucault 1969, 16). The historical author who supposedly brought stylistic uniformity and theoretical coherence has been replaced with something altogether more complex.

Baytiyeh and Pfaffman (2010) using a mixture of surveys, open ended questions and Likert scale questionnaires interviewed 115 Wikipedians. Their study shows that Wikipedians 'are largely driven by motivations to learn and create [...] altruism- the desire to create a public repository for all knowledge- is one of the most important factors' (Baytiyeh and Pfaffman 2010, 128). Hartelius (2010, 516) reports that a majority of Wikipedians are 'intellectuals in their late twenties and thirties ... typically male and English-speaking'. Their fundamental guiding principle in this endeavour is a 'neutral point of view'. This knowledge community is characterised by members who begin their work at the margins of *WP* (e.g., uploading images and proof reading) and move on to more complex tasks (e.g., maintenance of the website and writing), with the help of more experienced Wikipedians. The virtual space created is remarkably similar to Vygotsky's *zone of proximal development* through the application of Bakhtin's *dialogic interaction*. Hartelius shows how *WP* by promoting a chain of utterances challenges monologic, individualistic 'expertise' (Hartelius 2010, 505). *WP* encourages us to see 'truth' as forming through dialogue and rhetoric, that is rhetoric in the positive sense used by ancient Greeks and recently revived by Billig (1996). It also attempts to render superfluous the distinction between formal knowledge and everyday knowledge. It is these aspects of *WP* that set it apart from *EB* and perhaps even *EM*.

However, it would be naïve to suggest that collective authorship, anonymity, dialogic interaction, co-contructivism and constant editing have overcome issues of power imbalance. As Vugt has observed, 'Essentially, what is going on on the *pages* of Wikipedia in terms of politics is a struggle over voice, a struggle which only becomes visible when one decides to delve further into the wiki structure, i.e. the discussion and history pages' (Vugt 2010, 70). This struggle between and within the 75,000 Wikipedians who contribute to *WP*, the sixty-plus staff who run its day-to-day administration and Jimmy Wales who as founder shapes its evolution strategically, is not always visible but nevertheless a defining feature of the project. For example, *WP* decided to construct a 'social contract' for its Wikipedians in order to control editing. Some features of the software are 'available only to administrators, who are experienced and trusted members of the community' (Wikipedia, 'Wikipedia: Policies and Guidelines'). Some articles are blocked from public access when they become the site of ferocious editing wars. For example, the US president Barack Obama's page was blocked when 'birthers' (those who insist Obama is not a US citizen) changed Obama's birthplace from Hawaii to Kenya (Parvaz 15 January 2011).

METHOD

A qualitative approach is essential for comprehending the dynamics of encyclopaedic entries embedded in multi-layered discourses of knowledge. These texts have to be analysed for explicit meaning as well as hidden ideological roots. I, therefore, chose to combine a historical analysis of encyclopaedias with a 'close reading' of their contributions on three topics. The historical analysis has foregrounded the ontology, epistemology and political positions of encyclopaedias. Closed reading is a notion borrowed from the works of Moss and Shank (2002), Maingueneau & Angermüller (2007), and DuBois (2003).

Moss and Shank (2002) employ close reading to investigate computer mediated teaching and research interactions that occur online. Closed reading is preferred to coding strategies based on the following logic, 'One sense of close reading is the idea that crucial nuggets of insight are often infrequent, so there is a need to sift through the text looking for these sorts of nuggets. Relying solely on coding strategies, and especially coding software, tends to bury these infrequent responses, rather than bringing them to the surface where they can be studied'. These 'nuggets' are linked with others in complex patterns of interaction which a close reading can map out. The tradition of close reading expounded by Maingueneau & Angermüller (2007) emphasises the relation between discourse as text (intradiscursive) and discourse as activity (extradiscursive). This is certainly pertinent in a study of resources that have become, to use Hegelian inspired terminology, powerful tools-and-results of knowledge. *Tools*, in so far as they help us understand knowledge and *results* because, in time, they tend to form into self-constituting discourses that shape knowledge. Moreover, a close reading allows us to better understand the relationship between the encyclopaedic genre and the emergent narrative.

DuBois (2003) describes how close reading is critical and evaluative but it also takes chances when reading a text, since it uses creative imagination to forge linkage. This chance taking enhances its political efficacy. Close reading with its mix of modernist and postmodernist critical devices, thus, seems to be an appropriate method for assessing the intricacies of the text, its attributes as a genre and the extradiscursive factors shaping it.

My approach focuses on political credibility rather than accuracy. Francke and Sundin (2010) provide a useful definition of 'credibility' which I have adopted. It is a notion related to 'quality, trust, authority, and persuasion' (Francke and Sundin 2010). Credibility is further divided into three components, all of which were being assessed here: *source* credibility (i.e., our three chosen encyclopaedias); *message* credibility (the structure, style and content of entries); and, *media* credibility (here the credibility associated with either print or online publications).

I focused on three topics: Engels (in order to furnish an analysis of the popular biographical genre and a well known figure who divides opinion); Fascism (an ideological movement with extreme views which has been researched and discussed widely by numerous scholars); and, Social Psychology (a field I am personally acquainted with and feel drawn to). It is hoped the choice of topics has provided a reasonable representation of encyclopaedic entries, although I do not wish to deny the strong subjective element shaping the selection process. A number of obstacles and complications had to be addressed before data gathering could begin. For instance, a series of interesting topics had to be abandoned when it became obvious they were not equally regarded by the three encyclopaedias. *EB* does not have an entry on Sylvia Pankhurst or Lev Vygotsky. *EM* does not warrant the Zanj slaves' rebellion worthy of investigation.

A related problem was structural. Two of my encyclopaedias are organised around a small and a larger section. *EB* has Micro and Macro sections and the Marxist archive has a similar divide between *EM* and the rest of *MIA*. By contrast each entry in *WP* is whole but containing numerous hyperlinks, making the number of words for each topic uneven. I have dealt with this problem to the best of my ability, choosing appropriate topics with roughly similar word counts.

ANALYSIS

Friedrich Engels's historical biography

The *EB* entry on Engels (approx. 1980 words) is structured chronologically with a short 'factual' opening paragraph followed by four major subheadings (*Early life*, 1820-1842; *Conversion to Communism*, 1842-1845; *Partnership with Marx*, 1845-1883; *Last years*, 1883-1895), and a short bibliographical paragraph with recommendations for further reading.

The factual paragraph refers to Engels simultaneously as 'German Socialist philosopher' and (with Marx) as the founder of 'modern Communism' (p. 494). No indication is given as to whether the reader should treat socialism and communism as identical or two related aspects of the same movement (for a discussion of these issues see chapters 2 and 3 of Rubel and Crump 1987).

The early life section focuses on Engels's 'capacity for living a double life'- a curious choice of words that frames Engels as shadowy and suspect. This interpretation is reaffirmed when the reader is reminded of Engels's practice of publishing his journalistic articles under a pseudonym, without contextualising the action. In fact, this was (and to some extent still is) a common practice amongst radicals. For example, under Marx's editorship, the articles in *Neue Rheinische Zeitung* appeared without their author's name. This anonymity, besides discouraging unwanted scrutiny from security agencies, made the paper appear 'as the organ of a numberless and nameless public opinion' (Marx, quoted in Prawer 2011, 152).

Engels's growing interest in 'liberal and revolutionary works' put him at odds with his family's traditional values (p. 494). The Young

Hegelians helped turn an agnostic Engels into a 'militant atheist', a key phrase that is not explained. Engels was ripe for this transformation since 'his revolutionary convictions made him ready *to strike out in almost any direction*' (p. 404, emphasis added). The next section employs the religious term 'conversion' to describe Engels's break with the Young Hegelians and the adoption of communism. Ironically, Engels is portrayed as both over-sensitive in relation to Marx's casual response to the news of the death of Mary Burns (Engels's partner), and heartless for resisting marriage to Mary's sister, Lizzy Burns, until a deathbed 'concession' (p. 494). In fact, as Tristram Hunt (2010, 229) makes clear Marx showed staggering callousness on hearing of Mary Burns's death and Engels had every right to feel aggrieved. Hunt also describes Engels touchingly rushing to collect a priest in order to fulfil Lizzy's wish to die married. As Hunt writes, 'Engels placed the needs of Lizzy before ideological purity' (Hunt 2010, 271).

The section on his partnership with Marx depicts Engels as a man of substance but, nonetheless, a sidekick of the great Marx who also doubled-up on occasions as the 'hatchetman of the *partnership*' (p. 495). The shadowy and religious themes are developed further. Marx and Engels are mentioned as editors of a newspaper that '[appeared] in a democratic guise' during the Revolution of 1848 but was furnishing 'daily guidelines and incitements' (p. 495). The aim of Engels's correspondence with social democrats was to 'foster some degree of conformity among the *faithful*' and to sell *Das Kapital*-their 'Bible' (p. 405). One final point is the blurring of difference between 'economic' and 'material' interpretations of history, which is reminiscent of the blurring of distinction between 'socialism' and 'communism' mentioned above: 'Upon joining Marx in Brussels in 1845, Engels endorsed his newly formulated economic, or materialistic, interpretation of history, which assumed an eventual communist triumph' (p. 495).

The section on Engels's *Last Years* is noteworthy for its last sentence. Regarding some unmentioned critics of Engels who blame him for 'deviations' from 'true Marxism', *EB* refers the reader to the Marx-Engels correspondence as a way of dismissing the whole episode as a storm in a teacup (p. 495). This closing of a very productive avenue of research is to my mind the weakest aspect of *EB*'s entry on Engels.

WP's entry for Engels at approximately 2500 words is slightly longer than *EB*'s. The structure is less linear although just like *EB* it begins with a factual opening paragraph and ends with bibliography and further reading recommendations. *WP* chooses to segmentalise Engels's life based on geography with the following cities emphasised in his life's journey: Barmen, Manchester, Paris, Brussels, Cologne and London. The text includes 5 pictures (*EB* included only one). The existence of incomplete sub-headings and 'stubs' give the whole piece an impression of 'unfinalizability'. The opening paragraph is more informative than *EB*. For instance, Engels is introduced with more descriptive 'tags'. These tags or framing devices depict him as entrepreneur, social scientist, author, political theorist and philosopher.

The main body evaluates Engels in more positive terms than the preceding *EB* entry. Anonymous publishing by Engels are not explained as shadowy or underhanded. Rather anonymity is justified as a legitimate ethnographic method of analysis for someone investigating child labor and extreme impoverishment. Mary Burns is also described more warmly as 'a fierce young working woman with radical opinions ... who guided Engels through Manchester and Salford'. Quotes from Engels or Marx are utilised to provide a flavour of the ideas being discussed. Furthermore, *WP* provides information about Engels's military experiences as a volunteer during the 1989 uprising in South Germany missing from *EB*.

Engel's re-entry into Manchester business circles is described as an act of sacrifice which allowed Marx to live in relative comfort and complete *Das Kapital*. In *WP*'s estimation, Engels was not a mere sidekick of Marx but an original thinker in his own right, who contributed to our understanding of the rise of religion and family, the relationship between dialectical and historical materialism, and some of the most seminal peasant uprisings in medieval Europe. Moreover, his relationship with atheism and religion is more fully elaborated and his latter day pantheistic inclinations are alluded to. As part of assessing his legacy a number of his books are introduced and briefly contextualised. Tristram Hunt (2010) and Terrell Carver (1981) are again employed liberally to back up arguments but *WP* uses more and fresher sources compared to *EB*. Furthermore, Paul Thomas (1980) is employed to introduce a critical note regarding Engels's possible misinterpretations of Marx.

EM's treatment of Engels is arranged very differently from the preceding encyclopaedias. *EM* has chosen not to have a short article on Engels presumably since it already possesses a comprehensive archive of works by and on Engels at *MIA* (http://www.marxists.org/archive/marx/bio/index.htm). The archive is subdivided into four sections:

1. *Fredrick Engels*: containing a number of short biographies of Engels by Marx, Lenin and 19th century encyclopaedias. The contribution by Marx (1880) was published as an introduction to Engel's *Socialism: Utopian and Scientific* and reads like a friendly roll call of Engel's greatest theoretical and practical accomplishments (http://www.marxists.org/archive/marx/bio/engels/en-1893.htm).
Lenin's piece is an obituary written in 1895 (See http://www.marxists.org/archive/lenin/works/1895/misc/engels-bio.htm). It begins with Engel's own eulogy of Marx on occasion of the latter's funeral (*What a torch of reason ceased to burn/What a heart has ceased to beat!*). Like most obituaries it skews historical accuracy for a degree of myth-making. For instance, it claims 'From the time that fate brought Karl Marx and Frederick Engels together, the two friends devoted their life's work to a common cause'. Of course, we know that the first encounter was decidedly icy and that they warmed to each other gradually. Lenin's contribution is peppered with dogmatic assertions and economic determinism: 'Marx and Engels were the first to show that the working class and its demands are a necessary outcome of the present economic system ...' These assertions are mixed in with moments of wishful thinking by Lenin: 'These views of Marx and Engels have now been adopted by all proletarians who are fighting for their emancipation'. In a style reminiscent of Stalinist panegyrics, Lenin continues, '[Marx and Engels] taught the working class to know itself and be conscious of itself, and they substituted science for dreams'. He even claims somewhat fancifully that during the 1848 revolution, 'The two friends were the heart and soul of all revolutionary-democratic aspirations in Rhenish Prussia'.

The sombre tone of the abovementioned contributions are offset by Engels's own *Confession*- a series of humorous responses to a questionnaire. Thanks to the *Confession* we discover that Engels's idea of happiness was a bottle of Château Margaux 1848 and his idea of misery, going to the dentist! His favourite flower was Blue Bell and his favourite hot dish was Irish Stew.

2. *Recollections of Engel's Literary Interests*: this section compromises of two reminiscences by acquaintances of Engels. The first is Nikolay S. Rusanov, an early Russian populist who became

~ 146 ~

greatly influenced by Marx's *Das Kapital,* (See http://www.marxists.org/archive/marx/bio/engels/rusanov-literature.htm). The second is named Fanni Kravchinskaya (http://www.marxists.org/archive/marx/bio/engels/kravchinskaya-literature.htm), a less well-known friend. These are brief sketches that aim to portray Engels as a learned and wise father-figure to political refugees. They add little to our knowledge of the man or his ideas and seem to be included as a concession to leftist nostalgia.

3. *Collections*: begins with various media interviews between 1871-1893. Again Engels is portrayed as the all-knowing, all-seeing sage providing advice to the European proletariat, battling misinterpretations by the likes of Giovanni Bovio (an Italian parliamentarian), glorying in the success of German social democrats in the 1893 elections in a discourse eerily similar to contemporary post-election media analysis: 'We have gained 10 seats, said [Engels] ... On the first ballot we obtained 24 seats, and out of 85 of our men left in the second ballots, 20 were returned. We gained 16 seats and lost 6, leaving us with a net gain of 10 seats. We hold 5 out of the 6 seats in Berlin' (Daily Chronicle interviews Engels in 1893, see http://www.marxists.org/archive/marx/bio/media/engels/93_07.htm). This segment ends with Bakunin's impressions of Engels which is worth quoting since it represents a rare instance of critical commentary of Engels in *MIA/EM*, 'While [Marx's] devoted friend Engels was just as intelligent as he, he was not as erudite. Nevertheless, Engels was more practical, and no less adept at political calumny, lying, and intrigue' (Bakunin, http://www.marxists.org/reference/archive/bakunin/works/various/me bio.htm).

4. *Family of Marx & Engels*: an odd addition to the above sections with its selection of short biographies of various family members, showing for me once again that *MIA/EM* do not employ hyperlinks as astutely and organically as *WP*. The list includes references to Marx's wife, daughters and various son-in-laws but very little about Engels's lineage.

Fascism

Let us begin once more with *EB*'s Micropaedia entry, which at approximately 600 words is the shortest and least satisfying of the three entries (lack of space prevents us from investigating the Macropaedia entry which is significantly more substantial). The opening sentence confines the geographical boundaries of fascism controversially as, '*fascism*, a political movement that governed parts of central and eastern Europe during 1922-45' (*EB*, Micropaedia, 'fascism', p. 691). Yet of the three classical examples that are further elaborated, Italy, Japan and Germany, only the latter can fit the elusive tag 'central and eastern European'. *EB* follows this by characterising fascism as 'extreme right-wing nationalism,' '[contemptuous of] liberalism' and signifying a clear '[rejection] of Marxism and all left-wing ideologies' (p. 691).

The text then focuses briefly on the evolution of fascism within the three national identities mentioned above, without explaining the socio-cultural and economic conditions that led to the emergence of fascism. Finally, the term 'neo-fascism' is introduced rather confusingly as every manifestation of fascism since World War II. They are distinguished from fascists proper because 'unlike the fascists, [neo-fascists] tended to place more blame for their countries' problems on foreign immigrants rather than on leftists and Jews'. They were also less interested in territorial conquests and more 'obliged [to] portray their movements as democratic' (p. 691).

What is most fascinating about *EB*'s take on fascism is not what it says but what it leaves unsaid. Nowhere in this 600 word entry is the reader informed of the anti-working class, anti-women and homophobic tendencies of fascism. The sine quo non of fascism seems to be extreme nationalism with *many* forms of fascism also displaying 'virulent racism'. It is also noteworthy that the examples of fascism and neo-fascism furnished do not include any Anglo-Saxon country. It is as if *EB* is telling us fascism is the Other's doing which occasionally becomes 'our' problem.

At 1120 words the *EM* entry on fascism is more rigorous and informative (http://www.marxists.org/glossary/terms/f/a.htm). It is also pitched at a higher theoretical level. *EM* does not ignore the fact that fascism 'is an extreme form of capitalism' or that it comes to power 'through the sponsorship and funding of massive capitalists'. *EM* informs us that the social composition of fascism have historically 'been small capitalists, low-level bureaucrats of all stripes

... with great success in rural areas, especially among farmers, peasants, and in the city, slum workers'. *EM* draws attention to the support liberal countries gave nascent fascist movements as a bulwark against the USSR, 'until Germany's tanks were on the borders of England and France'. *EM* also distinguishes between fascists and neo-fascist, claiming that the former use working class discourse rhetorically in order to gain the masses support but the latter 'disdain any trace of Socialist/Communist terminology'. A cursory perusal through neo-fascist literature demonstrates the invalidity of this assertion since many still employ *plebeian* language to win the sympathy of workers. In provocative (and I would argue confused) terms *EM* refers to fascism's corporatism as a form of anarcho-syndicalism in reverse: 'Fascism championed corporate economics, which operated on an anarcho-syndicalist model in reverse: associations of bosses in particular industries determine working conditions, prices, etc. In this form of corporatism, bosses dictate everything from working hours to minimum wages, without government interference'.

EM concludes with a list of traits that add to *EB*'s rather limited characterisation of fascism. Here the hierarchal and religious tendencies of fascism are alluded to. However, the description of fascism as 'anti-modern' is more problematic. Even if we limit the definition of modernism to the art world, this ignores the rather ambivalent relationship of individuals like Goebbels with Jazz, Riefenstahl with modern filmmaking and Speer with modern architecture. If we employ a more expansive definition of modernism which including its economic aspects, then many fascists might be categorised as pro-modern. This conceptual slippage between 'modern', 'modernity' and 'modernism' detracts from what is a superior characterisation of fascism compared to *EB*.

At a staggering 18,500 words, the *WP* contribution on fascism is by far the longest of the three entries analysed here. I will be concentrating on a small section of this essay (around 2,000 words) which includes an introduction, etymology and various definitions of fascism (Wikipedia, 'Fascism').

The first paragraph contains two characterisations that many readers may disagree with. Fascism is defined as 'a *radical* and authoritarian *nationalist* political ideology' (my emphasis). The term 'radical' is hyperlinked to another webpage where it is correctly stated that 'historically, radicalism has referred exclusively to the radical left ... rarely incorporating far-right politics ...'

(http://en.wikipedia.org/wiki/Political_radicalism). It is even suggested that the current misuse of the term may have its roots in American political discourse where radicalism may refer to both extremes of the radical left and right. The opening paragraph also informs us that 'fascists seek to organize *a nation*' (my emphasis). This analysis may chime with both *EB* and *EM* but it fails to recognise that most forms of fascism are simultaneously nationalist and 'internationalist'.

On a more positive note, *WP* is sophisticated enough to distinguish between different varieties of fascism. Nazism, for instance, is hyperlinked as 'the ideology and practice of the Nazi party ... It was a unique variety of fascism that involved biological racism and anti-Semitism' (http://en.wikipedia.org/wiki/Nazism). We are also introduced to two fascist claims that to my knowledge are not mentioned by either *EB* or *EM*, namely, its claim to seek an 'organic community' and a 'trans-class economics'. Both these false claims are loaded with a multiplicity of interpretations beyond the scope of our analysis. I only note here that their mere inclusion by *WP* provides the analysis with added gravitas. Likewise, *WP* possesses enough space to not only discuss the etymology of the term 'fascist' (as do *EB* and *EM*) but significantly to elaborate on its symbolism, 'The symbolism of the fasces suggested *strength through unity*: a single rod is easily broken, while the bundle is difficult to break' (Wikipedia, 'Fascism', 'Etymology').

The next sub-section is concerned with various interpretations of fascism. It aims to give the impression that 'Since the 1990s, scholars including Stanley Payne, Roger Eatwell, Roger griffin and Robert O. Paxton have been gathering a rough consensus on the ideology's core tenets' (Wikipedia, 'Fascism', 'Definitions'). I find this statement problematic on two grounds; first, for an encyclopaedia with an anti-academic predilection, this section seems far too generous towards academia; and, more worryingly, it advocates a consensus that simply does not exist. In fact, many academic and non-academic theoreticians of fascism would consider the contributions of the abovementioned scholars atavistic (for a number of alternative interpretations of fascism see De Grand, 1995; Guerin, 1973; Ridley, 1988; Sohn-Rethel, 1987; Traverso, 1999; Vajda, 1976).

Social Psychology

EB's narrative structure on 'social psychology' is quite straight-forward: definition → subjects of study → methods of investigation → applications (see *EB Micropaedia,* 'Social Psychology', p. 922-23, approximately 600 words). The perennial conflict between mainstream and critical forms of social psychology (cf. Billig, 2008) is completely absent from *EB*'s account. Social psychology is restrictively defined as the '*scientific* study of human *behaviour* in its social and cultural setting' (p. 922, my emphasis). However, there is no hint that 'science' has both a narrow, positivist, experimental-oriented definition and a more expansive, complex and qualitative dimension.

The validation of the model derived from the 'hard sciences' is further underlined through focus on 'empirical methods'. *EB* claims that 'the pioneering [empirical] work in social psychology was done in the United States' (p. 922, italics added). This is problematic since it ignores parallel work in Europe and elsewhere (Hollway et al. 2007, 14). When it comes to categorising social psychology's subjects of study, *EB* reduces the range to mainstream topics such as 'social status', 'group membership', 'attitudes', and 'personality' (p. 922). The section explaining social psychology's approach to data gathering conflates methodology with method – a common occurrence. Disconcertingly, it also avoids linking methodology with epistemology or ontology, thus giving the impression that choosing one's data gathering approach is merely a matter of practicality.

EB concludes by citing social psychology's current applications as: social work, employee relations and advertising campaigns. Ominously social psychologists 'may be used to advise companies how to choose, train, and reward workers and how to organise production processes to lessen worker dissatisfaction' (p. 923).

The *WP* contribution for social psychology may be published on one webpage but it follows *EB*'s practice of separating an introductory 'Micropaedia' section (approx. 300 words) from a historical 'Macropaedia' one (approx. 4,700 words). I will focus on the former but a few aspects of the latter will be examined [http://en.wikipedia.org/wiki/Social_psychology_(psychology)].

The text certainly begins more promisingly than *EB*'s since the definition provided is more in tune with social psychology's subject of study: 'Social psychology is the scientific study of how people's thoughts, feelings and behaviours are influenced by the actual, imagined or implied presence of others'. This is already an improvement on *EB*'s over-emphasis on behaviour. True *WP* then goes on to define scientific as the 'empirical method of investigation' and behaviour, thoughts and feelings as 'measurable' psychological variables but at least *WP* problematises this by implying there are alternative perspectives.

Societal normalisation and its possible adverse effects are alluded to and the interdisciplinary nature of social psychology placed in the 'gap between psychology and sociology'. *WP* even alludes to the historical distinction between American and European forms of social psychology with the former focusing on the individual and the latter paying more attention to group phenomena.

The 'Macropaedia' section of the contribution contextualises social psychology historically. It inflicts a parental lineage on social psychology by referring to Kurt Lewin as 'the father of social psychology' (Wikipedia, 'Social Psychology', 'History'). We are informed that 'By the 1970s, however, social psychology in America had reached a crisis. There was heated debate over the ethics of laboratory experimentation, whether or not attitudes really predicted behavior, and how much science could be done in a cultural context' (ibid.). This is based on the academically reputable work of Kenneth Gergen (1973).

The distinction between *intra*personal and *inter*personal phenomena is both conventional and problematic. The former phenomena focus on issues of attitude, persuasion, social cognition, self-concept and cognitive dissonance. The latter embraces social influences, group dynamics, relations with others and interpersonal attraction. Brown explains how the study of intrapersonal relations, where 'group setting' involves merely the presence of another person, narrows the approach to social groups. Intrapersonal studies also happen to be the dominant tradition in social psychology (Brown 2007, 133). The other tradition, which emerged in the 1970s based on the works of Tajfel, Potter, Wetherell, and Billig, emphasises instead interpersonal dynamics. Unfortunately *WP*'s contribution reinforces this unnecessary demarcation.

The final section is a rather nondescript account of research methodology and ethics. The disappointing thing about the treatment of ethical issues is how closely *WP* follows convention in assuming today's researchers are more ethical thanks to rigorous checks conducted by ethical committees compared to the all-too-easily vilified Stanley Milgram and Philip Zimbardo.

EM does not have a specific entry on social psychology. Key psychology thinkers such as Pavlov, Freud, Mead, Jung, Vygotsky and Lacan are listed. The seminal schools of psychology that have shaped its internal dynamics are also expounded upon: Gestalt, behaviourism and psychoanalysis.

What I find impressive about the treatment of social psychology is the archives at *MIA* under the title 'Psychology and Marxism'. The webpage begins with a framing quote by Vygotsky, 'Psychology is in need of its own *Das Kapital* – its own concepts of class, basis, value etc. - in which it might express, describe, and study its object'. In order to explore the relationship between Marxism and Psychology the archives are subdivided into three sections:

1. Marxist Works (which can be found at http://www.marxists.org/subject/psychology/marxists.htm): consisting of two major groups of authors, Soviet Marxists and Western Marxists addressing psychology. Examples of the former group would be El'konin, Ilyenkov, Leontiev, Luria and Vygotsky, and the latter group are represented by Erich Fromm, Lucien Seve and Henri Wallon. Many books are available in pdf format for download.

2. Classics of Psychology (which can be found at http://www.marxists.org/subject/psychology/reference.htm): this section comprises of non-Marxist classical authors on psychology such as Wundt, Adler, Jung, Piaget, R. D. Laing and Chomsky. There is as yet no 21st century psychologist in these archives. In each case a key book by the author is made available for download.

3. Commentary (which are archived at http://www.marxists.org/subject/psychology/commentary.htm): consists of shorter texts by contemporary writers on previous themes. Many of these are famous neo-Vygotskians such as Fred Newman and Lois Holzman, Michael Cole, and Peter Jones.

DISCUSSION

Political credibility is projected very differently in encyclopaedias. *EB*, basing itself on positivist and empiricist epistemologies, pursues data in order to secure an abstract notion of bourgeois truth. *EB* conceals the chaotic, contradictory, messy process of knowledge building and presents the reader with a seemingly unambiguous product consisting of 'objective' units of information. This view of knowledge creates 'rigid facts, fragmented definitions and abstract classifications' (Pavlidis 2010, 95). The tone is impersonal in keeping with this avowed objectivity and the structure tends toward the classical, with a clear demarcation between beginning, middle and end of the narrative. As Kavanagh (2010, 238) writes: '[The style of such encyclopaedias] suggests that they present *facts*; they contain no questions or formulations that indicate uncertainty'. The final product is a *readerly* text (Barthes) with a *monologic* discourse (Bakhtin) which forecloses alternative interpretations.

EM by contrast nails its colours to the mast of proletarian struggle. It too seeks a mostly abstract notion of truth but one founded on historical materialism and the dialectical notion of class conflict. It represents a higher form of critical thinking which enhances our ability to 'perceive things as developing and changing ... [and] to perceive the interaction between opposite sides of the cognitive objects' (Pavlidis 2010, 75). Like *EB*, it is a mostly readerly text privileging monologic interaction, although by employing thousands of volunteers *EM* could lay claim to a measure of *writerly* and *dialogic* success. The outsider gains some insight into the internal decision making processes deployed at *EM* but it is also clear that the editorial board privileges Trotskyite interpretations over other forms of Marxism.

The epistemological foundation of *WP* incorporates post-structuralist relativism to critically evaluate subjects. Of the three encyclopaedias discussed here, *WP* is the most writerly and dialogic source. It may use mainly academic knowledge, as do *EB* and *EM*, but *WP* does not shirk from everyday knowledge. Truth and political creditability become a matter of protracted negotiation between academic and everyday knowledge. *WP,* as far as I can ascertain, seems genuinely interested in both the product and process of knowledge generation.

Of the dualities we discussed in the introduction, some have proved more real than others. It is clear for instance that the claim for objective, apolitical encyclopaedic work does not stand close scrutiny. After all, all encyclopaedias are political texts embedded in ideological suppositions. Furthermore, these ideological underpinnings carry with them a moral imperative. In setting out the aims of his *encyclopédie* Diderot was clear on this point, '... that our children, by becoming more educated, may at the same time become more virtuous' (Diderot quoted in Wernick 2006, 27). As with Grammarians of old, the new encyclopaedists make a play for our 'moral wisdom'. Encyclopaedias 'anticipate future knowledge, and accommodate as well as inspire the ongoing quest for knowledge' (de Vugt 2010, 65). Some encyclopaedias, even whilst privileging the expert, tend to be produced collaboratively so that at least the romantic notion of author-genius is challenged (ibid., p. 66). The online encyclopaedia also undermines the authority of the 'big individual author' but instead of killing authorship, it seems to have produced a more diffuse, ephemeral, anonymous, collective author.

Whilst the objective-political duality and the distinction between the individual-collective author have proved mostly fictive, other dualities seem to constitute real differences. The energetic efforts of *EB* to create an on-line version are testimony to the many advantages of an online presence: lower costs; regular updates; more efficient editing, to name but few. The free website was launched in 1999 but 'the appearance of the same information in a new medium, raised questions. The shift from printed to online encyclopaedias ... is not simply a relocation of content' (Hartelius 2010, 509). Unlike *WP* which is organically related to online research, *EB*'s online version feels ponderous. Ironically, the somewhat dubious and constructed distinction between modernist and postmodernist paradigms has proved fruitful throughout this analysis. *EB* consists of mostly modernist attributes whilst *WP* is characterised by a postmodernist method of knowledge generation. *EM* falls somewhere in the middle of these two stools.

My close reading has shown *EB*'s political credibility to be questionable. Whether depicting Engels as engaged in cloak and dagger political machinations, his alleged insensitivity in relation to female partners, or his assumed side-kick intellectual status compared to Marx, *EB*'s assessment of Engels seems at best uncharitable and at worst misleading. *EB* has ignored all the substantial criticisms radicals have directed at Engels over the years, in favour of inane journalistic innuendos and clumsy character assassination. On fascism, *EB* provides us with a deliberately restricted interpretation which conveniently fails to inform the reader of fascism's promotion of capitalism and its attacks on working class organisations. Instead we are introduced to a 'foreign' fascism devoid of ideological overlap with Anglo-Saxon liberalism. This convenient externalising of fascism skews historical knowledge for a self-deluding fairytale.

The most problematic *EB* entry, however, is its description of social psychology. We are given little indication of the '1970s crisis in social psychology' and the critical currents undermining confidence in experimentation and positivist interpretations ever since. The mainstream applications of social psychology as defenders of the status quo are normalised through a text shamelessly courting bourgeois respectability.

EM, in comparison to *EB*, displays a great deal of political nuance even though its overcomplicated organisation detracts somewhat from its achievements. Perhaps not surprisingly the entry on Engels is the least critical of the articles. *EM*'s political affinity for Engels as one of the 'fathers of Marxism' has prevented it from a balanced evaluation. The information vignettes on Engels are either propagandistic (e.g., Lenin's panegyrical obituary), sycophantic (e.g., literary sketches by the likes of Rusanov), or simply uninformative (e.g., pedantic family reports). The few critical remarks interspersed between all these files from Bakunin strike the reader as vindictive skulduggery by a known enemy rather than an attempt to provide a balanced assessment. The entry on fascism, on the other hand, is a strong piece full of relevant information. *EM* provides us with a reasonably comprehensive account of fascism in the space provided. Fascist characteristics are thoughtfully listed and explained. My only quibble is the conceptual slippage involving the term 'modernism' and the false analogy between fascist corporatism and anarcho-syndicalist forms of organisation.

The combined contributions of *EM/MIA* on social psychology make available many hard to come by texts. As social scientists we owe the editors a debt of gratitude for their selfless endeavours. However, even speaking as a fan of Vygotsky, I find the over-concentration on him and current neo-Vygotskian at the expense of other strands of Marxist Psychology a little disconcerting. The indefatigable browser is left with the distinct impression that although *EM/MIA* welcomes a dialogue about Marxism and Psychology, it prefers the key parameters to be predetermined in rather restrictive terms. Some readers may feel overwhelmed by the historical baggage attached to various concepts, and one must be frank here, the sterility of parts of the archived material.

In many ways *WP* represents the most fascinating of the three encyclopaedias, not necessarily because of its actual level of development but because of its potential to exceed previous knowledge trees. The contribution on Engels is written with warmth and a sophisticated political understanding. This may be related to *WP*'s more frequent use of descriptive tags for sketching biographies. *WP* also uses more images than *EB* and *EM,* which makes research more entertaining- a rather undervalued aspect of research work (cf. Francke and Sundin 2010). The entry on fascism strikes one as raw and incomplete. However, the increased space available to *WP* compared to the printed *EB* allows the former to discuss aspects of fascism such as 'organic community' and a 'trans-class economics'. Unfortunately these opportunities are not always taken advantage of and a certain amount of conceptual confusion persists. At times the sheer number of hyperlinks becomes distracting. The social psychology entry has a number of advantages over *EB* including better definitions of core concepts and a fuller historical narrative of the evolution of the discipline. Although *WP* does not underscore Marxist contributions to social psychology, it still manages a more critical assessment than *EB*'s rather conventional account.

CONCLUDING REMARKS

My preliminary study suggests that a combined survey of *EM* and *WP* entries should provide the inquisitive social researcher (whether teacher or student) with plenty of useful information as well as a critical orientation for demystifying capitalist social relations. The printed version of *EB*, however, seems to be losing the political credibility it once enjoyed. To put it another way, the dialectical method of *EM* and the dialogic approach of *WP* combined are far more instructive than the positivism of *EB*. Further investigation is essential before the results can be verified.

ACKNOWLEDGEMENTS
Thanks to a former-student, Mary Hanon, for her constructive criticisms of a draft version of this chapter.

REFERENCES

Anderson, B. (1990) *Imagined Communities: Reflections on the Origins and Spread of Nationalism*. London and New York: Verso.
Báez, F. (2008) *A Universal History of the Destruction of Books*. New York: Atlas & Co.
Barthes, R. (1974) *S/Z*. New York: Hill and Wang.
Baytiyeh, H. and Pfaffman, J. (2010) Volunteers in Wikipedia: Why the Community Matters. *Educational Technology & Society*, 13(2): 128-140.
Billig, M. (1995) *Banal Nationalism*. London, Thousand Oaks and New Delhi: Sage Publications.
Billig, M. (1996) *Arguing and Thinking: A Rhetorical Approach to Social Psychology*. Cambridge: Cambridge University Press.
Billig, M. (2008) *The Hidden Roots of Critical Psychology*. Los Angeles, London, New Delhi, Singapore: Sage Publications.
Brown, S. D. (2007) Intergroup processes: social identity theory. In D. Langdridge and S. Taylor (eds.) *Critical Readings in Social Psychology*, chapter 6. Maidenhead: Open University Press.
Caffentzis, G. (2008) *John Locke: The Philosopher of Primitive Accumulation*. No. 5. Bristol: Bristol Radical Pamphleteer.
Carver, T. (1981) *Engels*. Oxford, Toronto, Melbourne: Oxford University Press.
Cohen, N. (2007) Online Marxist archive blames China for electronic attacks, 5 February 2007, *The New York Times*. Available at http://www.nytimes.com/2007/02/05/technology/05iht-marx.4474381.html?_r=1 (accessed 12 January 2011).
Darnton, R. (1988) Philosophers Trim the Tree of Knowledge: The Epistemological Strategy of the Encyclopédie, in *The Great Cat Massacre and Other Episodes in French Cultural History*, chapter 5. London: Penguin Books.
De Grand, A. J. (1995) *Fascist Italy and Nazi Germany: The 'Fascist' Style of Rule*. London and New York: Routledge.
Empson, M. (2005) Marxism on the web. *International Socialism: A quarterly journal of socialist theory*. Available at http://www.isj.org.uk/index.php4?id=61&issue=105 (accessed 12 January 2011).
Encyclopaedia Britannica Corporate Site. *History of Encyclopædia Britannica and Britannica Online*. Available at http://corporate.britannica.com/company_info.html (accessed 28 February 2011).
Encyclopaedia Britannica (1898) *Negro*, 17: 316-318. The Werner Co., New York.

Encyclopaedia Britannica (1974/2010) *Engels*, Micropaedia, 15th edition, 494-495. Chicago/London/New Delhi/Paris/Seoul/Sydney/Taipei/Tokyo: Encyclopaedia Britannica Inc.

Encyclopaedia Britannica (1974/2010) *Fascism*, Micropaedia, 15th edition, 691-692. Chicago/London/New Delhi/Paris/Seoul/Sydney/Taipei/Tokyo: Encyclopaedia Britannica Inc.

Encyclopaedia Britannica (1974/2010) *Social Psychology*, Micropaedia, 15th edition, 922-923. Chicago/London/New Delhi/Paris/Seoul/Sydney/Taipei/Tokyo: Encyclopaedia Britannica Inc.

Foucault, M. (1969) *What is an Author?* Available at http://www.scribd.com/doc/20321761/foucault-1969-what-is-an-author-modernity-and-its-discontents (accessed 26 February 2011).

Fozooni, B. (due out, February 2012) Sport and the Islamic 'Revolution' in Iran. In J. Nauright and C. Parrish (eds.), *The ABC-CLIO Sports Around the World: History, Culture, and Practice (for MENA Region)*. Available at http://www.abc-clio.com/product.aspx?isbn=9781598843002 (accessed 14 November 2011).

Fozooni, B. (2007) Iranian Women and Football. *Cultural Studies,* 22(1): 114-133.

Francke, H. and Sundin, O. (2010) An inside view: Credibility in Wikipedia from the perspective of editors. *Information Research*, 15(3), paper colis 702. Available at http://informationr.net/ir/15-3/colis7/colis702.html (accessed 15 February 2011).

Gergen, K. (1973) Social psychology as history. *Journal of Personality and Social Psychology*, 26(2): 309-320.

Giles, J. (2005) Internet encyclopaedias go head to head. *Nature*, 438: 900-901.

Guerin, D. (1973) *Fascism and Big Business*. New York: Monad Press distributed by Pathfinder.

Hartelius, E. J. (2010) *Wikipedia* and the Emergence of Dialogic Expertise. *Southern Communication Journal*, 75(5), November-December: 505-526.

Hollway, W., Lucey, H. and Phoenix, A. (2007) *Social Psychology Matters*. Maidenhead: Open University Press.

Huvila, I. (2010) Where does the information come from? Information source use patterns in Wikipedia. *Information Research*, 15(3), Art. 433, available at http://informationr.net/ir/15-3/paper433.html (accessed 15 February 2011).

Hyland, P., Gomez, O. and Greensides, F. (eds.) (2003) *The Enlightenment: A Sourcebook and Reader*. London: Routledge.

Jandric, P. (2010) Wikipedia and education: anarchist perspectives and virtual practices. *The Journal for Critical Educational Policy Studies*, 8(2): 48-73. Available at http://www.jceps.com/PDFs/08-2-02.pdf (accessed 21 February 2011).

Kavanagh, N. (2010) 'What better advertisement could Australia have?' Encyclopaedias and nation-building. *National Identities*, 12(3): 237-252.
Maingueneau , D. and Angermüller, J. (2007) Discourse Analysis in France: A Conversation. *Forum: Qualitative Social Research*, 8(2), Art. 21, May, available at http://nbn-resolving.de/urn:nbn:de:0114-fqs0702218 (accessed 15 February 2010).
Marxist Internet Archive. *About the Encyclopaedia of Marxism.* Available at http://www.marxists.org/glossary/about/index.htm (accessed 27 February 2011).
Marxist Internet Archive. *Biography of Engels.* Available at http://www.marxists.org/archive/marx/bio/engels/en-1893.htm (accessed 27 February 2011).
Marxist Internet Archive. *Daily Chronicle Interviews Engels.* Available at http://www.marxists.org/archive/marx/bio/media/engels/93_07.htm (accessed 27 February 2011).
Marxist Internet Archive. *Fascism.* Available at http://www.marxists.org/glossary/terms/f/a.htm (accessed 27 February 2011).
Marxist Internet Archive. *Introduction: Marxist Internet Archive.* Available at http://www.marxists.org/admin/intro/index.htm (accessed 27 February 2011).
Marxist Internet Archive. *Fredrick Engels (by V. I. Lenin).* Available at http://www.marxists.org/archive/lenin/works/1895/misc/engels-bio.htm (accessed 27 February 2011).
Marxist Internet Archive. *Marx/Engels Biography.* Available at http://www.marxists.org/archive/marx/bio/index.htm (accessed 27 February 2011).
Marxist Internet Archive. *My Acquaintance with Engels (by N. S. Rusanov).* Available at http://www.marxists.org/archive/marx/bio/engels/rusanov-literature.htm (accessed 27 February 2011).
Marxist Internet Archive. *Recollections on Marx and Engels (by Mikhail Bakunin).* Available at http://www.marxists.org/reference/archive/bakunin/works/various/mebio.htm (accessed 27 February 2011).
Marxist Internet Archive. *Reminiscences (by Fanni Kravchinskaya).* Available at http://www.marxists.org/archive/marx/bio/engels/kravchinskaya-literature.htm (accessed 27 February 2011).
Moss, C. M. and Shank, G. (2002) Using Qualitative Processes in Computer Technology Research on Online Learning: Lessons in Change from 'Teaching as Intentional Learning'. *Forum: Qualitative Social Research*, 3(2), Art. 21, May. Available at http://nbn-resolving.de/urn:nbn:de:0114-fqs0202218 (accessed 15 February 2010).

Nature (2006) *Encyclopaedia Britannica and Nature: a response.* Available at http://www.nature.com/press_releases/Britannica_response.pdf (accessed 28 February 2011).

Parvaz, D. (2011) Loot it up: Wikipedia turns 10. *Aljazeera.net,* 15 January 20111. Available at http://english.aljazeera.net/indepth/features/2011/01/2011115717166553 85.html (accessed 15 January 2011).

Pavlidis, P. (2010) Critical Thinking as Dialectics: a Hegelian-Marxist Approach. *The Journal for Critical Educational Policy Studies,* 8(2); 75-102). Available at http://www.jceps.com/PDFs/08-2-03.pdf (accessed 12 February 2011).

Prawer, S. S. (2011) *Karl Marx and World Literature.* London, New York: Verso.

Ridley, F. A. (1988) *Fascism Down the Ages.* Brick Lane: Romer Publications.

Rubel, M. and Crump, J. (eds.) (1987) *Non-Market Socialism in the Nineteenth and Twentieth Centuries.* London: The MacMillan Press Ltd.

Sohn-Rethel, A. (1987) *The Economy and Class Structure of German Fascism.* London: Free Association Books.

Tankard, P. (2009) Reference Point: Samual Johnson and the Encyclopedias (The David Fleeman memorial Lecture, 2007). *Eighteenth-Century Life,* 33(3): 37-64.

Thomas, P. (1980) *Karl Marx and the Anarchists.* London, Boston and Henley: Routledge & Kegan Paul.

Traverso, E. (1999) *Understanding the Nazi Genocide.* London and Sterling, Virginia: Pluto Press.

Vajda, M. (1976) *Fascism as a Mass Movement.* London: Allison & Busby.

Wernick, A. (2006) Comte and the Encyclopedia. *Theory, Culture & Society,* 23(4): 27-48.

Wikipedia. *History of the Encyclopædia Britannica.* Available at http://en.wikipedia.org/wiki/History_of_the_Encyclop%C3%A6dia_Brit annica (accessed 4 January 2011).

Wikipedia. *Marxist Internet Archive.* Available at http://en.wikipedia.org/wiki/Marxists_Internet_Archive (accessed 12 January 2011).

Wikipedia. *Nazism.* Available at http://en.wikipedia.org/wiki/Nazism (accessed 12 January 2011).

Wikipedia. *Political radicalism.* Available at http://en.wikipedia.org/wiki/Political_radicalism (accessed 12 January 2011).

Wikipedia. *Wikipedia: Policies and Guidelines.* Available at http://en.wikipedia.org/wiki/Wikipedia:Policies_and_guidelines (accessed 12 January 2011).

Kiarostami Debunked!

Kiarostami continues to be an enigma for most cinephiles partly due to his own conscious attempts at concealment and prevarication. The article attempts to clarify his political, ideological and philosophical positions and contextualize his output within the dynamics of Iranian capitalism. Beginning with an investigation of his film techniques (including his use of framing, sound, image and music) I will discuss his attitude toward nationalism, psychology and religion. I end by suggesting reasons for his popularity outside Iran.

INTRODUCTION

It is widely accepted that premodern narration emphasized open-endedness and collective storytelling. The rise of modernist film-making, however, privileged a linear classical narrative, often related by an enigmatic auteur that many found irresistible. Origins and destinations need to be clearly demarcated in modernist narration. A fictive subjectivity is privileged as the agent of change. Both premodernity and postmodernity, in contrast and for different reasons, place subjectivity under erasure.

Although in some ways Kiarostami can be viewed as the epitome of Iranian modernism (Dabashi 2001, 33) his film-making methodology is at times closer to pre- and postmodern modes of investigation. Shunning simple cause-and-effect empirical relationships favoured by modernist ideology, he immerses himself ethnographically into his characters' environment and sketches 'thick' portraits of their lives for outsiders to dwell upon. Scripts are written only after location has been thoroughly investigated, a process that may take Kiarostami years to complete. This is reminiscent of the obsession with hermeneutics displayed by premodern and postmodern artistic productions and a far cry from modernism's preference for discursive brevity and precision. In films like *Under the Olive Trees* (1994) there is a 'studious attempt to eradicate the old boundary between unmediated *cinéma-vérité* and the shaping process of fiction film-making' (James 1997, 52). The 'golden rules', classical perspective and composition are all sacrificed towards this aim.

The initial aim of this paper is to question the classification of Kiarostami's cinema as modernist. By foregrounding various premodern and postmodern tendencies, I hope to offer a more coherent picture of his work. I look in detail at his film-making techniques. Finally, I turn my attention to his philosophical outlook and try to tease out various key attributes of his world-view.

KIAROSTAMI'S FILM TECHNIQUE

It would be counterproductive to reduce Kiarostami's film technique to a particular school of thought or artistic tendency. Certain techniques (e.g. the privileging of sound over image) may be categorized as premodern; some (e.g. his 'handling' of performers) could be viewed as scientific behavioural management and, therefore, associated with modernism; and still others (e.g. his love of repetition and non linearity) fit well with more recent postmodern concerns.

'Handling' performers

Kiarostami's reverence for daily life is such that filming schedule remains subordinate to its tempo. In an interview he claims,

> When I come on the set in the morning and I notice that my camera operator hasn't slept well, I avoid complex camera movements without letting him know. I do the same with the actors. If an actor has to play a sad scene and I notice he is in a better mood than on previous days, I alter the shooting schedule. (Kauffmann 1995, 29)

There may be a sense of bravado about such assertions but we dismiss Kiarostami's 'reverence' for life at our expense since, as it will be argued below, it is this mystic joy for life that is the key to understanding his films. For a director renowned for his 'humanism', the sheer scale of manipulative procedures employed is quite startling. In *Taste of Cherry* (1997) when he wanted the actor playing the Kurdish soldier to express amazement, '[Kiarostami] started to speak to him in Czech. At another point when [he] wanted him to look afraid, [Kiarostami] placed a gun in the glove compartment, and asked [the actor] to open it for a chocolate' (Rosenbaum 1997).

Related to this manipulative approach towards film-making is a predilection for pedagogic elitism. In his 'pre-revolutionary' phase (prior to 1979), 'society is treated like a child, in constant need of pedagogical advice and supervision' (Mir-Ehsan 1999, 108). Whilst socializing with his actors he gradually inserts ideas into their heads until they come to believe that certain ideas originated with them. It is only once Kiarostami's ideas are internalized by his actors that they can perform the dialogue *authentically*!

Sound

Another example of 'natural construction' is the soundtrack. At first it may sound amateurish, low-tech and raw but his technique of carefully constructed collage extends to the audial register. The same effect can be achieved by eliminating sound altogether, as he does in a number of scenes in *Close-Up* (1990). With regard to *The Wind Will Carry Us* (1999), Jones has commented,

> the careful modulation of birdsong, clucking hens, barking dogs, and windblowing through the grass, delicately, painstakingly ordered and placed to give the natural world a maximum of bewitching, mysterious presence ... (Jones 2000, 72)

Kiarostami once commented in an interview,

> Sound is far more important than image. In cinematography the aim is to achieve a two-dimensional representation. Sound adds a third dimension to the image by compensating for its shortcomings ... sound is so important to me that I occasionally jest, 'we're off to record sound but we'll take a cameraman with us just in case'. (Translated from Pir-Poshteh 1997, 83)

This sense of 'naturalness' is enhanced through the use of 'real-time' photography and pyscho- geographic landscapes that seem to project the inner feelings of the protagonists (again parallels with Antonioni and Rossellini are very strong here). Kiarostami uses Nature's rhythm during editing, as did Tarkovsky and Dovzhenko. The contrast between tension and relaxation, spring and winter, day and night, sustains interest.

Image

Rosenbaum has observed,

> the closest thing Kiarostami has to a visual signature might be termed the cosmic long shot ... [whilst] the sound of the characters' dialogue remains in the foreground, recalling long-shot-like panels in comic books accompanied by dialogue bubbles. (Rosenbaum 1997, 6)

One immediately thinks of the Situationist technique of *detourned* comic strips and paintings. The *detournement* of aesthetic elements refers to 'the integration of present or past artistic production into a superior construction of a milieu ... a method which testifies to the wearing out and loss of importance of [old cultural spheres]' (Knabb 1989, 45–46). These long-shot representations of reality ease effortlessly into representations of the means of representation and back again. Kauffmann (1998, 25) notes,

> Like Ozu and Antonioni, with whom he has rightly been compared, Kiarostami seems to look at film not as something to be made, but to be inhabited, as if it were there always, like the world, waiting to be stepped into, without fuss.

However, the operative term here is 'seems to', for a careful examination demonstrates how hard he has to work in order to achieve 'naturalness' in his films. For instance, in *Where is my Friend's Home?* (1987), Kiarostami took a great deal of time painting the village with bright colours to create the desired ambience. As Mulvey (1998, 26) observes, here 'one thinks of Minnelli spraying the cornfields yellow for *Lust for Life* or Ophuls painting the road red for *Lola Montès*.'

One of Kiarostami's truisms governing the practice of film-making is that too much aesthetic beauty is counterproductive, 'The scenes that are less cinematically arrogant, they interest me more. When I edit my movies, I come upon perfectly framed, nice-looking close-ups, and I say, *This is too cinematic*' (Kiarostami quoted in

Lopate 1996, 38). On the other hand, we must remember that, Kiarostami is also a photographer who pays great attention to composition and lighting. In general, cinematography *is* immensely important to him.

A key feature of his cinematography is minimalism. By concentrating on the bare minimum required to depict 'reality', minimalism has the unfortunate side effect of downplaying history - a criticism that also applies to Kiarostami. His minimalism is best exemplified by *Ten* (2002), a film shot entirely from inside a car, with minimum camera movement, colour, scripting and direction. In fact, Kiarostami is on record as claiming,

> If anyone were to ask me what I did as a director on this film, I'd say, 'Nothing and yet if I didn't exist, this film wouldn't have existed'. (Kiarostami quoted in *Pride*, 2003, 2)

Music

Kiarostami normally avoids music, as it tends to elicit an emotional response from the audience. A number of observations with this regard are pertinent. First, Iranian audiences are, by and large, not as well versed in either western or eastern musical traditions, and may miss the historical connotations of a chosen score. There are a number of historical reasons for this lack of musical knowledge: (1) many of the leading film-makers in the 1970s and 1980s were from a theatrical background and, consequently, did not pay film music much attention; (2) the ban on most forms of musical discourse after the victory of Islamic fascism meant film-makers preferred alternative modes of communicating their intention (Naficy 2002, 28); and (3) the perennially slow editing rhythm of so many Iranian films makes music's ability to enhance tension redundant. Even when used, music is not integral to the scene but more often than not acts as background 'decor'. It is quite possible that with the recent revival of interest in both western and eastern music amongst the youth (Naficy 2002, 58), film music will also become more sophisticated in the future.

Kiarostami's aesthetics are partially forged through his struggle against melodrama, a genre that makes no distinction between real human emotions and *emotionalism* as an ideology of audience manipulation. At times the marginalization of music combined with self-reflective techniques creates an unfortunate dualism between emotion and intellect in his films.

Camerawork and composition

One remarkable aspect of Kiarostami's camerawork is that the audience cannot rely on a universal language for deciphering his message. They cannot even be granted the sop of identifying with the characters since Kiarostami uses remarkably few point-of-view shots. Each film is made in a different context and thus employs a unique syntax, which has to be learnt in the process of viewing. The audience is, therefore, not reduced to passive consumers but is forced to engage productively with the film. When asked if he has a preference for long shots or close-ups, Kiarostami replies,

> To me, a close-up doesn't necessarily mean that I'm close to the person. In every movie I made, the implication would be different. In *And Life Goes On* (1992), the use of longshots made more sense. If I were to use close-ups, it would have meant you were dependent on following one person ... The film is really more about a society rebuilding itself, so it's a longshot movie. (quoted in Lopate 1996, 40)

Composition is determined by feeling and instinct and not through the application of rigorous scientific criteria. It is instructive to note that he began his career as an art student, then a graphics artist. He then made commercials and designed title sequences and, finally, he tried his hand at directing. In fact, the ideal situation calls for the viewer choosing the lens irrespective of its composition by the director. Dabashi (2001, 49) has gone as far as claiming that irony is Kiarostami's chief 'optics' and that his aesthetics are determined by the tension between his ability to 'remain on the verge of abandoning a culture without entering another'. What is beyond doubt is the influence of painting and photography on his film-making practice. He imagines visual images from daily life first and then works them into a sequence. The sequence then becomes a plot. The choice between close-ups and long shots is usually subordinated to content,

> In *Close-Up* [perhaps his most outstanding 'docudrama' which effortlessly dismantles the 'real'] we had two cameras

in the courtroom scene. One is just a longshot to follow the proceedings of the court. The other one is our camera, an artistic camera, which is basically focused on Sabzian in closeup. The logic behind those two different shots is that the Law always has to be in a longshot, meaning that you have to look after the interests of everybody. (Lopate 1996, 40)

One final reason for using long shots is to help the non-professional crew relax into their characters. Working with non-professionals has meant adopting improvisation as a basic technique, '... I don't give dialogue to the actors, but once you explain the scene to them, they just start talking, beyond what I would have imagined' (Kiarostami quoted in Kauffmann 2000, 28).

Repetition

Kiarostami's other authorial hallmark is the use of repetition. Postmodernist critics are very fond of this aspect of his work. In *Where is my Friend's Home?* (1987), the child protagonist wanders repeatedly over an alien terrain before he succeeds in finding his friend's house. As Williamson (1999, 93) has correctly noted the 'use of repetition stylistically counters the idea that children should have only one chance'. The repetition also points to the difficulties some of the actors have in being both themselves and not themselves. In *And Life Goes On* (1992) for instance,

the character Hossein, the persistent suitor, repeatedly mis-speaks his lines when they do not correspond to his lived experience: he repeats, over and over, that the number of family members he lost in the earthquake was twenty-five, rather than sixty-five, the number his character is directed to say. (Williamson 1999, 97)

Kiarostami prefers working with non-professionals precisely because they tend to double-up as scriptwriter and director. He explains this point further in an interview with Hamid (1997, 22): 'As soon as [nonprofessional actors] cannot say a line of dialogue, which is probably badly written anyway, or they can't act a scene, they somehow give me this message that there is something wrong in my work - so without knowing it they are correcting my script ...'. This spontaneous approach to scripting takes into account the element of chance (surrealism) and emotional accidents. As with Raphael (1483–1520) who believed the painter should take advantage of accidental paint droplets on the canvas instead of hiding them, Kiarostami too has a Sufi-surreal reverence for chance encounters. Finally, he prefers non-professionals because he is desperate 'to show us that the ordinary people he uses as actors can be just as difficult as Hollywood stars' (James 1997, 52). Other modernist techniques employed will be more familiar to western audiences. In *Under the Olive Trees* (1994) for example,

> Kiarostami deploys not only the device of an actor speaking directly to the audience (in the faux documentary moment) but also reveals the cinematic apparatus through real-time shots and repetition. These combine to effectively create a 'writerly' text. Kiarostami uses both the returned gaze of his actors and the returned gaze of the cinematic apparatus to alienate and educate his viewers. (Williamson 1999, 103)

No sooner has he flirted with modernism than he reverts back to a premodern theme. The courtship ritual initiated and perpetuated by the suitor, Hossein, without response from his intended bride, 'might well be seen to rely too much on bullying and hectoring ... [but this is because] it comes from a tradition in which persistence in courtship is as much a virtue as it is in the medieval European Romance, and should be judged accordingly' (James 1997, 52).

It is easy to mistake this obsessional 'pre-modern' courtship with 'post-modern' stalking. If the ending of the film is deliberately left inconclusive it is because Kiarostami takes seriously the right of the viewer to be a co-creator with him. Now all this may sound like old hat to western art-house audiences brought up on Brechtian alienating devices, Barthesian writerly texts and Bakhtinian dialogism. However, in a climate of absolutism and intolerance orchestrated by Islamic fascism it was a gambit as vital as it was daring.

PHILOSOPHICAL OUTLOOK

Premodern influences

Despite his urbane sophistication and familiarity with both Italian neorealism and French New Wave, Kiarostami is first and foremost an *Iranian* artist. I am convinced of his sincerity when he contends that Brechtian distanciation techniques such as showing the film crew have been arrived at independently of Brecht,

> I found distanciation in *Taaziyeh* ... Although everything happens so simply in *Taaziyeh*, the audience is very much involved ... this year I went to a village near Tehran to watch a *Taaziyeh*. In the scene of Yazid and Imam Hossein's battle, Imam Hossein's sword suddenly became bent because it was made of very cheap, soft metal. Yazid went to him and took his sword and put it on a big stone and straightened it with another stone and gave it back to him and then they continued fighting ... these things really helped me. I saw how nothing could affect this scene. (Kiarostami interviewed by Hamid 1997, 24)

Taaziyeh is the traditional folk theatre depicting the Shi'a account of the murder of Imam Hossein, the grandson of Mohammad by his (Sunni) rival Yazid, which is performed each year on the anniversary of the event. The premodern impact of *Naqqali* (public storytelling), *Rou-Hozi* (popular theatre) and *Taaziyeh* (passion play) continue to invigorate Kiarostami's art (Dabashi 2001, 38).

Ironically many Iranians have championed Kiarostami's cinema for its alleged 'atheism'. Kiarostami's enigmatic and at times guarded response to persistent questions about his beliefs has only added to the speculation. The Sufi-influenced film critic, Mir-Ehsan (1999, 113), for instance, has argued that Kiarostami's philosophical outlook has ideological affinities with the notion of 'divine atheism',

> I must return to the comparison of Kiarostami's work with sacred art. A cinema that can manifest the heretical in the mundane, questions both the sacred and the profane. It advances the intellectually challenging notion of 'divine atheism', based on the mystic teachings of Hafez and Ibn Arabi, as an alternative to both intolerant theism and its Western mechanical negation, atheism.

Kiarostami himself has been very careful to maintain a fog of ambiguity over his views on religion, perhaps understandably given the nature of the theocratic regime. We can, however, state categorically that the influence of premodern Persian philosophy of Avicenna and the Zoroastrian/Sufi doctrine of Suhrewardi have greatly shaped his outlook. In a different era this could have been a distinct disadvantage limiting Kiarostami's relevance to a western audience but since the advent of 'postmodernity', these philosophical hangovers have turned into positives. Persian premodernity's emphasis on cyclical time, hermeneutics, repetition and symmetry in the arts, and its refusal to draw a sharp dividing line between body and soul or the physical and metaphysical have found strong echoes in a western culture tired of the arrogant boasts of science and technology. As Mir-Ehsan (1999, 109–13) observes,

> This is a world-apart from the ideological straitjacket of a neo-realism grounded in 'objectivity' and the pursuit of absolute 'truths'. This outlook is deeply hostile to the positivism inherent in neo-realism. Instead it chooses to rely on the New Hermeneutics and a pluralistic world view ... Kiarostami is the inheritor of an Eastern art tradition which foregrounds deconstruction and multiple-narration, features most notable in *Close-Up* ... These techniques have allowed Kiarostami to 'distance' himself from emotionalism and the quagmire of political expediency that feeds off it.

Modernist impact

None of this is to deny the influence of Europe. Readily admitting the influence of neo-realism he explains the kinship succinctly: '... it's more a question of congruence of taste than ... a decision to follow their example' (Kiarostami quoted in Aufderheide 1995, 32). Kiarostami came to neorealism tangentially and more from the perspective of the Persian modernist poet, Nima, than European cinema (Dabashi 2001, 48). The congruence he talks about between present-day Iran and post-World War II Italy is both socio-economic as well as artistic. Religion as a determining mediating factor in both societies adds to the parallels.

One of his latest films, *The Wind Will Carry Us* (1999), is steeped in allusions about modern disorientation. Cheshire has observed these references with typical shrewdness,

> In the wilderness far beyond the city, where such dramas of initiation always take place, Behzad [the protagonist film-maker of *The Wind Will Carry Us*] gains sudden access to the vertical and, thus, the chance of a genuine ascent. Yet he is

profoundly disoriented. Around him are allusions connecting this domain to Abraham and the mystical spring called zamzam, Joseph and the well, Jacob and his Ladder, the cosmic crypt or cave (not unlike Plato's) that recurs in Islamic mysticism and, most important of all, the Miraj, the Prophet Mohammad's bodily ascent into heaven. But instead of these signs, Behzad repeatedly heeds only that faulty messenger of the flatland, his cell phone. (Cheshire 2000, 12)

One recurring technique employed by Kiarostami is to have characters that are never shown. *The Wind Will Carry Us* (1999), for instance, is about people who do not exist - the old woman who is dying, the ditchdigger who is heard but not seen. Kiarostami has commented, 'The movie does have a physical essence to it, but it also has a non-physical or spiritual side. We don't see some characters, but we do feel them. This shows there is a possibility of being without being' (quoted in Kauffmann 2000, 28). Similarly,

what speaks to us the loudest in *The Taste of Cherry* is the 'unheard', in the same way that the most privileged imagery is the 'unseen'. The gradual 'fading' of the main character, parallels the structuring of the film through a kind of long-drawn-out 'fade'. (Mir-Ehsan 1999, 110)

Laura Mulvey (2000, 63) has argued with regard to *The Wind Will Carry Us* (1999) that characters are deliberately not shown because 'to see is not necessarily to understand, and the implication might be - the demand for everything to be seen is simply the other side of censorship's coin'. The forced veiling of women under the ayatollahs has resulted not so much in a blind attempt to imitate the West but to discover a third path. The idea that women are objectified in the West through over-exposure and in the East through concealment is one that many Iranian intellectuals would agree with. By not showing intimate moments between lovers, Kiarostami is not only being true to the reality of a society that frowns upon public displays of erotic affection but is also pointing out that there are moments of intimacy that should not be filmed.

None of this should deter us from questioning Kiarostami's traditionalist outlook on women. As Farahmand (2002, 100) has argued, 'female roles in his films are depicted either as over-sentimental and therefore blameworthy (the absent mother in

Homework, 1989), or as cold, aggressive, unaffectionate and thus tolerable (*Through the Olive Trees*)'.

A modernized mysticism

The clash between premodern Iranian cultural values and a modernist Europe has resulted in a modernized mysticism in Kiarostami's outlook. There are affinities here with the Christian mysticism of Tarkovsky especially in films such as *Solaris* (1973) and *Stalker* (1979) and Pasolini's extradiegetic technique of creating a spiritual ambience in *The Gospel According to St Matthew* (1964). And here is where children as spiritual guides play such a decisive role for him. Again a quote from Kiarostami himself can be instructive,

> In Eastern philosophy, we have this belief that you don't ever set foot in unknown territory without having a guide. The kid in [*And Life Goes On*] was acting more rationally, and the father was not rational. The kid has accepted the instability and the illogic of the earthquake, he is just living on. (In Lopate 1996, 38)

Here is the Sufi kernel at the heart of Kiarostami's world-view. The serene and totally rational coming to terms with life 'as it is' instead of a 'utopian' vision of 'life as could be'. This aspect of his work divides critics more than anything else. One of the reasons Kiarostami is sometimes shunned by the dispersed 'communities' of Iranians opposed to the Islamic regime is precisely to do with his quietism in the face of intolerant bigotry - a quietism which chimes well with a very petty bourgeois brand of Sufism that has been gaining ground in the last two decades throughout the Middle East but especially within Iran. In *And Life Goes On* (1992) he makes a comparison between earthquakes and revolutionary transformation. He is of the opinion that 'revolutions do not alter essential values, merely displace them' (quoted in Pir-Poshteh 1997, 63). Conversely cinema, if it is true to the Sufi technique of initiation, can do precisely that, 'In my opinion,' asserts Kiarostami, 'cinema and all the arts ought to be able to destroy the mind of their audience in order to reject the old values and make it susceptible to new values' (Hamid 1997, 24).

Humorous quietism

In his defence one could mention that at least his quietism is tinged with a certain humanistic optimism and dry humour - rare commodities in a society where austerity and seriousness are fetishized by official ideology. He is on record as saying, 'I'd rather look at the positive side of daily life than the negative, which makes me sleepless and nervous' (quoted in Aufderheide 1995, 32). This attitude chimes with the 'optimist' wing of Italian neo-realism (Visconti and Fellini). Fellini, for example, portrays human emotions without veering into emotionalism in *La Strada* (1954). Occasionally Kiarostami has fallen into the trap of emotionalism and sentimentalism as for example in *Two Solutions for One Problem* (1975) but, by and large, he has managed to steer away from such cheap stunts (Dabashi 2001, 49).

Italian neo-realism emerged *after* the defeat of fascism whereas Kiarostami has been labouring first under the Shah's dictatorship and lately under an ultra-right Islamic regime with numerous affinities to European fascism. Given this major difference, a great deal of his optimism can be mistaken for conformity and worse - collaboration with reactionaries. For instance, when he blithely repeats one of the current myths about Iranian audiences, one is inclined to take his comments with a pinch of salt,

> Before the revolution [1979], religious people didn't go to the movies because they didn't feel safe there. They now can go to see movies that don't have sex and violence in them as much as before and they can relax. (Kiarostami quoted in Aufderheide 1995, 33)

Here the weight of historical evidence is against Kiarostami. First, religious people *did* attend cinemas before the 'revolution'. One of the main attractions was a steady diet of melodrama, sex and violence that the commercial cinema screened. The cinema had become a powerful competitor to the mosque. Gradually after the 'revolution' a myth was created that cinemas had been 'unsafe' environments for pious believers before the 'revolution'. Also Kiarostami neatly sidesteps the arson attacks carried out by religious fanatics on cinemas (in one notorious incidence in the southern city of Abadan some 400 cinema-goers were burnt alive at Cinema Rex). It could reasonably be argued, therefore, that it was irreligious audiences that felt unsafe and under threat as a result of waves of mindless moral crusades waged by religious purifiers.

I do not believe it is possible to apologize for Kiarostami's comments on grounds that he is trying not to offend the regime. Kiarostami is usually quite forthright in interviews and speaks his mind (almost) without holding back. Subjects as sensitive as authoritarianism, sexism, drinking and the infamous fatwa against Salman Rushdie are discussed by him (and other Iranian film-makers) openly. It is true that at times he may be 'economical with the truth' or 'play with the interviewer' but his views on religion and cinema, as stated in the above quote, are consistent with his admiration for religious passion plays. As for 'sex and violence', Kiarostami has on numerous occasions denounced this trend in Hollywood and native pre-1979 film-making which he rather naively associates with '*film-e mobtazal*' (degenerate and/or trite film).

Additionally, we are perfectly entitled to enquire as to why most religious people might feel uncomfortable discussing sexual matters and how this mentality impacts on their world-view. Kiarostami finds these issues too problematic and on the few occasions when a space has opened up he has refused to participate in the debate, preferring instead a mysterious silence.

Individualism and non-conformity

His defenders have pointed out that in *Where is My Friend's Home?* (1987), Kiarostami encourages individuals to break rules that are anathema to their beliefs, that in *Homework* (1989) he attacks the disciplinarian educational system in Iran and its collusion with religiosity and in *Taste of Cherry* (1997) he puts under erasure the concept of suicide and, finally, in *The Wind Will Carry Us* (1999) he questions the after-life. Yet these mild philosophical enquiries should be seen within a background of daily social struggles within Iran against theocracy. The militant proletarian demonstrations attacking symbols of religious authority and the subversive subculture ridiculing Islamic capitalism are the reality which provides Kiarostami with a semi-autonomous space to express himself.

Other forms of non-conformity are discerned in *Ten* (2002). The obnoxious little kid berating his mother for breaking up the family unit is reminiscent of school children described by Valerie Walkerdine in her book, *Schoolgirl Fictions* (1990). These children verbally abuse their female teacher using sexist language they have absorbed from patriarchy. Only in the case of *Ten*, given the mother's patronizing and deceitful brand of bourgeois feminism that is incessantly shoved down the kid's throat, it is little wonder that he rebels. Our sympathies vacillate between the mother (a victim of patriarchy) and the son (a victim of bourgeois disciplining), finally rejecting both characters as equally odious. The only person fascinating enough to hold the attention and worthy of respect is, of course, the sexworker. The unseen prostitute enjoys her work. At some stage she bursts into halting English to denounce patriarchal discourse by demanding, 'Sex, love, sex!' She refuses to feel guilty and declares herself 'smarter' than the woman driver who is summarily dismissed as an 'idiot'. Understanding perfectly the nature of her work, she sees sex as exchange value, no more: 'It's just an exchange ... you're [you, bourgeois women are] wholesalers. We [us, working-class women] are retailers'. In a culture where (almost) everyone aims to be a moral guardian, the prostitute's brazen subversion of all mores is refreshing and perhaps the only saving grace of *Ten*.

Within this context the postmodern cynicism regarding 'truth' and 'justice' has no place. Even in the midst of devastation and despair, Kiarostami sees hope and beauty. A European artist who earnestly talks about art as a mission would be laughed out of court. Kiarostami, on the other hand, can reintroduce these arguments into a European discourse about film-making, as he is perceived to be 'authentic',

> We live in a world without values, a world full of falsity. I think the mission of art should be to discover the truth of life. By this I mean getting closer to the essence of humans and all of my films are attempts in this direction. (Quoted in Pir-Poshteh 1997, 65)

DISCUSSION

Political dimension

In an interview with *Cineaste* Kiarostami innocently claims,

> My technique is similar to collage. I collect pieces and put
> them together. I don't invent material. I just watch and take it
> from the daily life of people around me. (Aufderheide 1995,
> 32)

There is some truth in this assertion but it is hardly a complete
explanation of his continuing appeal. Mulvey (1998, 25) believes
'Kiarostami's cinema is about curiosity, directly engaging the
spectator's desire to know, decipher and understand.' Kiarostami
himself considers his work to be highly political although some may
not share his definition of 'political'. 'I think that any work of art is a
political work', he asserts in an interview with Hamid (1997, 22),
'but it's not party political ... I think surprisingly that those films
which appear non-political, such as poetic films, are *more* political
than films known specifically as *political* films' [original emphasis].

Let us not forget that Kiarostami was born in an era influenced by
social realism and anti-colonial sentiments (Dabashi 2001, 37). In
1980 during life-and-death political power struggles and the
impending Iran-Iraq war, Kiarostami was making a film about dental
hygiene (*Toothache*, 1980). For him the dentures in *Toothache* are
more real than the reality exploding around him.

Close-Up for instance cannot help but cross explicitly political
contours on its way towards a reformulation of fantasy and reality.
The class dimension of *Close-Up* is reminiscent of Pasolini's
Teorema (1968) where the Terrance Stamp character exposes
bourgeois mores by playing members of a family against each other,
exposing their inner desires and hidden hostilities. Perhaps a closer
analogy would be with Fred Schepisi's *Six Degrees of Separation*
(1993) 'in which a wealthy family is gulled by a man claiming to be
Sidney Poitier's son', or Scorsese's *The King of Comedy* (1983)
where Robert De Niro impersonates Jerry Lewis.

Ironically he is on record as claiming that his films do not have a
message. He enjoys quoting Francois Truffaut on the subject, 'If you
have a message for the spectators, go to the post office and send them
a telegram' (quoted in Nayeri 1993, 28). It is difficult to take this
statement at face value. There has always been a certain didacticism
about Kiarostami's work. This is as true of the early phase of his
work where children are encouraged to develop psychologically
along a continuum as stage-managed as Piaget's, as it is of the latter,
more subtle, phase of his pedagogic film-making. Yet it is true that
he no longer rams his 'message' down the audience's throat. The

switch to a more sophisticated mode of communication is a real one. As he makes clear in another part of the interview,

> Cinema is no longer a storytelling medium. That period is gone. It's not a novel with images. It's not the manipulation of the audience's emotions. It's not educational, it's not entertainment, it doesn't trigger guilt feelings in the audience. The best form of cinema is one which poses questions for the audience. (Nayeri 1993, 28)

This philosophy explains the numerous moments of silence and inactivity during his films when viewers are given the opportunity to reflect.

Ideological dimension

Kiarostami makes a stark distinction between those artists who draw inspiration from life and those who limit themselves to artistic representations,

> One draws inspiration either from books and novels, or directly from life itself. I always think that directors who look for stories in books are like those Iranians who live next to a stream full of fish, but eat out of tins. (Nayeri 1993, 27)

This statement should also be interpreted as an assault on urban consciousness. With *The Wind Will Carry Us*, for instance, Kiarostami launches a sustained lyrical attack on the speciousness of urban consciousness through poetry. Those who know Kiarostami intimately suggest that he is far more literate and engaged with the history of cinema that he lets on. There is obvious bravado in his claim that he watches few films. Moreover, Dabashi (2001) amongst others have traced Kiarostami's love of modern Persian poetry and its continuing influence on his works. However, despite his borrowings from literature and film history there is a certain contempt for cinema which may seem ungrateful, given how cinema has been generous to Kiarostami. He sees cinema as atavistic because it lacks the abstractions of other arts like painting and music. There are no (or fewer) blanks to be filled in by the spectators.

It could be argued that despite his jet-setting lifestyle, his nationalistic outlook has limited Kiarostami's understanding of the world we live in. Most western critics, perhaps applying positive discrimination, tend to ignore his parochialism. Sometimes this is achieved by completely denying his cultural background. For example, when Laurent Roth insists on interpreting the veiled shyness of female characters such as Tahereh in *Under the Olive Trees* in Lacanian terms, we are thrown back to a colonial discourse of 'Otherness'. Ironically, at other times, the western critic shields Kiarostami from criticism by applying an extreme form of cultural relativism. We are discouraged from confronting Kiarostami's elitist and nationalistic outlook on the grounds that his work has to be understood within the nuanced landscape of Iran. Both approaches have the unfortunate consequence of reifying Kiarostami as the 'Other', whilst silencing both 'internal' and 'foreign' critics of his work. Kiarostami is very clear regarding the contradictions in his reception by European critics,

> On the one hand, in their encounter with Iranian cinema, they look at it as a culture which is healthy and humane and in a way also poetic. On the other hand, they view it as a culture of terrorism. The conflict between these two views has caused this reaction, which makes people unwilling to acknowledge my Iranian background. (Quoted in Hamid 1997, 22)

Nationalistic dimension

Nowhere is Kiarostami's parochialist world-view more obvious than when he tackles 'non-Iranian' topics. *Certified Copy* (2010), his first feature shot outside Iran, begins intriguingly but seems to run out of steam. Its emotional plane is deliberately sabotaged by Kiarostami in favour of an intellectual debate that never rises above mediocre observations about art, copies and authenticity. Likewise, *ABC Africa*'s (2001) failure to come to terms with the complexities of Aids, its socio-economic and cultural imperatives is a dire warning that Kiarostami can only be trusted to deliver when the subject matter emanates from the cultural soil of Iran. Kiarostami does not seem to appreciate the objectification that NGOs, newscasters and charities have subjected the 'African' to. At times his film resembles the worst aspects of the stereotypical depiction of suffering and pain found in western media. The occasional scene of children playing joyfully fails to overcome the clichéd nature of the enterprise. The failure of *ABC Africa* is partly due to the fact that the suffering of the children has no unequivocal cause. In his early films Kiarostami could furnish an indirect critique of dogma (e.g. *The Wind Will Carry Us*), authority (e.g. *Where is My Friend's Home?*), and discipline (e.g. *Homework*). Sadri (1996, 2) has remarked,

> Kiarostami's idealism consists in the insight that the tyranny of grownups and authority figures, like the logic of social domination and status privileges (e.g. in *Under the Olive Trees*) finally crumble in the face of the efforts of unyielding heroes.

The destructive powers of Aids permits of no heroic fight-back, especially not in poor regions of the world such as Africa. Hence the film's indecisiveness results from the shortcomings of Kiarostami as a thinker. Jones (2000, 72) asks,

> Is Kiarostami's aesthetics becoming as narrowly defined as Antonioni's had become by the mid-sixties, or Wender's by the early eighties? Because as thrilling as [*The Wind Will Carry Us*] is, it also feels a little cozy, a work of self containment rather than self-discovery.

European dimension

I have tried in this paper to contextualize Kiarostami within the cultural and artistic milieu of his native Iran in order to show both his strengths and weaknesses. I have also been keen to demonstrate most of the markers western critics recognize as modernist or postmodernist techniques in Kiarostami's work, devices such as Brechtian distanciation, neo-realist non-professional acting, French New Wave spontaneity and outdoor shooting, surrealism's chance encounters, and Situationist psycho-geography and drifting have been arrived at independently. I have also pointed out various premodernist influences that usually go unnoticed, such as *Taaziyeh* (passion plays).

None of this is surprising given the complexities of Iranian capitalism and the way 'progress' has been cramped into a shorter time frame. Williams (1973) talked of *dominant, residual* and *emergent* cultural forms. Iranian capitalism combines premodern residual cultural forms (expressed in themes around 'honour'), dominant modernist cultural forms (expressed in themes around the 'dignity' of labour), and finally emergent postmodernist cultural forms (expressed around themes such as 'authenticity'). Kiarostami's strength is mostly due to the ease with which he crosses these boundaries, mixing themes and metaphors in an open-ended and dialogic tapestry. On his journey he aims (and sometimes succeeds) in reaching a situation 'where the problems of the character and the problems of the spectator become one and the same' (Dalby 1997, 41).

Psychological dimension

Let us conclude by revisiting the role children play in Kiarostami's cinematic oeuvres. After all, since 1968 the Institute for the Development of Children and Young Adults has produced some twenty of his shorts and features. Iranian psychologists (in particular developmental psychologists) have traditionally been a reactionary lot (Rejali 1994). Child psychologists have been at pains to exclude what they see as westernization, a coded term standing for 'sinful' behaviour. In this regard religious and secular forces have combined to 'socialize' working-class children and to 'protect' upper-class ones. It is this notion of moral guardianship and its disciplinary apparatus that Kiarostami has been at pains to critique. For instance *Case No. 1, Case No. 2* (1979) 'which condemned high schoolers who rat on their neighbours, so flummoxed officials of the new Islamic regime that they first gave it an award, then banned it' (Cheshire 1996, 5). In *Traveller* (1972) 'a masterful depiction of childhood cruelty' (Cheshire 1996, 5), he places the blame squarely on the Iranian character rather than aspects of nature (bad dog in *Where is My Friend's Home?* Or earthquake in *And Life Goes On*), or societal forces in general (oppressive educational traditions in *Homework*). The stages theory of development, with its liberal connotations influenced by Piaget is posited as an alternative to the paternalistic moralism of both right- and left-wing doctrinaires.

This dalliance with developmental psychology represents yet another reason for Kiarostami's positive reception in the West. However, as Erica Burman (2001, 5) has made clear in her devastating critique,

> Developmental psychology as a modern, western (minority-world) discipline has been wedded to an individualist model of child development that treats the baby or child as an isolated unit of development. Heir to both romantic and functionalist traditions within its Euro-American context of formulation, within this paradigm the child develops according to regular, predictable patterns (sometimes described as stages) that are presumed to be largely universal in their structure.

There is in Kiarostami an unfortunate fetishization of childhood (more accurately boyhood) as the privileged site of development. As Dabashi (2001, 52) observes, 'For Kiarostami adults are finished realities, children realities in making'. The rediscovery of Vygotsky and Voloshinov in recent years has undoubtedly damaged this liberal consensus in the West (Collins 1999; Newman and Holzman 1993; Ratner 1991) and it is a matter of time before its effects are echoed within Iran. In fact, Vygotsky and a number of 'neo-Vygotskians' have already been translated into Farsi and incorporated into a number of leading academic psychology and language courses by, amongst others, Behrooz Azabdaftari (see Vygotsky 1988 and 1999). Hopefully these efforts will enable the next Kiarostami to have a more sophisticated understanding of children and development.

IN CONCLUSION

Kiarostami has weathered the storm of 'revolution', censorship and trade boycott better than most. In the process he has provided us with a rare glimpse into a complex culture that seems on the verge of yet another cataclysmic transformation. How he is going to cope with a post-Islamic Iran is a question only time will tell.

ACKNOWLEDGEMENT

Ian Parker (Manchester Metropolitan University) has patiently read various versions of this paper. I would like to acknowledge his criticisms as well as the comments made by my two anonymous reviewers at *New Cinemas*. The study was made possible thanks to a generous scholarship from the Department of Psychology and Speech Pathology at Manchester Metropolitan University.

FILMOGRAPHY (FEATURES)

1972   *Mosafer/Traveller* (+scr)
1978   *Gozaresh/The Report* (+scr)
1986   *Avaliha/First Graders* (+scr)
1987   *Khaneh-ye Doust Kojast?/Where is my Friend's Home?* (+scr)
1989   *Mashg-e Shab/Homework* (+scr)
1990   *Nama-ye Nazdik/Close-Up* (+scr)
1992   *Va Zendegi Edameh Darad/And Life Goes On* (+scr)
1994   *Zir-e Derakhktan-e Zeitoun/Under The Olive Trees* (+scr/prod)
1997   *Taameh-e Gilas/Taste of Cherry* (+scr/prod)
1999   *Special Ceremony*
1999   *Bad Mara Khahad Bord/The Wind Will Carry Us* (+scr/prod)
2001   *ABC Africa* (+scr)
2002   *Ten*
2010   *Certified Copy* (+scr)

REFERENCES

Aufderheide, P. (1995) Real Life is More Important than Cinema: an interview with Abbas Kiarostami. *Cineaste*, 21(3): 31–33.

Burman, E. (2001) Beyond the Baby and the Bathwater: Postdualistic Developmental Psychologies for Diverse Childhoods. *European Early Childhood Education Research Journal*, 9(1): 5–22.

Cheshire, G. (1996) Abbas Kiarostami: a cinema of questions. *Film Comment*, July–August, 32(4): 34–40.

Cheshire, G. (2000) How to read Kiarostami. *Cineaste*, Fall, 25(4): 8.

Collins, C. (1999) *Language, Ideology and Social Consciousness: Developing a Sociohistorical Approach*. Aldershot, Brookfield USA, Singapore and Sydney: Ashgate.

Dabashi, H. (2001) *Close Up Iranian Cinema: Past, Present and Future*. London and New York: Verso.

Dalby, A. (1997) Kudos at Cannes. In *The Middle East*, July–August, 269: 40–41.

Debord, G. (1956/1989) Theory of Dérive. In Ken Knabb (ed.), *Situationist Internationalist Anthology*. California: Bureau of Public Secrets, pp. 50–54.

Farahmand, A. (2002) Perspectives on Recent (International acclaim for) Iranian Cinema. In Richard Tapper (ed.), *The New Iranian Cinema: Politics, Representation and Identity*. London and New York: I. B. Tauris, pp. 86–108.

Hamid, N. (1997) Near and Far. *Sight and Sound*, February, 2: 22–24.

Issa, R. and Whitaker, S. (1999) *Life and Art: The New Iranian Cinema*. London: British Film Institute.

James, N. (1997) Through the Olive Trees. *Sight and Sound*, January, p. 52.

Jones, K. (2000) The Wind Will Carry Us: Review. *Film Comment*, March, 36(2): 72.

Kauffmann, S. (1995) Through the Olive Trees. *The New Republic*, 20 March, 212(12): 28–30.

Kauffmann, S. (1998) Taste of Cherry. In *The New Republic*, 13 April, 218(15): 24–25.

Kauffmann, S. (2000) Stanley Kauffmann on Films: A Homeland. *The New Republic*, August, 14: 28.

Knabb, K. (1989) *Situationist Internationalist Anthology*. California: Bureau of Public Secrets.

Lopate, P. (1996) Kiarostami close up. *Film Comment*, July–August, 32(4): 37–40.

Mir-Ehsan, M. (1999) Dark Light. In Rose Issa and Sheila Whitaker (eds.), *Life and Art: The New Iranian Cinema*. London: BFI, pp. 105–14.

Mulvey, L. (1998) Kiarostami's uncertainty principle. *Sight and Sound*, June, 6: 24–27.

Mulvey, L. (2000) *The Wind Will Carry Us*. *Sight and Sound*, October, 10: 63.

Naficy, H. (2002) Islamizing Film Culture in Iran: A Post-Khatami Update. In Richard Tapper (ed.), *The New Iranian Cinema: Politics, Representation and Identity*. London and New York: I. B. Tauris, pp. 26–65.

Nayeri, F. (1993) Iranian Cinema: What Happened in Between. *Sight and Sound*, December, 12: 26–27.

Newman, F. and Holzman, L. (1993) *Lev Vygotsky: Revolutionary Scientist*. London and New York: Routledge.

Pir-Poshteh, M. (1997) *Tarhi az doost [Portrait of a Friend]*. Tehran: Rowzaneh Publications.

Pride, R. (2003) Taking Stock: Abbass Kiarostami counts down to *Ten.* Available at http:// www.newcitychicago.com/chicago/2408.html (accessed on 10 September 2004).

Ratner, C. (1991) *Vygotsky's Sociohistorical Psychology And Its Contemporary Applications*. New York: Plenum Press.

Rejali, D. M. (1994) *Torture and Modernity: Self, Society, and State in Modern Iran*. Boulder, San Francisco and London: Westview Press.

Rosenbaum, J. (1997) Fill In The Blanks. *The Chicago Reader: On Film* Available at http://www.chireader.com/movies/archives/1998/0598/05298.html (accessed on 18 August 2004).

Sadri, A. (1996). Searchers: The New Iranian Cinema. *The Iranian*, Abadan Publishing Co.

Tapper, R. (2002) *The New Iranian Cinema: Politics, Representation and Identity*. London and New York: I. B. Tauris.

Vygotsky, L. S. (1988) *Thought and Language [Tafak-kor va Zaban]* (trans. Behrooz Azabdaftari), Tabriz: Neema Publications.

Vygotsky, L. S. (1999) *Mind in Society [Zehn va Jame'eh]* (trans. Behrooz Azabdaftari). Tehran: Fatemi Publications.

Walkerdine, V. (1990) *Schoolgirl Fictions*. London: Verso.

Williams, R. (1973) Base and superstructure in Marxist cultural theory. *New Left Review*, 82 (November–December).

Williamson, C. (1999) Art Matters: the films of Abbas Kiarostami. In Rose Issa and Sheila Whitaker (eds.), *Life and Art: The New Iranian Cinema*. London: BFI, pp. 90–104.

INDEX

Auftakt 4
Get ahead in German

Transcript Booklet